Critiquing Transhumanism

Critiquing Transhumanism

The Human Cost of Pursuing Techno-Utopia

Julie Miller

 Public Philosophy Press

Copyright © 2022 Julie Miller

Public Philosophy Press, Phoenix, Arizona
www.publicphilosophypress.com

All rights reserved

Catologing-in-Publication Data available from the Library of Congress

Paper ISBN: 978-1-7365424-6-0
Ebook ISBN: 978-1-7365424-7-7

Cover Design: Virginia De La Lastra
Typesetting: Matthew Hicks

For my husband Buzz

Just as there would be no Tale of the Ring without
Samwise Gamgee,
there would be no tale of Critiquing Transhumanism without
Buzz Miller.

Contents

Chapter 1: Transhumanism: A History of The Very Idea 1

Chapter 2: Transhumanism, Artificial Intelligence, and
Superintelligence: Believe it or Not? 33

Chapter 3: Artificial General Intelligence and Creativity:
How *BRUTUS* Fails the Lovelace Test. 75

Chapter 4: Transhumanism and the Metaphysics of the
Human Person 115

Chapter 5: Transhumanism's Superlongevity:
A Tolkienian Critique 157

Chapter 6: Transhumanism's Superhappiness:
Making Dystopian Fiction A Reality 189

Chapter 7: Conclusion 219

Bibliography 233

Index. 259

Chapter One

Transhumanism: A History of The Very Idea

"Transhumanism and posthumanism are both future-oriented intellectual projects. This is strange territory for an historian; the future is definitely a foreign country. Yet, if anything has a past the future does..."[1]

Alison Bashford

Introduction

IN ITS BROADEST SENSE, transhumanism is the view that humanity's problems can and should be solved through science and technology.[2] Humanity's chief problems, on this view, derive from our biological, cognitive, and psychological limits. Transhumanists, therefore, seek to overcome these limits through applying science and technology to human persons. And this, they propose, will eventually lead to a new species labeled "posthumans."[3]

Transhumanists envision a techno-utopia sometimes referred to as a triple 'S' civilization of superintelligence, superlongevity, and superhappiness, a future where there is a gradual blurring of the tradition-

---

1   Alison Bashford, "Julian Huxley's Transhumanism," in Marius Turda, editor, *Crafting Humans: From Genesis to Eugenics and Beyond* (Goettingen: V&R unipress, 2013), 154.

2   Max More, "The Extropian Principles version 3.0, A Transhumanist Declaration," (1998), *MROB.com*, The Extropian Principles, v. 3.0 at MROB (accessed March 15, 2020).

3   Ibid.

al bounaries between human persons and machines.[4] This transition is sometimes referred to as the Double Blur, or the two-pronged pursuit to build machines to be persons (then surpass humans), and at the same time to transform human persons into machines through artificial technological enhancements.[5]

Transhumanism is rooted in three central ideas: a desire to control nature and transcend human limitations, a mechanistic world picture, and a technological view of progress. These three ideas, combined with a materialist philosophy of mind and persons, undergird and drive the belief that machines can be persons and that humans can and should be artificially enhanced to transcend current limitations in cognition, biology, and psychology to become posthumans.

Scientific discoveries and technological innovations have been the main agents of change in society since at least the seventeenth century.[6] Early modern scientists and philosophers, such as Johannes Kepler, Robert Boyle, Francis Bacon, and Rene Descartes, characterized the universe as a vast machine that was rational, knowable, explainable, and open to study, and the human body was seen as part of that machinery. Increasingly, there developed a focus on the practical value of scientific knowledge and its application, not only to overcome nature but also to overcome human limitations. Thus, the world of science and the world of technology were coupled, a relationship which Lewis Mumford analogized as "science acting as captain and technology as the soldier."[7]

The transhumanists are convinced their projects of superintelligence, superlongevity, and superhappiness are metaphysically possible based

---

4   David Pearce, "What is Transhumanism? The 3 Supers," *Institute for Ethics and Emerging Technologies*, (September 16, 2014), What is Transhumanism? – the 3 Supers (accessed March 15, 2020).

5   Selmer Bringsjord and David A. Ferrucci, *What Robots Can and Can't Be* (Dordrecht, The Netherlands: Kluwer Academic Publishers, 1992), 4.

6   See the following resources: Lewis Mumford, *Technics and Civilization* (Chicago: University of Chicago Press, 2010); Hans Jonas, *Philosophical Essays: From Ancient Creed To Technological Man* (Englewood Cliffs, NJ: Prentice-Hall, Inc., 1974); Jacques Ellul, "On the Aims of A Philosophy of Technology," in Robert C. Scharff and Val Dusek, editors, *Philosophy of Technology* (UK: John Wiley & Sons, 2014); George Grant, *Technology and Empire: Perspective on North America* (Toronto: House of Anansi, 1969); Langdon Gilkey, *Religion and the Scientific Future: Reflections on Myth, Science, and Theology* (New York: Harper & Row, 1970).

7   Mumford, *Technics and Civilization*, 52.

on their assumed materialism.[8] This materialist assumption is the primary focus of my critique of transhumanism because, first of all, it conflates epistemological materialism (how we know things) with ontological materialism (nature of ultimate reality). This philosophical mistake developed in part because empirical methods were so successful in gaining knowledge about the physical world it was assumed these same methods would be equally successful in gaining knowledge about man, including the mind and emotions. Ontological materialism aims to close the gap between nature and the human person by reducing man to the same level of scientific explanation as physical objects. Therefore, transhumanism's techno-utopian worldview is, first of all, committed to a strictly physical story about reality and how things came to be. Transhumanists see this story as complete and comprehensive, meaning all physical effects have only physical causes. It is from this mistaken view of human persons as merely complex matter arranged according to the impersonal laws of physics and as the product of evolution that transhumanists boldly pursue their projects of superintelligence, superlongevity, and superhappiness.

My thesis for this entire project is threefold. First, I will critique transhumanism and argue that its failed materialist philosophy of mind and human persons exposes the metaphysical impossibility of its techno-utopia. Next, I will show the dehumanizing effects of pursuing the projects of superintelligence, superlongevity, and superhappinesss by critiquing them through the lens of selected literature and their failed philosophy.[9] My critiques will show how transhumanism's failed materialist philosophy of mind and persons reveals the impossibility and human cost of its triple "S" civilization. Finally, I will demonstrate that this failed materialism points to the need for an alternative metaphysics. I suggest returning to ancient philosophy, namely the Aristotelian metaphysical picture of reality.[10] This

---

8   J. P. Moreland & William Lane Craig, *Philosophical Foundations for a Christian Worldview* (Downers Grove, Illinois: IVP Academic, 2003), 50, 257, 497, and 503. There are no clear criteria which can be applied mechanically to determine whether a proposition is metaphysically possible/impossible. I take metaphysical possibility to mean broad logical possibility in terms of actualizability. Metaphysical possibility is not the same as conceivability, which means you can imagine it can occur. Rather, for something to be a real possibility, there has to be an actual potential or ability for it to occur.

9   Chapter five critiques transhumanism's superintelligence and superlongevity from a Tolkienian perspective and chapter six critiques the project of superhappiness from selected dystopian literature.

10   Metaphysics is the science of the first principles of being, the fun-

ancient road is paved with three relevant foundational ideas: essentialism, teleology, and virtue-based human flourishing, each of which offers wisdom to face the challenges of transhumanism. My thesis is loosely based on this advice from C. S. Lewis: "Progress means getting nearer to the place you want to be. And if you have taken a wrong turn, then to go forward does not get you any nearer. If you are on the wrong road, progress means doing an about-turn and walking back to the right road; and in that case the man who turns back soonest is the most progressive man."[11] My aim is to provide the reader with good reasons to turn back from transhumanism and return to the ancient road that leads to human flourishing.

The History of Transhumanism

The word "transhuman," according to *The New Shorter Oxford English Dictionary*, means "beyond what is human; superhuman."[12] A leading expert on transhumanism, Natasha Vita-More,[13] further clarifies the meaning of transhuman as "an evolutionary transition from being biologically human toward our merger with technology."[14] As these definitions suggest, transhumanists are above all focused on the future and not on the past, or their own past specifically. However, as historian Alison Bashford aptly says, "If anything has a past the future does."[15] Thus, to understand the very idea of transhumanism it is important to begin with how transhumanists perceive and interpret their own history.

Transhumanist leaders Max More, Nick Bostrom, and James J. Hughes provide histories of transhumanism, each mentioning similar key figures

---

damental issues in ontology, such as causation, substance, essence, modality, identity, persistence, and teleology.

11   C. S. Lewis, *Mere Christianity* (New York: HarperCollins Publishers, 1980), 28-29.

12   "Transhuman," Lesley Brown, editor, *The New Shorter Oxford English Dictionary: On Historical Principles* (Oxford: Clarendon Press, 1993), 3369.

13   Humanity+ Management Team, *Humanityplus.org*, https://humanityplus.org/about/management/ (accessed February 2, 2020). Natasha Vita-More, Ph.D. is the executive director of Humanity+ and a Professor at the University of Advancing Technology.

14   Aleksandra Przegalinska, "Design to Expand Human Potential - Interview with Natasha Vita-More," *The Creativity Post* (June 4, 2014), https://www.creativitypost.com/article/expanding_human_Potential_an_interview_with_natasha_vita_more (accessed February 2, 2020).

15   Alison Bashford, "Julian Huxley's Transhumanism," 154.

and ideas.[16] Since most transhumanist literature focuses on the application of future emerging technologies, one could easily get the impression that their ideas have appeared ex nihilo in the latter twentieth century. This perception is implied by their self-stories, which, for the most part, give only a brief nod to key historical figures of transhumanist thought.

In truth, transhumanism is firmly rooted in ideas from ancient literature, the Renaissance, the Enlightenment, and the early twentieth century eugenics movement. This history reveals transhumanism's core tenets as extensions of three historical ideas: a desire to control nature and the human condition, a mechanistic and materialist picture of the world, and a technological view of progress. Later chapters will demonstrate that transhumanism's commitment to carry to completion the materialistic metaphysical picture of reality by remaking humans into posthumans is based on a profound philosophical mistake.

Ancient Literature

The Epic of Gilgamesh

The fundamental ambition of transhumanism is to improve the human condition by applying technology to "eliminate aging and to greatly enhance human intellectual, physical, and psychological capacities."[17] For transhumanists, this aspiration is seen as a modern expression of the ancient longing to overcome human limitations. They cite *The Epic of Gilgamesh*, the oldest of epic literature, as the first record of the human desire for immortality.

According to the tale, the Sumerian King Gilgamesh of Uruk becomes distraught about his own mortality after witnessing the death of his close

---

16   See accounts of transhumanism's histories: Nick Bostrom, "A History of Transhumanist Thought," *Journal of Evolution and Technology*, Vol. 14, Issue 1 (April 2005), 1-25, https://www.nickbostrom.com/papers/history.pdf (accessed February 2, 2020); Max More, "Philosophy of Transhumanism," in Max More and Natasha Vita-More, editors, *The Transhumanist Reader* (West Sussex, U.K.: Wiley-Blackwell, 2013), 8-15; James J. Hughes, "The Politics of Transhumanism and the Techno-Millennial Imagination, 1626-2030," *Zygon Journal of Religion and Science*, Vol. 47, No. 4 (December, 2012), https://www.trincoll.edu/Academics/centers/TIIS/Documents/Hughes--April%203.pdf (accessed February 2, 2020).

17   "What is Transhumanism?" The Transhumanist FAQ, *Humanityplus.org*, https://humanityplus.org/philosophy/transhumanist-faq/ (accessed February 24, 2020).

friend Enkidu. "How can I rest, how can I be at peace? Despair is in my heart. What my brother is now, that shall I be when I am dead. Because I am afraid of death I will go as best I can to find Utnapishtim whom they call the Faraway, for he has entered the assembly of the gods."[18] Gilgamesh sets out on a perilous journey to find the secret of eternal life from the ageless Utnapishtim, the survivor of the Great Flood. Utnapishtim tells Gilgamesh of a plant that grows at the bottom of the ocean that will make him young again. Gilgamesh retrieves the plant, but before he can eat it, a snake steals it. Having failed in his quest for immortality, Gilgamesh returns to the city of Uruk and finds meaning in life by becoming a good king to the people. Transhumanists are inspired to pursue radical life extension by the fact that the earliest record of human culture includes this longing for eternal life.[19]

Prometheus Bound

Transhumanists are often criticized and accused of hubris for their desire to transcend human limitations, a reaction similarly represented in ancient Greek mythology. Citing the tragedy *Prometheus Bound* by Aeschylus, transhumanists identify with Prometheus, who is punished by Zeus for stealing fire to give to humans. As humanity's benefactor, Prometheus taught men all kinds of civilizing arts and technology to overcome nature, such as language, writing, mathematics, architecture, agriculture, astronomy, metallurgy, and medicine. He is portrayed as the savior of mankind and the source of man's reason and progress, allowing them to escape the tyranny and destruction of Zeus.[20]

Transhumanists sympathize with Prometheus, who endured underserved punishment from Zeus for improving man's condition. In Simon Young's *Transhumanist Manifesto* he says, "Prometheus symbolizes the innate human drive to increase knowledge and abilities, even at the expense

---

18   Nancy Katherine Sandars, translator, *The Epic of Gilgamesh*, *Assyrian International News Agency: Books Online*, chapter 4, 16, http://www.aina.org/books/eog/eog.pdf (accessed February 15, 2020).

19   The transhumanist project of radical life extension will be investigated in chapter 5. In brief, the desire for eternal life is best explained by Christian theism, which understands this desire as part of our human nature because our destiny is with God in the afterlife; according to Ecclesiastes 3:11, God has set eternity in the hearts of men.

20   Aeschylus, "*Prometheus Bound*," in Mortimer Adler, editor, *The Great Books of the Western World* (Chicago: Encyclopedia Britannica, 1990) 40, 45- 46.

of present pains."[21] Transhumanists also find it significant that ancient Greek literature presents human progress in a positive light, as a way to overcome the forces of nature.

Daedalus and Icarus

Transhumanists reference the myth of "Daedalus and Icarus" from Ovid's epic poem *Metamorphoses* as yet another example of a skilled inventor and craftsman who is harshly treated yet overcomes nature with technology. Daedalus, a brilliant Athenian inventor, and his son Icarus find themselves imprisoned on the island of Crete after angering King Minos, who had blocked their escape by land or sea. Determined to escape by air, Daedalus carefully fashions wings by securing feathers with strings and wax, resembling the curvature of the wings of a bird. The artificial wings allow Daedalus and Icarus to escape the island of Crete, but their liberation soon ends in disaster. Icarus ignores his father's warnings and flies too close to the sun, which melts the wax of his wings and he drowns in the ocean.[22] Transhumanists focus on the success of Daedalus' "wing" technology to enhance human capabilities while downplaying the potential risks. Overall, they believe the benefits of technology will outweigh the bad consequences.

In summary, transhumanists cite these select ancient literary figures to suggest that the human desires for physical immortality, improving the human condition, and technological enhancements are innate because "they are as ancient as our species itself."[23] However, this idea that humans have innate desires that are universal conflicts with the transhumanist view that human beings have no fixed nature, essence, or teleology. Rather, human beings are just one point along a blind evolutionary pathway.[24] As Bostrom argues, our human nature is nothing more than "a half-baked beginning that we can learn to remold in desirable ways."[25]

---

21   Simon Young, *Designer Evolution* (New York: Prometheus Books, 2006), 39.

22   Ovid, "Daedalus and Icarus," *Metamorphoses Book VIII*, translated by Sir Samuel Garth, John Dryden, et al, *The Internet Classics Archive*, http://classics.mit.edu/Ovid/Metam.mb.txt (accessed February 25, 2020).

23   Nick Bostrom, "A History of Transhumanist Thought," *Journal of Evolution and Technology*, Vol. 14, Issue 1 (April 2005) (accessed February 28, 2020).

24   Max More and Natasha Vita-More, *The Transhumanist Reader*, 4.

25   Nick Bostrom, "Transhumanist Values," *Journal of Philosophical Research*, Vol. 30, 3-14, *nickbostrom.com*, https://www.nickbostrom.com/ethics/values.html (accessed Feb. 27, 2020).

The Early Renaissance

The early humanist phase of the Renaissance began in fifteenth century Italy.[26] Because the Greek and Latin classics had been recovered and made available, a new style of humanistic education arose that inspired intellectual developments in various philosophies and philosophies of nature, including Platonist, Neo-Platonist, Aristotelian, anti-Aristotelian, Stoic, and skeptic.[27] The spirit of the times was marked by individualism, self-development, and a feeling of discovery and adventure.[28]

The Alchemists

Transhumanists applaud this shift in focus away from Medieval Scholasticism's emphasis on the other-worldly and religious authority to the this-worldly ideal of the well-rounded autonomous human person.[29] Max More regards the early alchemists, like Paracelsus (1493-1541) and Nicholas Flamel (1330-1418), as proto-transhumanists because they searched for such things as the Elixir of Life, the Philosopher's Stone, the cure for diseases, and immortality.[30] In the spirit of the Renaissance, the alchemists combined man's creativity with philosophical speculation, an interest in science, and magic to promote human development. From this period, transhumanists identify Count Giovanni Pico della Mirandola as their intellectual predecessor.[31]

Count Giovanni Pico della Mirandola (1463-1494)

Pico della Mirandola was an eclectic philosopher who sought to synthesize Greek, Hebrew, Muslim, and Christian thought.[32] When he was only twenty-four years old, he delivered his "Oration on the Dignity of Man" in Rome.[33] Russell Kirk contends that the "Oration lives as the most succinct

---

26 Frederick Copleston, S. J., *A History of Philosophy: Volume III: Late Medieval and Renaissance Philosophy* (New York: Doubleday, 1993), 207.
27 Ibid., 18.
28 Ibid., 18, 208-210.
29 Bostrom, "A History of Transhumanist Thought," 2.
30 Max More and Natasha Vita-More, *Transhumanist Reader*, 9.
31 Ibid., 2.
32 Giovanni Pico della Mirandola, translated by A. Robert Caponigri, *Oration on the Dignity of Man* (New York: Regnery Publishing, 1984), xii.
33 Ibid., xiii. Pico submitted 900 theses to Rome (three were close to heresy), but the disputation was forbidden by the ecclesiastical authorities. The "Oration" is considered the Preface to his larger work.

expression of the mind of the Renaissance;" other scholars refer to it as the manifesto of humanism.[34] In the "Oration," Pico expressed what he believed was the essence of humanism, that God gave Man great powers, and with those powers, free will, "to turn his faculties to the praise and improvement of noble human nature."[35] He describes God as the Supreme Maker who creates Man with an indeterminate image. "We have given you, Oh Adam," God says in Pico's view, "no visage proper to yourself, nor any endowment properly your own, in order that whatever place, whatever form, whatever gifts you may, with premeditation, select, these same you may have and possess through your own judgment and decision."[36] Pico argues against the deterministic view of human actions, believing that man has the free will to choose what he wills himself to be. He imagines God saying to man:

> I have placed you at the very center of the world, so that from that vantage point you may with greater ease glance round about you on all that the world contains. We have made you a creature neither of heaven nor of earth, neither mortal nor immortal, in order that you may, as the free and proud shaper of your own being, fashion yourself in the form you may prefer. It will be in your power to descend to the lower, brutish forms of life; you will be able, through your own decision, to rise again to the superior orders whose life is divine.[37]

Transhumanists disregard the Christian humanist view that the dignity of human nature is the gift of God. They prefer to interpret Pico's claim as support for their own anthropology, that man's nature is not to have a nature. We can be, rather, anything we decide to be.[38] Even though Pico did not seek to dethrone God, Russell Kirk notes, "the seeds of *hubris*" were sown, which in the end would become the aspiration of contemporary transhumanists. The goal of the Renaissance humanist was to become a truly noble human person. The transhumanist goal, in contrast, is endless expansion into higher forms that will replace the idea of God.[39] As Kirk

---

34   Giovanni Pico della Mirandola, translated by A. Robert Caponigri, *Oration on the Dignity of Man* (New York: Regnery Publishing, 1984), xi, xiii.
35   Ibid., xv.
36   Ibid., 7.
37   Ibid., 7-8.
38   Bostrom, "A History of Transhumanist Thought," 2.
39   Max More, "Transhumanism: Towards a Futurist Philosophy," (1996),

explains, "By the dignity of man, Pico della Mirandola meant the high nobility of disciplined reason and imagination, human nature as redeemed by Christ, the uplifting of the truly human person through an exercise of soul and mind. He did not mean technological triumph."[40] In Max More's words, transhumanism means: "No more gods, no more faith, no more timid holding back. Let us blast out of our old forms, our ignorance, our weakness, and our mortality. The future is ours."[41]

The English Renaissance

Francis Bacon (1561-1626)

Francis Bacon was a leading figure in natural philosophy in the transitional period between the Renaissance and the early modern era. He is best known for developing a new scientific methodology based on rigorous empirical observation, experimentation, and induction. He replaced Aristotle's ontological approach to nature with a much more narrow empirical approach.[42] This is not to say that Bacon refuted Aristotle's view, but instead sought to replace it with a new conception of knowledge. Max More sees Francis Bacon as a precursor to transhumanism, claiming, "The realization of transhumanist goals—or perhaps even the full articulation of the philosophy—would not be possible before the development and use of the scientific method."[43] More has even suggested that transhumanists should drop the Western Christian calendar for a new one in which year zero would be the year in which Bacon's famous work, the *Novum Organum*, was published."[44]

For Bacon, the true ends of knowledge were to aid man in exercising power to overcome the necessities and miseries of humanity.[45] This was an intentional departure from Aristotle's aim of wisdom, which was the result

---

more@extropy.org (accessed March 1, 2020), 6.

40 Mirandola, *Oration*, xvii.
41 More, "Transhumanism: Towards a Futurist Philosophy," 6.
42 Aristotle's ontological approach was concerned with the principles of being and the fundamental issues of causation, substance, essence, modality, identity, persistence, and teleology.
43 Max More and Natasha Vita-More, *The Transhumanist Reader*, 9.
44 Max More, "H+: True Transhumanism," *Metanexus* (February 5, 2009), https://metanexus.net/h-true-transhumanism/ (accessed March 4, 2020).
45 Francis Bacon, *The Great Instauration*, preface, *Constitution Society*, https://www.constitution.org/bacon/instauration.htm (accessed March 5, 2020).

of a theoretical understanding of the formal and final causes of Being. Bacon considered the search for formal and final causes to be a hindrance to natural philosophy, largely because he thought it was vain and unfruitful to the betterment of mankind.[46] Bacon's new methodology focused on real physical causes, meaning material and efficient causes, which were of value in extending human power over nature.[47] Bacon summarized his ideas with this aphorism: "Knowledge and human power are synonymous, since the ignorance of the cause frustrates the effect; for nature is only subdued by submission, and that which in contemplative philosophy corresponds with the cause, in practical science becomes the rule."[48] That is to say, the value of knowledge is measured by its practical productivity, meaning the practical applications of knowledge are the whole fruit of science. Contemporary transhumanist Max More epitomizes Bacon's dictum in his "Letter to Mother Nature" by vowing to conquer nature by means of science. By discovering nature's methods, transhumanists will be able to take nature's place to perform nature's methods for themselves.[49]

Transhumanists have a mechanistic picture of the world, meaning all of nature can be modeled after a machine. If you need to fix something, you take apart its components and find out the causal connections. Hence, for transhumanists, all problems can be solved scientifically, in an immediate quantifiable way. Bacon's experimental method reflects this mechanistic view of nature; he says this method actually "penetrates the more secret and remote parts of nature, in order to abstract both notions and axioms from things by a more certain and guarded method."[50]

It is obvious why transhumanists see Francis Bacon as a pivotal figure in their ideological history. Like none before him, Bacon symbolizes the three core tenets of transhumanism: a desire to control nature and human persons, a mechanistic picture of the world, and a technological view of progress. The transhumanist projects to remake humans with emerging

---

46   Francis Bacon, "The Advancement of Learning," in Mortimer Adler, editor, *The Great Books of the Western World, Vol. 28* (Chicago: Encyclopedia Britannica, Inc., 1990, 17.

47   Francis Bacon, "Novum Organum," in Mortimer Adler, editor, *The Great Books of the Western World, Vol. 28* (Chicago: Encyclopedia Britannica, Inc. 1990), 107.

48   Ibid.

49   Max More and Natasha Vita-More, eds., *Transhumanist Reader*, 449-450.

50   Bacon, "Novum Organum," 108.

technologies are seen as the ultimate fruit of the power of scientific knowledge that Bacon championed.

Rene Descartes (1596-1650) and early scientists

Descartes expanded on Bacon's mechanistic view in his *Treatise of Man*, wherein he compares the working machine of the body to a clock's movements. He writes, "I desire you to consider, I say, that these functions imitate those of a real man as perfectly as possible and that they follow naturally in this machine entirely from the disposition of the organs—no more nor less than do the movements of a clock or other automaton, from the arrangement of its counterweights and wheels."[51] Descartes believed that the mechanistic knowledge of the material world, including the human body, could be employed and adapted to make mankind "masters and possessors of nature."[52]

Following Bacon and Descartes, other early scientists and philosophers rejected the Aristotelian philosophy of nature and replaced it with a picture of the universe as a vast machine. On this view, the world is rational, knowable, explainable, open to study, and the human body is part of that machinery. Philosopher Edward Feser says of this view, "All natural objects are essentially the same one kind of thing, namely fundamental particles in different configurations."[53] To be clear, Aristotle did not deny that the universe and natural objects are in some respects machine-like. But for the Greek philosopher, this is only part of a complete explanation. For Aristotle, Feser explains, "to be part of the "natural" order of things *just is to* have a substantial form and intrinsic teleology."[54] The mechanistic view is a sharp departure from Aristotle's view because, for him, nature is strictly *not* a machine, despite the superficial similarities. No one downplays the scientific achievements that have resulted from this mechanistic point of view, but it is legitimate to take exception when this view is set up as the absolute and all-sufficient form of explanation. In the chapters that follow, I will explain how bringing the whole of human nature under a materialistic ontology is a philosophical mistake and has created recalcitrant

---

51   Rene Descartes, translated by Thomas Steele Hall, *Treatise of Man* (New York: Prometheus Books, 2003), 113.

52   Rene Descartes, *Discourse on Method*, in Mortimer Adler, editor, *The Great Books of the Western World, Volume 28* (Chicago: Encyclopedia Britannica, 1990), 285.

53   Edward Feser, *Aristotle's Revenge: The Metaphysical Foundations of Physical and Biological Science* (Germany: editiones scholasticae, 2019), 46.

54   Ibid., 43.

problems in contemporary philosophy of mind and anthropology that cannot be solved by materialism.

The Enlightenment

Denis Diderot (1713-1784) and Jean LeRond d'Alembert (1717-1783)

Transhumanist James Hughes credits Francis Bacon's work as the beginning of the Enlightenment, a period from the late seventeenth to nineteenth century, characterized by an ambition for intellectual and scientific knowledge in order to empower humans to improve society and their individual lives.[55] The crowning work that represents Enlightenment thought is the twenty-eight volume French *Encyclopédie* (1751-1772), edited by Denis Diderot and Jean LeRond d'Alembert. It aimed to be "a reference work for all topics related to the arts and sciences—and to be a militant undertaking, spreading Enlightenment ideas in order to found a new order of things."[56] Inspired by Bacon's emphasis on the practical uses of scientific knowledge, the *Encyclopédie* was the first of its kind to describe and systematize the mechanical arts, what is now called technology, which they thought had been a neglected subject compared to science. They hoped to bring to light the hidden ideas of technology and to encourage research in the mechanical arts. In the *Preliminary Discourse to the Encyclopédie*, Diderot and d'Alembert express their dismay that the names of inventors, the benefactors of mankind, are almost all unknown, whereas conquerors are known to everyone. Their goal was to bring the inventor's names to the public's attention.[57] Perhaps their desire to honor inventors was partly inspired by Bacon's novel *New Atlantis*. On Bacon's fictional utopian island of Bensalem, the ruling scientific elite are devoted to the study and practical

---

[55] James Hughes, "The Politics of Transhumanism and the Tecno-Millennial Imagination, 1626-2030," *Zygon Journal*, Vol. 47, 759 (December 2012), *Wiley Online Library*, https://onlinelibrary.wiley.com/doi/abs/10.1111/j.1467-9744.2012.01289.x (accessed March 6, 2020).

[56] Diderot and D'Alembert, Encyclopédie, "Bulletin," *Classiques Garnier*, https://classiques-garnier.com/editions-bulletins/Encyclopedie_Diderot_D-Alembert_WEB.pdf, (accessed March 6, 2020).

[57] Jean-Baptiste Le Rond d'Alembert, *Preliminary Discourse to the Encyclopedie*, Richard N. Schwab and Walter E. Rex, translators (Ann Arbor, Michigan: University of Michigan Library, 2009), https://quod.lib.umich.edu/d/did/did2222.0001.083/--preliminary-discourse?rgn=main;view=-fulltext;q1=Jean+Pestre (accessed March 7, 2020).

application of science. They have a prestigious gallery displaying the statues of all the principal inventors in history.[58]

Denis Diderot was a committed materialist and an atheist by the time he wrote his two works *Conversation between D'Alembert and Diderot and D'Alembert's Dream* (1769).[59] In both works, which are creative dialogues, he expresses a mechanistic, materialistic, and atheistic view of the origin of the universe, the human body, psychology, and morality.[60] He also suggests radical ideas, such as a theory of evolution, the possibility of deliberate eugenic experiments, and animal-human hybrids. He held firmly to his revolutionary views, amidst conservative criticism and government censorship; his boldness even led to his arrest and imprisonment at Vincennes for three months.[61]

Marquis de Condorcet (1743-1794)

French Enlightenment thinker Marquis de Condorcet promoted the ideas of power over human nature, indefinite progress, and extended lifespans. In his 1795 book *Outlines of an Historical View of the Progress of the Human Mind*, Condorcet reveals a Baconian optimism about a future that links knowledge with power over nature:

> May it not be expected that the human race will be meliorated by new discoveries in the sciences and the arts, and, as an unavoidable consequence, in the means of individual and general prosperity; by farther progress in the principles of conduct, and in moral practice; and lastly, by the real improvement of our faculties, moral, intellectual and physical, which may be the result either of the improvement of the instruments which increase the power and direct the exercise of those faculties, or of the improvement of our natural organization itself?[62]

---

58 Francis Bacon, *New Atlantis*, in Mortimer Adler, editor, *The Great Books of the Western World, Volume 28* (Chicago: Encyclopedia Britannica, 1990), 214.

59 Denis Diderot, *Rameau's Nephew/D'Alembert's Dream*, translated by Leonard Tancock (London: Penguin Books, 1966), 137-138.

60 Ibid., 137-233.

61 Mortimer Adler, editor, "Denis Diderot," in *Great Books of the Western World, Volume 34* (Chicago: Encyclopedia Britannica, Inc., 1990), 254.

62 Marquis de Condorcet, *Sketch for a Historical Picture of the Progress of the Human Mind: Tenth Epoch*, translated by Keith Michael Baker. *Daedalus*, 133, no.3, 2004. http://www.jstor.org/stable/20027931 (accessed March 1, 2020).

Condorcet died before this book was published, but it became the inspiration for future generations of thinkers in their understanding of the idea of progress and human enhancement. It is important to notice that his vision for the future is about improving the material, physical, and moral conditions of humanity. But in no way is he advocating the transhumanist goal of ending humanity in order to usher in a new species of posthumans. In addition, his view of progress does not necessarily mean immortality:

> Would it even be absurd to suppose this quality of melioration in the human species as susceptible of an indefinite advancement; to suppose that a period must one day arrive when death will be nothing more than the effect either of extraordinary accidents, or of the slow and gradual decay of the vital powers; and that the duration of the middle space, of the interval between the birth of man and this decay, will itself have no assignable limit? Certainly man will not become immortal; but may not the distance between the moment in which he draws his first breath, and the common term when, in the course of nature, without malady or accident, he finds it impossible any longer to exist, be necessarily protracted?[63]

Even though transhumanists laud Condorcet's progressive vision of the future, he is not as radical as the transhumanists in their view of perpetual progress. To this point, philosopher George Santayana (1863-1952) says, "Progress, far from consisting in change, depends on retentiveness. When change is absolute there remains no being to improve and no direction is set for possible improvement; and when experience is not retained, as among savages, infancy is perpetual. Those who cannot remember the past are condemned to repeat it."[64] On Santayana's view, transhumanism's progress toward a posthuman species represents absolute change with no being, or self, left to improve.

At the core of transhumanist thought is the importance of the individual self that wills self-transformation, which is rooted in Renaissance indi-

---

63   Marquis de Condorcet, *Sketch for a Historical Picture of the Progress of the Human Mind: Tenth Epoch*, translated by Keith Michael Baker. *Daedalus*, 286, no.3, 2004. http://www.jstor.org/stable/20027931 (accessed March 1, 2020)

64   George Santayana, *The Life of Reason or The Phases of Human Progress* (New York: Charles Scribner's Sons, 1906), 284, quoted in Charles T. Rubin, *Eclipse of Man: Human Extinction and the Meaning of Progress* (New York: New Atlantis Books, 2014), 43.

vidualism and the concept of individual rights from the Enlightenment. Although transhumanists consider themselves as ideological descendents of the Enlightenment, their project for radical enhancements reveals a metaphysical problem of the self and personal identity. In chapter four, we will investigate transhumanism's philosophy of human persons and their "patternist" view of the self, but for now I suggest that their materialistic view of the self is not sufficient to account for personal identity over time.[65]

Nineteenth Century

Charles Darwin (1809-1882)

The transhumanists understand and filter their Enlightenment ideas of rationality, the scientific method, individual rights, and progress, through an evolutionary lens. Darwin's explanation of his naturalistic theory in his 1859 *Origin of Species* made it plausible for transhumanists to view the current version of humanity as an early phase, rather than the endpoint of evolution. In his theory of biological evolution, Charles Darwin concluded that humans gradually evolved by natural selection sifting random natural variations from the lower animals. Natural species, then, are not fixed.[66] His theory abandons the traditional notion that human beings are uniquely created by God with a fixed nature and purpose by reducing "the organic and human world" to the physical laws governing the inorganic universe.[67]

"If human beings are constituted of matter obeying the same laws of physics," writes transhumanist Nick Bostrom, "then it should, in principle, be possible to learn to manipulate human nature the same way we manipulate external objects."[68] Simon Young describes transhumanism as "Designer Evolution," meaning human beings are the creative designers, recognizing and enhancing their own physical form by manipulating biological material. Designer Evolution is to Darwinism as a fashion design-

---

65 Susan Schneider, "Future Minds: Transhumanism, Cognitive Enhancement and the Nature of Persons," *Neuroethics Publications*, (July 1, 2008), 1-14, https://repository.upenn.edu/cgi/viewcontent.cgi?article=1037&context=neuroethics_pubs (accessed March 8, 2020).

66 Charles Darwin, *Descent or Origin of Man*, in Mortimer Adler, editor, *Great Books of the Western World, Volume 49* (Chicago: Encyclopedia Britannica, Inc., 1990), 253.

67 Victor Ferkiss, *Nature, Technology, and Society: Cultural Roots of the Current Environmental Crisis* (New York: New York University Press, 1993), 59.

68 Bostrom, "A History of Transhumanist Thought," 4.

er is to a blind, amateur seamstress.[69] Ironically, transhumanists accept blind evolution as man's origin, but reject it for man's future.

Frederich Nietzsche (1844-1900)

Another nineteenth century predecessor of transhumanism is Frederich Nietzsche. Even though Bostrom claims that there are only superficial similarities between the posthuman and the Nietzschean vision of the Ubermensch, or overman, Max More maintains that Nietzsche directly influenced his early thinking about transhumanism. There are Nietzschean quotes and concepts in More's seminal essay "Transhumanism: Towards a Futurist Philosophy" and his original transhumanist statement, "The Principles of Extropy."[70] Nietzsche's doctrine of the will-to-power in human beings suggests that by self-transformation the human species will evolve.[71] Nietzsche's character Zarathustra declares, "And life itself confided this secret to me: 'Behold,' it said, 'I am that which must always overcome itself.'"[72] In his essay "Why I Am So Wise," Nietzsche says, "My humanity is a constant self-overcoming."[73]

In Max More's essay on transhumanism, he quotes Nietzsche's character Zarathustra to challenge the contemporary religionist, "I teach you the overman. Man is something that is to be overcome. What have you done to overcome him?" Transhumanists resonate strongly with the Nietzschean image of humanity's self-overcoming through their will-to-power. More reasons that, even though Nietzsche had little to say about technology, he

---

69 Young, *Designer Evolution*, 27-30, 305.

70 Max More, "Transhumanism: Towards a Futurist Philosophy," *Scribd*, 1990, https://www.scribd.com/doc/257580713/Transhumanism-Toward-a-Futurist-Philosophy, (accessed March 8, 2020); Max More, "Principles of Extropy," Humanity+ pedia, 1990, https://hpluspedia.org/wiki/Extropian_principles#1990_Original_Extropian_Principles, (accessed March 8, 2020). More's four principles of extropy are: boundless expansion, self-transformation, dynamic optimism, and intelligent technology.

71 Frederich Nietzsche, "Guilt, Bad Conscience, and the Like," *On the Genealogy of Morals and Ecce Homo*, translated by Walter Kaufmann and R. J. Hollingdale (New York: Vintage Books, 1989), 78-9.

72 Frederich Nietzsche, "Thus Spake Zarathustra: Part II Self-Surpassing," *Gutenberg.org*, https://www.gutenberg.org/files/1998/1998-h/1998-h.htm#link2H_4_0040 (accessed on March 9, 2020).

73 Frederich Nietzsche, "Why I Am So Wise," *On the Genealogy of Morals and Ecce Homo*, translated by Walter Kaufmann and R. J. Hollingdale (New York: Vintage Books, 1989), 233.

would likely be enthusiastic about using current technologies as a means of self-overcoming.[74] He also agrees with Nietzsche that nihilism is merely a transitional stage that will be left behind.[75] Nietzsche's vision of the overman was meant to provide meaning for scientifically minded people who had abandoned belief in God and the afterlife.[76] Similarly, More offers a transhumanist vision of the posthuman to give meaning to scientifically-minded people today.[77]

Twentieth Century

Transhumanists trace their most recent history to three British scientists, sometimes referred to as the prophets of transhumanism: John Burdon Sanderson Haldane (1892-1964), John Desmond Bernal (1901-1971), and Sir Julian Sorell Huxley (1887-1975).[78] Transhumanists embrace the futuristic insights of these British scientists, but are quick to make disclaimers, since all three are associated with the eugenics movement of the early twentieth century. Transhumanists unequivocally condemn the eugenics crimes perpetrated by the racist Nazi totalitarian regime, yet it is still evident they agree with the underlying aim of eugenics, which is "to use scientific methods to make the best of the inherited component for the health and wellbeing of the children of the next generation."[79] After all, transhumanists are working to bring about a new era where scientists can modify DNA to rewrite the code of nature and ultimately create new genetic species.[80]

---

74   Max More, "The Overhuman in the Transhuman," *Journal of Evolution & Technology*, Vol. 21, Issue 1 (January 2010), 3, https://jetpress.org/v21/more.htm (accessed March 8, 2020).
75   Ibid., 2.
76   Nietzsche, "Thus Spake Zarathustra," 309.
77   Ibid., 2.
78   Hava Tirosh-Samuelson, "Engaging Transhumanism," in Gregory R. Hansell and William Grassie, editors, *H+/-: Transhumanism & Its Critics* (Philadelphia: Metanexus Institute, 2011), 20-21.
79   Alison Bashford, "Where Did Eugenics Go?" in Alison Bashford and Philippa Levine, editors, *The Oxford Handbook of the History of Eugenics* (New York: Oxford University Press, 2010), 541.
80   Rachel Armstrong, "Alternative Biologies," in Max More and Natasha Vita-More, editors, *The Transhumanist Reader* (West Sussex, UK: John Wiley & Sons, Inc., 2013), 103.

Transhumanists distance themselves from past eugenics by stressing the importance of liberal individualism. For example, "The Transhumanist Declaration" states their opposition to authoritarian social control and their promotion of decentralization of power and respect for individual autonomy and rights.[81] In Nick Bostrom's "Transhumanist Values," he opposes "centrally planned efforts to create better people (e.g., the eugenics movement and Soviet totalitarianism), which shows that we need to be wary of collective decision-making in the field of human modification."[82] Even though transhumanists advocate individual rights in their official rhetoric, it will be made clear in subsequent chapters that transhumanists find it increasingly difficult to defend individual rights as their techno-utopian projects progress.

Transhumanists repudiate Nazi eugenics as if that period represents the totality of eugenics history. But, as historian Alison Bashford argues, "Eugenics functioned as often through liberal governments, as it did through authoritarian coercion, arguably more so."[83] Certainly the experience of Nazism reduced the attractiveness of eugenic policies, but there was no sudden abandonment of eugenics ideology after World War II. For example, existing eugenic journals continued to publish after 1945. They just changed their titles: *Eugenics Quarterly* changed its name to *Social Biology* and *The Eugenics Review* was renamed the *Journal of Biosocial Science*.[84] There is a continuous history of eugenics, but it is usually divided into two eras. The first era (1870-1950) is called "old eugenics" and the current era

---

81   "The Transhumanist Declaration," (March 2009), *Humanityplus.org*, https://humanityplus.org/philosophy/transhumanist-declaration/ (accessed March 9, 2020). Principle #6 states, "Policy making ought to be guided by responsible and inclusive moral vision, taking seriously both opportunities and risks, respecting autonomy and individual rights, and showing solidarity with and concern for the interests and dignity of all people around the globe. We must also consider our moral responsibilities towards generations that will exist in the future."

82   Nick Bostrom, "Transhumanist Values," *Review of Contemporary Philosophy*, Vol. 4, (May 2005), https://www.nickbostrom.com/ethics/values.html (accessed March 9, 2020). Principle #5 Derivative Values.

83   Alison Bashford, "Julian Huxley's Transhumanism," in Marius Turda, editor, *Crafting Humans: From Genesis to Eugenics and Beyond* (Goettingen: V & R Unipress, 2013), 154-5.

84   Alison Bashford, "Where Did Eugenics Go?" in Alison Bashford and Philippa Levine, editors, *The Oxford Handbook of The History of Eugenics* (New York: Oxford University Press, 2010), 542.

(1950-present) is called "new genetics," reflecting the advent of molecular biology.[85] Spanning the gap between the two eras, the works of Haldane, Bernal, and Huxley link the ideology of eugenics with contemporary transhumanism.

John Burdon Sanderson Haldane (1892-1964)

Population geneticist J. B. S. Haldane taught that our future society could be shaped by eugenics and saw the biologist, or today's genetic engineer, "as the most romantic figure on earth at the present day."[86] In 1923, he envisioned advancements in biology that would be the beginning of humans directing their own evolution for their benefit. He prophesied that negative eugenics would prevent the transmission of diseases like syphilis and insanity and progress in medicine would eradicate infectious diseases.[87] He foretold the invention of ectogenesis, now called in vitro fertilization, which would make selective breeding possible.[88] Haldane realized that his prophecies appeared "indecent and unnatural," but he firmly believed that biological inventions "begin as a perversion and end as a ritual supported by unquestioned beliefs and prejudices."[89] This must be an encouragement to transhumanists as they wait for their futuristic ideas to be fully appreciated. They respect Haldane as a visionary who was convinced that scientific knowledge would continue to progress and revolutionize human life.

John Desmond Bernal (1901-1971)

J.D. Bernal, Haldane's colleague, was a crystallographer and molecular biologist who imagined a similar future where science would transform all aspects of society. In his 1929 book *The World, the Flesh, and the Devil*, he anticipated that the mechanism of evolution would be superseded by directly altering the "germ plasm," a process now called genetic engineering, to "perhaps even manage to produce new species with special potentialities."[90] He expected that men would eventually conquer and colonize space

---

85   Alison Bashford, "Where Did Eugenics Go?" in Alison Bashford and Philippa Levine, editors, *The Oxford Handbook of The History of Eugenics* (New York: Oxford University Press, 2010), 541.

86   J. B. S. Haldane, "Daedalus: or Science and the Future," A paper read to the Heretics, Cambridge, on February 4th, 1923, Marxists.org, https://www.marxists.org/archive/haldane/works/1920s/daedalus.htm (accessed March 11, 2020).

87   Ibid., 12-13.

88   Ibid., 14.

89   Ibid., 10-11.

90   J. D. Bernal, *The World, the Flesh, and the Devil*, (1929) Marxist.org,

in genetically modified cyborg bodies.[91] Breaking with organic evolution, the cyborg man would replace organs and limbs with artificial mechanical parts.[92] Bernal pictured a final state where bodies are left behind. Only the most important organ, the brain, would be preserved with its nerve connections, immersed in a cylinder of cerebro-spinal fluid.[93] It could then be possible to connect the brains of two or more people to form a compound brain for co-operative thinking.[94]

Transhumanists imagine a similar future, including rewriting our DNA by genetic engineering, space colonization, cyborg bodies, post-biological mind uploading, brain-machine interfacing, the Global Brain, and the creation of a post-human species.[95] Bernal argued that his beliefs about the future were not pure speculation, but rather based on his "analysis of causes acting in the present."[96] The fundamental causes that informed Bernal's views of the future were the constant development and application of knowledge, religion being replaced with science, and man's desires being seen as the chief agent of change in the universe.[97] It is as if transhumanists use Bernal's playbook to explain the reasons for their views, which are likewise based on powerful emerging technologies and man's desire to improve the human condition through applied reason and science.[98]

Sir Julian Sorell Huxley (1887-1975)

The third prophet of transhumanism, evolutionary biologist Sir Julian Huxley, is the closest ideological antecedent to contemporary transhumanism, not only because he is credited with coining the term "transhumanism," but also because Huxley considered himself the midwife of transhumanism, delivering a new ideology to the world.[99] In his 1957 book

---

https://www.marxists.org/archive/bernal/works/1920s/soul/, chapters 3 "The Flesh," (accessed March 11, 2020).

91 J. D. Bernal, *The World, the Flesh, and the Devil*, (1929) Marxist.org, https://www.marxists.org/archive/bernal/works/1920s/soul/, chapters 2 "The World" and 3 "The Flesh," (accessed March 11, 2020).

92 Bernal, *The World, the Flesh, and the Devil*, chapter 3, "The Flesh."

93 Ibid.

94 Ibid.

95 Max More and Natasha Vita-More, *The Transhumanist Reader*, 103, 235, 113-114, 131-2, 4.

96 Bernal, *The World, the Flesh, and the Devil*, chapter 6, "Possibility."

97 Bernal, *The World, the Flesh, and the Devil*, chapter 1, "The Future."

98 Max More and Natasha Vita-More, *The Transhumanist Reader*, 3-4.

99 Julian Huxley, *New Bottles For New Wine* (New York: Harper & Brothers

New Bottles for New Wine, Huxley developed the idea of transhumanism, which he describes this way:

> The human species can, if it wishes, transcend itself—not just sporadically . . . but in its entirety, as humanity. We need a name for this new belief. Perhaps transhumanism will serve; man remaining man, but transcending himself, by realizing new possibilities of and for his human nature. "I believe in transhumanism": once there are enough people who can truly say that, the human species will be on the threshold of a new kind of existence, as different from ours as ours is from that of Pekin man. It will at last be consciously fulfilling its real destiny.[100]

While some hold that humanity is the climax of evolution, Huxley argued that modern man is not the final product of evolution, but only a temporary phase in the process.[101] He announced a new categorical imperative, "that man's destiny, his duty and privilege in one, is to continue in his own person the advance of the cosmic process of evolution."[102] Extending Huxley's imperative, transhumanists suggest that parents have a moral duty to use genetic engineering methods to ensure their child-to-be will be as healthy as possible.[103] David Pearce implies something similar in his book *The Hedonistic Imperative*, where he writes, "Future parents who decide, whether in deference to God or Nature, to decline gene-therapy for a child they know will likely grow up depressive, for example, may be open to accusations of child-abuse."[104]

Owing to Huxley's view of man as a "highly imperfect creature, carrying a heavy burden of genetic defects and imperfections," eugenics plays a central role in advancing the human species; negative eugenics for preventing the spread of defective genes and positive eugenics for raising human and

---

Publishers, 1957), 17, 256, 259, 260.

100 Julian Huxley, *New Bottles For New Wine* (New York: Harper & Brothers Publishers, 1957), 17.

101 Ibid., 44-45.

102 Ibid., 103.

103 "Why transhumanists advocate human enhancement as ethical rather than pre-WWII eugenics?" Transhumanist FAQ, *Humanityplus.org.*, https://humanityplus.org/philosophy/transhumanist-faq/,(accessed March 13, 2020).

104 David Pearce, *The Hedonistic Imperative* (available online), chapter 3, Section 3.3 "Good Code Gets Better," https://www.hedweb.com/hedethic/hedon3.htm#code (accessed March 1, 2020).

performance to a new level.¹⁰⁵ Huxley took great pains to distance his views from the unscientific doctrine of Nazi eugenics based on race. He argued against it in three official documents, all of which he either authored or signed: "'Race' in Europe" (1936), "The Geneticists' Manifesto" (1939), and "UNESCO: Its Purpose and its Philosophy" (1946).¹⁰⁶ Transhumanists, likewise, condemn coercive eugenic policies and strongly reject any policies based on racialist and classist assumptions.¹⁰⁷ This seems motivated by pragmatism since this kind of moral stance has no basis in their materialist philosophy. Still, they realize that state-sponsored coercive eugenics is not culturally acceptable.

Huxley was still a lifelong champion of eugenics as an agenda for social reform. In the "Geneticists' Manifesto," he advocated for legalization and development of birth control, voluntary sterilization, contraception, abortion, and artificial insemination¹⁰⁸ and eugenic insemination by deliberately preferred donors (E.I.D.).¹⁰⁹ Unlike Huxley, transhumanists prefer to aim their enhancement projects toward individuals rather than toward society as a whole.

For man to fulfill his destiny, Huxley thought people would need to be convinced that science is the gateway for securing knowledge and human

---

105   Julian Huxley, *Evolutionary Humanism* (New York: Prometheus Books, 1992), 268.

106   Julian Huxley, "'Race' in Europe," (1936), Rare Books and Manuscripts, https://digital.kenyon.edu/rarebooks/16 (accessed March 13, 2020); "The Geneticists' Manifesto," 1939, The Seventh International Congress of Genetics in Edinburgh, *And You Haven't Seen Anything Yet...*, https://sniadecki.wordpress.com/2015/01/19/thegeneticists-manifesto-1939/ (accessed March 12, 2020), Signers of the Manifesto: A. E. Crew, J. S. Huxley, J. B. S. Haldane, H. J. Müller, S. C. Harland. J, Needham, L. T. Hogben, P. Child, C. L. Huskins, P. R. David, W. Landaurer, G. Dahlberg, H. H. Plough, Th. Dobzhansky, E. Price, R. A. Emerson, J. Schultz, C. Gordon, A. G. Steinberg, John Hammond, C. H. Waddington; Julian Huxley, "UNESCO: Its Purpose and Its Philosophy," UNESCO.org, UNESDOC Digital Library, https://unesdoc.unesco.org/ark:/48223/pf0000068197 (accessed March 13, 2020).

107   "Why transhumanists advocate human enhancement as ethical rather than pre-WWII eugenics?" Transhumanist FAQ, *Humanityplus.org.*, https://humanityplus.org/philosophy/transhumanist-faq/ (accessed March 13, 2020).

108   "The Geneticists' Manifesto," 1939, The Seventh International Congress of Genetics in Edinburgh, *And You Haven't Seen Anything Yet...*, https://sniadecki.wordpress.com/2015/01/19/thegeneticists-manifesto-1939/ (accessed March 12, 2020).

109   Huxley, *Evolutionary Humanism*, 272.

progress. He pointed to Francis Bacon and his successors as exemplars of the scientific outlook, which embraces a desire to control nature, a mechanistic picture of the world, and a technological view of progress. Huxley described Bacon's scientific outlook this way:

> [Bacon's] primary idea of science is . . . the idea that by investigating natural phenomena, however apparently insignificant, men could attain new realms of knowledge and acquire new possibilities of control over nature—together with the general idea resulting from Newton's great work—the conception of the physical universe as a machine—those ideas so dominated the general attitude and so transformed the intellectual climate that it was natural for people to think technologically, in terms of inventing new techniques for the better handling of old problems, and of a general extension of man's control over nature.[110]

Within a decade of Huxley's challenge for people to adopt a scientific outlook, a 1960's group known as the Up-Wingers had formed based on that very idea.

Contemporary Transhumanism

F. M Esfandiary (1930-2000)

The Up-Wingers were founded by F. M. Esfandiary, who legally changed his name to FM-2030 in the mid-1970's to reflect his confidence that he would be alive in the year 2030. Esfandiary was a professor of future studies at the New School for Social Research in New York, who enticed a select group with his transhumanist ideas by calling attention to the possibility and desirability of using science and technology to advance human evolution.[111]

In Esfandiary's 1973 book *Up-Wingers: A Futurist Manifesto*, he touted the promise of scientific progress and the resulting benefits to humanity. His vision of the future sounds very much like the futures depicted by Haldane, Bernal, and Huxley in the 1920's, except Esfandiary's future seems more attainable because of the advances underway in biology, genetics, physics, astronomy, medicine, and computer science. He advocated redesigning our bodies by genetic engineering, becoming cyborgs by incorporating

---

110   Huxley, *New Bottles for New Wine*, 255.
111   Bostrom, "A History of Transhumanist Thought," 13.

machine replacements, overcoming death, cryonics, evolving beyond our bodies to become posthuman, and space colonization.[112]

Esfandiary enthusiastically promoted eugenics saying, "Human life is too precious to leave to chance . . . We must give each newborn a chance to start life with healthy genes."[113] His ideal future society was more extreme than his predecessors because he thought marriage and family should be eliminated. Esfandiary pictured children genetically engineered from embryos, grown in artificial wombs, and cared for in Child Center Homes.[114] His aim was Universal Planned Procreation and Universal Life: "Let every newborn belong biologically and socially to the whole world."[115] FM-2030 died of pancreatic cancer at the age of sixty-nine, but his body is frozen using vitrification at the Alcor Life Extension Foundation in Arizona where he is waiting to be reawakened when science has advanced enough to restore him to good health.[116]

Robert Ettinger (1918-2011)

Robert Ettinger, the Father of Cryonics, launched the cryonics movement with his 1964 book *The Prospect of Immortality*, which appealed to a wide audience. In it, he explained that at very low temperatures it is possible to preserve the dead with essentially no deterioration, indefinitely.[117] Ettinger was convinced that it was only a matter of time before science would succeed in reaching the goal of physical immortality. However, since some of us do not have much time, a cryonics program should be implemented so that we can be rescued after we die.[118] People responded positively and in 1976, he founded the Cryonics Institute, whose mission is to extend human lifespans by preserving the body using existing cryogenic technol-

---

112 F. M. Esfandiary, *Up-Wingers: A Futurist Manifesto*, (1973), E-Reads, https://slowlorisblog.files.wordpress.com/2015/05/esfandiary-up-wingers-a-futurist-manifesto.pdf, (accessed on March 13, 2020).

113 Esfandiary, *Up-Wingers*, Part 2, "Beyond Family: Universal Life."

114 Ibid.

115 Ibid.

116 Douglas Martin, "Futurist Known as FM-2030 Dead at 69," *The New York Times* (July 11), 2000, https://www.nytimes.com/2000/07/11/us/futurist-known-as-fm-2030-is-dead-at-69.html (accessed March 14, 2020).

117 Robert Ettinger, *The Prospect of Immortality*, 1962, cryonics.org, https://www.cryonics.org/images/uploads/misc/Prospect_Book.pdf (accessed March 14, 2020), 11.

118 Robert Ettinger, *Man to Superman: The Startling Potential of Human Evolution—and How to Be Part of It* (New York: St. Martin's Press, 1972), 280.

ogies with the goal of revival by future science.[119] Ettinger died in 2011 at the age of ninety-two and his body is frozen at the Cryonics Institute.[120] By making his ideas about immortality and cryonics accessible to the public, Ettinger laid the groundwork for contemporary transhumanism.

Max More

In 1988, philosopher and transhumanist Max More, with T. O Morrow, published the first transhumanist magazine called *Extropy: Vaccine for Future Shock*, later renamed *The Journal of Transhumanist Thought*. The term extropy expresses the opposite of entropy and is a metaphor meaning "a drive for improvement."[121] In 1990, More articulated the transhumanist philosophy in his "Principles of Extropy," which provides a basic framework of seven precepts for improving the human condition: perpetual progress, self-transformation, practical optimism, intelligent technology, open society, self-direction, and rational thinking.[122]

More founded the Extropy Institute in 1991, a transhumanist think tank based on his 1990 definition of transhumanism: "A philosophy of life (such as an extropian perspective) that seeks the continuation and acceleration of the evolution of intelligent life beyond its currently human form and human limitations by means of science and technology, guided by life-promoting principles and values."[123] After Eric Drexler introduced the concept of nanotechnology in his book *Engines of Creation* in 1986, explaining the possibility of repairing cell damage caused from freezing, the Alcor Life Extension Foundation, a cryonics non-profit organization, began to gain attention and members. Max More became the President and Chief Executive Officer of Alcor in 2011.

---

119 Cryonics Institute, https://www.cryonics.org/about-us (accessed March 15, 2020).

120 Emma Brown, "Robert Ettinger, founder of the cryonics movement, dies at 92," (July 24, 2011), *The Washington Post*, https://www.washingtonpost.com/local/obituaries/from-phyics-teacher-to-founder-of-the-cryonics-movement/2011/07/24/gIQAupuIXI_story.html (accessed on March 14, 2020).

121 Max More, "The Philosophy of Transhumanism," in Max More and Natasha Vita-More, editors, *The Transhumanist Reader*, 5.

122 Max More, "The Extropian Principles 3.0," (1998), *extropy.org*, https://mrob.com/pub/religion/Extro_prin.html (accessed March 15, 2020).

123 Max More, "The Philosophy of Transhumanism," in *Transhumanist Reader*, 3.

Nick Bostrom and David Pearce

With the growth of transhumanism, various organizations formed across America, such as FM-2030's UpWingers, Max More's Extropians, and Eric Drexler's Foresight Institute. In 1998, British philosophers Nick Bostrom and David Pearce founded the World Transhumanist Association (WTA) to bring transhumanists together under one organization that reflected the same central themes, values, and identity. In 2008, they rebranded WTA as Humanity Plus to project a more humane image. It currently boasts 6,000 members from more than 100 countries.[124] Nick Bostrom also serves as the director of the Future of Humanity Institute at Oxford University and utilitarian David Pearce seeks to abolish suffering through genetic engineering and nanotechnology.

The Transhumanist Declaration, originally crafted in 1998, reflects Max More's Extropian Principles by promoting the use of science and technology to "broaden human potential by overcoming aging, cognitive shortcomings, involuntary suffering, and our confinement to planet Earth."[125] Humanity Plus organizes an annual TransVision conference and in 1998, established the publication of a peer-reviewed academic online journal called the Journal of Evolution and Technology.[126] While Humanity Plus gathers together the broad currents of the transhumanist movement, other organizations exist for particular transhumanist issues, such as life extension, nanotechnology, artificial intelligence, and the Singularity (which I explain below).[127]

Transhumanists expect radical enhancements in human cognition with the extension of technology into the domain of thought. They look to advancements in artificial intelligence to not only provide human-machine interfaces, but also to develop artificial general intelligence, which are machines with human-level intelligence or better.[128] Artificial Intelli-

---

[124] "About Humanityplus," *Humanityplus.org*, https://humanityplus.org/about/ (accessed March 15, 2020).

[125] "The Transhumanist Declaration," *Humanityplus.org*, https://humanityplus.org/philosophy/transhumanist-declaration/ (accessed March 15, 2020).

[126] Journal of Evolution and Technology, *jetpress*, https://www.jetpress.org/ (accessed March 15, 2020).

[127] See Appendix A for a list of transhumanist related institutions and organizations.

[128] Ben Goertzel, "Artificial General Intelligence and the Future of Humanity," in Max More and Natasha Vita-More, editors, *The Transhumanist Reader*, 128.

gence researchers and futurists such as Marvin Minsky,[129] Ray Kurzweil,[130] Eric Drexler,[131] Frank Tipler,[132] and Hans Moravec[133] express transhumanist themes alongside their overall goal of creating an autonomous, artificially intelligent species.

Vernor Vinge and Ray Kurzweil

The idea of a rapid acceleration in technological change that leads to an artificial intelligence explosion is referred to as the technological Singularity.[134] The technological Singularity, as opposed to a singularity in physics, is the point at which a greater-than-human machine intelligence, multiplying exponentially, would make everything about our world unpredictable.[135] Transhumanists generally agree that mathematician and computer scientist Vernor Vinge is one of the first to propose the idea of a techno-utopian Singularity event.[136] Vinge's presentation at the 1993 VISION-21 Symposium, which was sponsored by NASA, was entitled "The Coming Technological Singularity: How to Survive in the Post-Human Era."[137] He described the Singularity as a time when "greater-than-human intelligence drives progress, and that progress will be much more rapid. In fact, there seems no reason why progress itself would not involve the creation of still more intelligent entities—on a still-shorter time scale."[138]

---

[129] See Marvin Minsky, *The Emotion Machine: Commonsense Thinking, Artificial Intelligence, and the Future of the Human Mind* (New York: Simon & Schuster, 2006).

[130] See Ray Kurzweil, *The Age of Spiritual Machines: When Computers Exceed Human Intelligence* (New York: Viking 1999).

[131] See Eric K. Drexler, *Engines of Creation* (Garden City, NY: Anchor Press/Doubleday, 1986).

[132] See Frank J. Tipler, *The Physics of Immortality: Modern Cosmology, God and the Resurrection of the Dead* (New York: Doubleday, 1994).

[133] See Hans P. Moravec, *Mind Children: The Future of Robot and Human Intelligence* (Cambridge, MA: Harvard University Press, 1988).

[134] Anders Sandberg, "An Overview of Models of Technological Singularity," in Max More and Natasha Vita-More, editors, *The Transhumanist Reader*, 376-7.

[135] Vernor Vinge, "Technological Singularity," in Max More and Natasha Vita-More, editors, *The Transhumanist Reader*, 35.

[136] Ibid., 377.

[137] Vernor Vinge, "The Coming Technological Singularity: How to Survive in the Post-Human Era," verbatim transcript, *NASA Technical Reports Server*, https://ntrs.nasa.gov/archive/nasa/casi.ntrs.nasa.gov/19940022856.pdf (accessed March 15, 2020).

[138] Ibid., 1.

Vinge predicts we will have superhuman intelligence within thirty years, or the year 2023.[139]

For artificial intelligence researcher Ray Kurzweil, the singularity will be the beginning of his envisioned utopia. He predicts that superintelligent machines will enable him to transition to a completely non-biological existence by brain-porting himself to a hardware medium. This would mean "scanning his brain, capturing all of the salient details, and reinstantiating the brain's state in a different—most likely much more powerful—computational substrate."[140] This kind of bodiless existence is one way transhumanists plan to achieve physical immortality, but some might choose to be uploaded into a virtual simulated body, which allows interactions with people in the world.[141]

The overall aim of transhumanism is dependent on the successful development of artificial general intelligence and superintelligence. In the next chapter I will argue that artificial general intelligence is metaphysically impossible because it is based on a materialist philosophy of mind, which is false and self-defeating.[142]

Conclusion

Transhumanists are fixated on the future. Even the names of their organizations reflect their ambition and focus: *The Future of Humanity Institute*, *Foresight Institute*, *Extropy Institute*, *Humanity Plus*, and *Alcor Life Extension Foundation*. Because transhumanism depends on the use of cutting-edge technologies, one might suppose that transhumanism is unique or original. However, by investigating their influential key historical figures, I

---

139   Vernor Vinge, "The Coming Technological Singularity: How to Survive in the Post-Human Era," verbatim transcript, *NASA Technical Reports Server*, 1, https://ntrs.nasa.gov/archive/nasa/casi.ntrs.nasa.gov/19940022856.pdf (accessed March 15, 2020).

140   Ray Kurzweil, *The Singularity is Near: When Humans Transcend Biology* (New York: Penguin Books, 2005), 324.

141   "Transhumanist FAQ - What is uploading?" *Humanityplus.org.*, https://humanityplus.org/philosophy/transhumanist-faq/ (accessed on March 15, 2020).

142   There are no clear criteria which can be applied mechanically to determine whether a proposition is metaphysically possible/impossible. I take metaphysical possibility to mean broad logical possibility in terms of actualizability. Metaphysical possibility is not the same as conceivability, which means you can imagine it can occur. Rather, for something to be a real possibility, there has to be an actual potential or ability for it to occur.

have shown that contemporary transhumanism has roots deep in the history of ideas.

Transhumanism represents the culmination of three historical ideas: a desire to control nature and human persons, a mechanistic picture of the world, and a technological view of progress. As evidenced by *The Epic of Gilgamesh*, the desire to control nature has the oldest pedigree. Yet all three central tenets of transhumanism can be traced back to Francis Bacon. The transhumanist road leads to the techno-utopian projects of superintelligence, superlongevity, superhappiness, and eventually to posthumanity. In the ensuing chapters I will give reasons to reject transhumanism and show that these projects will not succeed because they are based on a materialist philosophy of mind and human persons. Transhumanism's philosophical mistake requires a return to the right road that leads to human flourishing instead of extinction. This involves recognizing that the wrong turn was the rejection of Aristotle's philosophy of nature, a rejection which began in full force with Bacon. To return to the right road will mean embracing a metaphysical picture of the world that includes essences, teleology, and a virtue-based philosophy of human flourishing.

APPENDIX A

Organizations that Support the Transhumanist Vision

Accelerating Future https://acceleratingfuture.com/
Alcor Life Extension Foundation https://alcor.org/
Anders Transhuman Resources https://www.aleph.se/Trans/
Applied Foresight Network https://dl.acm.org/citation.cfm?id=1823144
Artificial General Intelligence Research Institute http://www.agiri.org/
Betterhumans http://betterhumans.com/
Cryonics Institute https://cryonics.org/
Extropy Institute http://www.extropy.org/
Future Human Evolution Gateway https://www.visionlearning.com/en/library/Biology/2/Future-of-Human-Evolution/259
Genetics & Public Policy Center https://www.pewtrusts.org/en/projects/archived-projects/genetics-and-public-policy-cente
Immortality Institute http://www.imminst.org/about
Institute for Ethics and Emerging Technologies https://ieet.org/
Institute for the Study of Accelerating Change http://accelerating.org/
Journal of Evolution and Technology https://jetpress.org/
Mormon Transhuman Association https://transfigurism.org/
Singularity for Artificial Intelligence https://su.org/
Upwingers https://hpluspedia.org/wiki/Up-Wingers:_A_Futurist_Manifesto

Chapter Two

Transhumanism, Artificial Intelligence, and Superintelligence: Believe it or Not?

"The survival of man depends on the early construction of an ultraintelligent machine ... Let an ultraintelligent machine be defined as a machine that can far surpass all the intellectual activities of any man however clever ... An ultraintelligent machine could design even better machines; there would then unquestionably be an "intelligence explosion," and the intelligence of man would be left far behind. Thus, the first ultraintelligent machine is the last invention that man need ever make, provided that the machine is docile enough to tell us how to keep it under control."[1]

Irving John Good

Introduction

BEN GOERTZEL is a prominent artificial intelligence researcher and Chairman of the Board of Humanity+, the international transhumanist organization.[2] He sums up the transhumanist consensus

---

1 Irving John Good, "Speculations Concerning the First Ultraintelligent Machine," Conference on the Conceptual Aspects of Biocommunications, October 1962, University of California, Los Angeles, Draft of this monograph (May 1964), 1 and 3. http://acikistihbarat.com/dosyalar/artificial-intelligence-first-paper-on-intelligence-explosion-by-good-1964-acikistihbarat.pdf (accessed March 28, 2020). Irving John Good (1916-2009) was a British statistician and cryptologist who worked with Alan Turing at Bletchley Park during WWII to break the German encryption system called Enigma, which helped defeat Hitler. Later, Good and Turing built and programmed one of the first electrical computers.

2 "Humanity+ Board of Directors," *Humanity+*, https://humanityplus.

about superintelligence in four core beliefs, which correspond to the convictions of Irving J. Good in 1964: (1) Superintelligence is very likely possible, according to known physics; (2) A very likely path to superintelligence is the creation of machines that can improve themselves and increase their own intelligence, e.g., self-modifying software programs; (3) In most cases, the future trajectory of a self-improving, superhuman intelligence will be very hard for human beings to predict; (4) If one creates a human-level artificial general intelligence with certain human-friendly goals, and allows it to self-modify freely, the odds are high that it will eventually self-modify into a condition where it no longer pursues the same goals it started out with.[3]

Just as Good believed the survival of man was dependent on the development of an ultraintelligent machine, Goertzel likewise argues that "humanity's near future well-being, and perhaps survival, critically depends on getting some help from very smart artificial general intelligence (AGI)."[4] Good's optimism was tempered by his concern that an ultraintelligent machine would have to be "docile enough to tell us how to keep it under con-

---

org/about/board/ (accessed March 29, 2020). In addition to serving as Chairman of the Board of Humanity+, Ben Goertzel is CEO of AI software company Novamente LLC and bioinformatics company Biomind LLC. He is the leader of the open-source OpenCog Artificial General Intelligence software project and Chief Technology Officer of biopharma firm Genescient Corp. He is director of Engineering of the digital media firm Vzillion Inc. and an advisor to the Singularity University and Singularity Institute. He serves as Research Professor in the Fujian Key Lab for Brain-Like Intelligent Systems at Xiamen University, China and general Chair of the Artificial General Intelligence conference series.

3   Ben Goertzel, "Superintelligence: Fears, Promises and Potentials," Journal of Evolution & Technology, Vol. 24 Issue 2 (November 2015), 55-87, https://jetpress.org/v25.2/goertzel.htm (accessed March 28, 2020).

4   Howard E. Gardner, The Mind's New Science: A History of the Cognitive Revolution (United States: Basic Books, 1985) 140-1. Artificial General Intelligence (AGI), often referred to as "strong AI," means the appropriately programmed computer really is a mind in the sense that computers, given the right programs, can be literally said to understand and have other cognitive states. The narrow version of AI, often referred to as "weak AI," means the programmed computer simulates human intelligence as an expert tool in a specific domain with restricted applicability. Examples of "weak AI" would be the Deep Blue chess-playing computer program, the Watson Jeopardy-playing computer program, driverless cars, spam filters, computer programs that diagnose medical conditions.

trol."[5] Similarly, transhumanists are optimistic regarding the benefits of a superintelligent machine, but voice concerns that a self-modifying superintelligence could be an existential risk to humanity.[6]

The intelligence explosion that Good anticipated is what transhumanists now call the Singularity, which they believe will be the result of the realization of AGI. In fact, Goertzel's work focuses solely on AGI because it plays a special role as the main catalyst of radical change leading to the Singularity.[7] The progress of the emerging technologies that undergird the transhumanist projects of superintelligence, superlongevity, and superhappiness are dependent on the success of AGI in bringing about the Singularity. Goertzel writes, "The Singularity is going to involve a variety of different technologies, including genetic engineering, nanotech, novel computing hardware, quantum computing, robotics, brain-computer interfacing, and a lot more."[8] Achieving AGI is the pivotal step in reaching the Singularity and transhumanists are wholly committed to it, as seen in their numerous think tanks and research labs that are focused entirely on achieving it.[9]

Three cognitive scientists have voiced serious skepticism about the transhumanist belief in AGI and the coming Singularity event. In their 2012 paper, "Belief in The Singularity is Fideistic," Selmer Bringsjord, Alexander Bringsjord, and Paul Bello categorize the Singularity as a religious event because it is weighty, unseen, and temporally removed, which are qualities belonging to the realm of religion.[10] They argue that belief in

---

5   Good, "Speculations Concerning the First Ultraintelligent Machine," 3.
6   Nick Bostrom, Superintelligence: Paths, Dangers, Strategies (Oxford, UK: Oxford University Press, 2014), 140-154. Although transhumanists agree that the development of a superintelligence is very likely possible in the near future, they disagree on the degree of risk it poses to humanity and how to mitigate the risks.
7   Ben Goertzel, "Artificial General Intelligence and the Future of Humanity," in Max More and Natasha Vita-More, editors, *The Transhumanist Reader* (West Sussex, UK: John Wiley & Sons, Inc., 2013), 129.
8   Ibid., 129.
9   "A Timeline of Transhumanism," The Verge, https://www.theverge.com/a/transhumanism-2015/history-of-transhumanism (accessed March 29, 2020). Transhumanist AGI research centers include: Singularity University, Machine Intelligence Research Institute, Novamente, Center for Applied Rationality, Thiel Fellowship, Global Brain Institute, OpenCogBot, and The Future of Life Institute.
10 Selmer Bringsjord, Alexander Bringsjord, and Paul Bello, "Belief in The

the Singularity is not supported by empirical evidence or rational arguments and therefore, they conclude that proponents of the Singularity are fideists.[11]

There continues to be vigorous debate over whether it is reasonable to believe that the Singularity will likely happen. Transhumanists predict the Singularity event is near because they believe the achievement of AGI is imminent. For this reason, I begin my investigation of transhumanism by critiquing the philosophy of AGI. I will argue that belief in the Singularity is not reasonable based on the metaphysical impossibility of AGI. In my examination and critique of AGI, I will demonstrate that its current limits will remain recalcitrant, not due to any deficiency in technological advancement, but because the assumed materialist philosophy of mind is false. To make my case I will first offer a history of the origin of modern AI and its intellectual antecedents. Second, I will investigate the materialist foundations of AGI, including some reasons for the rise of the materialist philosophy of mind in the twentieth century. Third, I will explain and critique the philosophy of AGI in relation to its major theories: the principle of causal closure, functionalism, and computationalism. Finally, I will suggest a way forward for AGI researchers and transhumanists. My argument is:

1. If AGI is metaphysically possible, then the materialist philosophy of mind is possible.
2. The materialist philosophy of mind is false and self-defeating.
3. Therefore, AGI is metaphysically impossible.[12]

Singularity is Fideistic," (January 25, 2012), 5-6, RPI.edu, http://kryten.mm.rpi.edu/SB_AB_PB_sing_fideism_022412.pdf (accessed April 19, 2020).

11   Selmer Bringsjord, Alexander Bringsjord, and Paul Bello, "Belief in The Singularity is Fideistic," (January 25, 2012), 14, RPI.edu, http://kryten.mm.rpi.edu/SB_AB_PB_sing_fideism_022412.pdf (accessed April 19, 2020).

12   J. P. Moreland & William Lane Craig, *Philosophical Foundations for a Christian Worldview* (Downers Grove, Illinois: IVP Academic, 2003), 50, 257, 497, and 503. There are no clear criteria which can be applied mechanically to determine whether a proposition is metaphysically possible/impossible. I take metaphysical possibility to mean broad logical possibility in terms of actualizability. Metaphysical possibility is not the same as conceivability, which means you can imagine it can occur. Rather, for something to be a real possibility, there has to be an actual potential or ability for it to occur.

The Necessity of Critiquing AGI

Even though AI may seem like a topic that would only attract the interest of scientists and computer geeks, it has increasingly captured the attention of the public and mainstream media. For example, the *Wall Street Journal* published one hundred and sixty-five articles featuring AI related content in the three month period ending March 31, 2020.[13] Whereas the coverage of AI in the media frequently focuses on the huge impact that it will have on a reader's daily life, little, if any, attention is devoted to the fact that many of the big questions of life converge on the subject of AI. Accordingly, it is necessary for us to identify and thoughtfully engage the philosophical issues that are intertwined with the new scientific discipline we call AI. The big questions of life that can easily be seen lurking beneath the surface in any serious discussion about AI are: What is a person? What is consciousness? What is the mind/body relationship? What is human intelligence? Can an artificial machine be a person? The aim of this chapter is to provide answers to some of these questions.

Generally speaking, AGI research programs assume a materialist philosophy of mind, evidenced by the three theories that undergird their research: the principle of causal closure, functionalism, and computationalism. The term 'materialism' has been used in diverse ways in philosophy; however, traditionally in philosophy of mind it represents a mechanistic view, meaning that mental states are either dependent on or reduced to physical states. In other words, materialism entails that there is no aspect of the mind that cannot be ultimately explained by physical forces.[14]

Historically, some scientific theories have generally been held as valid long before they were confirmed by empirical evidence. For example, the CERN Hadron Collider confirmed the existence of the Higgs particle that

---

13   *The Wall Street Journal*, three month period ending March 31, 2020, *WSJ. com*, https://www.wsj.com/search/term.html?KEYWORDS=Artificial%20Intelligence%20or%20AI, (accessed April 20, 2020). Article titles included: "Deep Genomics Gathers $40 Million for AI-Based Drug Discovery" on January 7, 2020; "Tech Will Rule These '20's, Too" on January 5, 2020; "Conceptualizing AI in Human Terms Is Misleading" on February 7, 2020; "What Office Life Might Look Like in the Year 2030" on March 5, 2020; Additionally, there were five Mutual Funds that have "Artificial Intelligence" in their name.

14   Victor Reppert, "The Argument from Reason," in William Lane Craig and J. P. Moreland, editors, *The Blackwell Companion to Natural Theology* (West Sussex, UK: John Wiley & Sons Ltd, 2009), 344-6.

had long been predicted by the Standard Model.[15] Similarly, those who hold the materialist philosophy of mind look to neuroscience and AGI for empirical evidence for their philosophy. In other words, the success of the AGI project could be conceived as a way of confirming the materialist philosophy of mind.

A History of Artificial Intelligence

The Origin of Modern AI

In 1956, a select group of scholars, trained primarily in mathematics and logic, gathered at Dartmouth College in Hanover, New Hampshire for an eight-week summer conference to brainstorm about the possibility of programming computers to behave and think intelligently.[16] Their aim was clearly stated in the grant application to the Rockefeller Foundation:

> The study is to proceed on the basis of the conjecture that every aspect of learning or any other feature of intelligence can in principle be so precisely described that a machine can be made to simulate it. An attempt will be made to find how to make machines use language, form abstractions and concepts, solve kinds of problems now reserved for humans, and improve themselves.[17]

This conference was the brainchild of John McCarthy (1927-2011), who envisioned it as a "two month, ten man study" to investigate a subject so new he had to invent a new term: Artificial Intelligence (AI).[18] Today AI has morphed into an interdisciplinary project that includes engineering, cognitive science, mathematics, linguistics, psychology, and neuroscience.

Intellectual Antecedents of AI

Whereas the modern AI project has a relatively brief history beginning in 1956 at the Dartmouth Conference, the intellectual origins of AI go back

---

15   Roger Trigg, *Beyond Matter: Why Science Needs Metaphysics* (West Conshohocken, PA: Templeton Press, 2015), 54 and 88.

16   Gardner, The Mind's New Science, 30. The notable participants were: John McCarthy, Marvin Minsky, Herbert Simon, Allen Newell, Nathaniel Rochester, Claude Shannon, and John Nash.

17   John McCarthy, "Dartmouth AI Project Proposal," August 31, 1955. LivingInternet.com, https://www.livinginternet.com/i/ii_ai.htm (accessed March 20, 2020).

18   Gardner, *The Mind's New Science*, 30.

at least to Rene Descartes (1596-1650), who contemplated the limitations of the automata of his day.[19] These clockwork machines resembling the human body could imitate human actions, so Descartes proposed something akin to today's Turing Test, which tested the machine's use of language and reason as sufficient evidence to recognize the difference between the machine and the human person.[20] On the basis of Descartes' mind/body dualism, this test showed that the "rational soul could not be in any way derived from the power of matter."[21]

Contrary to Descartes' dualistic view of the mind and body as separate substances, Thomas Hobbes (1588-1679) argued for a thoroughgoing materialism. On this view, Hobbes viewed mental processes, including reasoning itself, as reducible to the established principles of matter in motion.[22] Foreshadowing the modern computational theory of mind, Hobbes described reasoning as computation, he writes, "For reason, in this sense, is nothing but reckoning (that is, adding and subtracting) of consequences of general names agreed upon for the marking and signifying of our thoughts."[23] He explained that propositions are formed by adding the subject and predicate and syllogisms are formed when logicians add propositions.[24]

Inspired by Hobbes, Gottfried Leibniz (1646-1716) advanced the idea that logical reasoning could be reduced to computation. He connected concepts with numbers by applying reasoning about numbers to reasoning about concepts. He dreamed of a machine that could evaluate logical expressions the same way machines proved mathematical expressions.[25]

---

19   Rene Descartes, "Discourse on Method," in Mortimer Adler, editor, *The Great Books of the Western World*, Volume 28 (Chicago: Encyclopedia Britannica, Inc., 1990), 283-4.

20   Ibid. Descartes' method of testing is seen as the earliest version of the Turing Test.

21   Ibid., 284.

22   E. A. Burtt, *The Metaphysical Foundations of Modern Science* (New York: Dover Publications, Inc., 2003), 126-127.

23   Thomas Hobbes, "Leviathan: Of Man," in Mortimer Adler, editor, *The Great Books of the Western World, Volume 21* (Chicago: Encyclopedia Britannica, Inc., 1990), 58.

24   Ibid., 58.

25   Bruno Woltezenlogel Paleo, "Leibniz's Characteristica Universalis And Calculus Ratiocinator Today," *ResearchGate*, December 2016, https://www.researchgate.net/publication/311456139_Leibniz's_Characteristica_Universalis_and_Calculus_Ratiocinator_Today (April 1, 2020).

This approach was an early precursor to what we have today—logical reasoning encoded as binary arithmetical computations. Leibniz said with optimism, "If controversies were to arise, there would be no more need of disputation between two philosophers than between two accountants. For it would suffice to take their pencils in their hands, to sit down with their slates and say to each other: Let us calculate."[26]

Cambridge mathematician Charles Babbage (1791-1871) designed a calculating machine he called the Difference Engine based on the idea that individual teeth on a cogwheel stood for numbers. The meshing of the cogwheels arranged in vertical columns would carry out the arithmetical calculation.[27] Motivated in part by Lady Ada Lovelace, Babbage developed the Analytical Engine, which was meant to supersede the Difference Engine. He envisioned it to be the size of a small steam locomotive, containing 20,000 cogwheels with thousands of gear-shafts, camshafts, and power transmission rods. The entire operation of the Analytical Engine was controlled by a punched-card system, borrowed from the punched card method of the Jacquard loom.[28] The invention of the card system was a preview of how computers today are programmed using binary digits as units of information.[29] The Analytical Engine was never built because the British government withdrew funding before it became a reality.[30]

Thereafter, British mathematicians George Boole (1852-1862), Alfred North Whitehead (1861-1947), and Bertrand Russell (1872-1970) worked to figure out the basic laws of thought and ground them in principles of logic. Boole's logic system was two-valued, meaning any logical expression could be expressed as either "1," meaning true or "0," meaning false.[31] Whitehead and Russell carried Boole's work further by demonstrating that the roots of mathematics are founded in the basic laws of logic.[32] These

---

26 Bertrand Russell, translator, *The Philosophy of Leibniz* (London: George Allen and Unwin, 1958), 170, quoted in Bruno Woltenzenlogel Paleo, "Leibniz's Characteristica Universalis And Calculus Ratiocinator Today," *ResearchGate*, December 2016, 1, https://www.researchgate.net/publication/311456139_Leibniz's_Characteristica_Universalis_and_Calculus_Ratiocinator_Today (accessed April 1, 2020).

27 James Essinger, *Ada's Algorithm: How Lord Byron's Daughter Ada Lovelace Launched the Digital Age* (New York: Melville House Publishing, 2015), 88-89.

28 Ibid., 115-118.

29 Ibid., 119.

30 Ibid., 156-161

31 Gardner, *The Mind's New Science*, 143.

32 Ibid., 143.

ideas are exemplified today in computer programs, where coded instructions are thought of in terms of formal logic rather than arithmetic.[33]

In 1950, the ideas, groundwork, and dreams of the previous three hundred years about the relationship between human thought and machines were realized when the British mathematician and code-breaker Alan Turing invented the general calculating machine. His legendary paper "Computing Machinery and Intelligence" posed this provocative question, 'Can machines think?'[34] Six years later, at the Dartmouth Conference, AI was inaugurated as an independent research field aimed at answering Turing's daunting question.

According to participant Herbert Simon, this conference marked the genesis of a new scientific approach to understanding the human mind: the information processing paradigm.[35] That is, an approach that understands intelligence in terms of processes. "At the root of intelligence are symbols, with their denotative power and their susceptibility to manipulation . . . Intelligence is mind implemented by any patternable kind of matter."[36] In their 1961 paper "Computer Simulation of Human Thinking," Allen Newell and Herbert Simon write, "The brain and the computer are both general-purpose symbol-manipulating devices and the computer can be programmed to execute elementary information processes functionally quite like those executed by the brain."[37] In other words, both the brain and the computer are systems that process information to solve problems using rules and symbolic logic.

---

33   Gardner, *The Mind's New Science*, 144.

34   Alan M. Turing, "Computing Machinery and Intelligence," *Mind* Vol. 49, (1950): 433. https://home.manhattan.edu/~tina.tian/CMPT 420/Turing.pdf (accessed February 15, 2020). He proposed a test of computer intelligence he called the "imitation game," which is now called the Turing Test. For a computer to pass the test and be considered reasonably intelligent, the machine output would have to be indistinguishable from a human's responses in the same situation.

35   Herbert Simon, "Cognitive Science: the Newest Science of the Artificial," *Cognitive Science* Vol. 4, (1980): 34. https://onlinelibrary.wiley.com/doi/pdf/10.1207/s15516709cog0401_2 (accessed February 25, 2020).

36   Ibid., 35.

37   Allen Newell and Herbert A Simon, "Computer Simulation of Human Thinking," The Rand Corporation: Computer Science Department, P-2276 (April 20, 1961): 9. http://www.bighole.nl/pub/mirror/www.bitsavers.org/pdf/rand/ipl/P-2276_Computer_Simulation_Of_Human_Thinking_Apr61.pdf (accessed March 4, 2020).

The Materialist Foundation of AGI

The Scientific Revolution and the Rise of Materialism

I contend that AGI has gone wrong on first principles; that is to say, they are mistaken in their assumption of a materialist philosophy of mind. Therefore, a preliminary question to investigate is: How did the study of mind and intelligence come to embrace the philosophy of scientific materialism? In other words, why have today's philosophers of mind taken the view that the human mind ought to be explained strictly in terms of physical processes, properties, and causes?

As shown in chapter one, Francis Bacon's interest in the practical control of nature through the knowledge of causes by scientific empirical methods galvanized a shift from the classical metaphysics of the Middle Ages to the metaphysics of modern scientific materialism. Philosopher E. A. Burtt analyzes this philosophical revolution and the ultimate triumph of the modern scientific view of the world in his book *The Metaphysical Foundations of Modern Science*.[38] According to Burtt, the shift involved transformations in three essential conceptions: reality, causality, and the human mind.[39]

First, according to the modern scientific view, the real world is fundamentally micro-particles—molecules, atoms, electrons, protons, quarks, etc., all moving according to the laws of nature, which can be stated in mathematical forms. No longer is reality understood as whole substances with internal forms, teleology, and ultimate qualities that could be known by observation and experience. Second, the Aristotelian understanding of internal formal and final causes were rejected as explanations and replaced by efficient physical causes based on mechanism.[40] Finally, as the mechanical picture of the world developed, later thinkers (e.g., after Descartes and Pascal) deleted God as the final external cause. With God out of the picture, the understanding of the mind as an immaterial substance was also excluded from the materialistic picture of the world.[41] It seemed plausible to believe that the mind would yield to a purely physical explanation.

During the ensuing four hundred years, the discoveries, predictions, and the success of science, particularly in physics, established the legit-

---

38   E. A. Burtt, *The Metaphysical Foundations of Modern Science* (New York: Dover Publications, Inc., 2003).

39   Ibid., 303.

40   Ibid., 303.

41   Ibid., 310-325.

imacy of the scientific materialistic view of the world. However, this does not mean that all debates in the philosophy of mind have been settled in favor of materialism.[42] The very fact that the project of naturalizing the mind continues today reveals the weakness of the materialist philosophy of mind. This ongoing debate has not been confined only to philosophers and neuroscientists by any means. Key figures defending classical humanism, such as Irving Babbitt, Paul Elmer More, T. S. Elliot, C. S. Lewis, and G. K. Chesterton, harshly critiqued materialism because it reduced persons to things to be studied as part of nature.[43]

Irving Babbitt (1865-1933), the intellectual leader of the New Humanists, fought to maintain and honor the distinction between man and nature against the scientism and progressivism in the academy. He quotes Ralph Waldo Emerson's *Ode, Inscribed to William H. Channing* to describe the distinction between man and nature to underscore his argument against the overreach of scientific materialism into other academic disciplines:

There are two laws discrete,
Not reconciled,
Law for man, and law for thing.
The last builds town and fleet,
But it runs wild,
And doth the man unking.[44]

Babbitt adds to Emerson's lament, "Man himself and the products of his spirit, language, and literature, are treated not as having a law of their own, but as things, as entirely subject to the same methods that have won for science such triumphs over phenomenal nature."[45]

Chesterton (1874-1936) championed the classical view of man's essential nature and purpose in *The Everlasting Man*: "It is not natural to see man as a natural product. It is not common sense to call man a common object of the country or the seashore. It is not seeing him straight to see him as an

---

42 Debates regarding consciousness, personal identity, reason, intentionality, qualia, etc. are ongoing.

43 Michael D. Aeschlman, *The Restitution of Man: C. S. Lewis and the Case against Scientism* (Grand Rapids, Michigan: William B. Eerdmans Publishing Company, 1983), 62-72.

44 Irving Babbitt, *Literature and the American College: Essays in Defense of the Humanities* (New York: Houghton, Mifflin, and Company, 1908), preface.

45 Ibid., 30.

animal. It is not sane. It sins against the light; against that broad daylight of proportion which is the principle of all reality."[46]

C. S. Lewis (1898-1963) likewise argued against reducing persons to things in *The Abolition of Man*, "We reduce things to mere Nature," he wrote, "in order that we may 'conquer' them ... But as soon as we take the final step of reducing our own species to the level of mere Nature, the whole process is stultified, for this time the being who stood to gain and the being who has been sacrificed are one and the same."[47]

Despite ongoing vigorous debate, materialism has been the mainstream position in the philosophy of mind since at least the beginning of the twentieth century, but not because philosophers or neuroscientists proved it.[48] Materialism's dominance in the philosophy of mind rests largely on the belief that modern science has been successful in applying the materialistic mechanical model of explanation to every other phenomenon in the universe, so they reasonably expect that materialism is capable, in principle, of explaining the mind. And yet, materialists have not shown how specific aspects of mind, such as qualia, consciousness, reason, and intentionality, are purely material properties that cannot exist apart from some physical substrate. As will be seen, these aspects of the mind represent the recalcitrant limits of AGI.

The Advance of Materialism in the Twentieth Century

The materialist approach to the study of mind and intelligence thrived in the twentieth century and was motivated, in part, by the following movements of the time: (1) the Vienna Circle's unity of science, (2) John Dewey's science-ification of the academic disciplines, (3) E.O. Wilson's consilience and the unity of knowledge, and (4) the authority of science in the culture. An examination of each one will help us grasp the widespread influence and propagation of materialism.

The Unity of Science: The Vienna Circle

A group called The Vienna Circle (hereafter referred to as "the Circle") began as an informal intellectual club of philosophers, scientists,

---

46   G. K. Chesterton, *The Everlasting Man* (New York: Dodd, Mead and Company, 1925), 20.

47   C. S. Lewis, *The Abolition of Man* (New York: HarperCollins, 1974), 71.

48   Three primary materialist theories developed: Behaviorist Theory (1920-50), Identity Theory (1950-60), and Functionalist Theory (1970-).

and mathematicians, but became an organized international movement in 1929, the year the Circle published their manifesto entitled "The Scientific Conception of the World."[49] The manifesto stated that the primary goal of the Circle was to advocate "a scientific conception of the world" that opposed metaphysical philosophy. One of their goals was to unify the sciences, eliminating the usual boundary between the two kinds of things researched: non-organisms and organisms. In the manifesto they argue:

> The aim of scientific effort is to reach the goal, unified science, by applying logical analysis to the empirical material. Since the meaning of every statement of science must be statable by reduction to a statement about the given, likewise the meaning of any concept, whatever branch of science it may belong to, must be statable by stepwise reduction to other concepts, down to the concepts of the lowest level which refer directly to the given.[50]

Rudolf Carnap, a leader of the Circle, considered physics and biology in their wider sense as representing the sciences of non-organisms and organisms, respectively. In his essay "Logical Foundations of the Unity of Science," he argues that a law of physics is meant to be universally valid without restriction; the law applies to the processes in organisms as well as inorganic matter. The biologist needs the laws of physics to explain biological processes. "Therefore, biology presupposes physics, but not vice

---

49   Members of the Circle listed in the Manifesto: Gustav Bergmann, Rudolf Carnap, Herbert Feigl, Philipp Frank, Kurt Gödel, Hans Hahn, Viktor Kraft, Karl Menger, Marcel Natkin, Otto Neurath, Olga Hahn-Neurath, Theodor Radakovic, Moritz Schlick, and Friedrich Waismann. Hans Hahn, Otto Neurath, and Rudolf Carnap, "Wissenschaftliche Weltauffassung. Der Wiener Kreis," 1929, English translation: "The Scientific Conception of the World: The Vienna Circle," in Sahotra Sarkar, Series Editor, *Science and Philosophy in the Twentieth Century, Volume I: The Emergence of Logical Empiricism: from 1900 to the Vienna Circle* (New York: Garland Publishing, 1996), 340.

50   Hans Hahn, Otto Neurath, and Rudolf Carnap, "Wissenschaftliche Weltauffassung. Der Wiener Kreis," 1929, English translation: "The Scientific Conception of the World: The Vienna Circle," in Sahotra Sarkar, Series Editor, *Science and Philosophy in the Twentieth Century, Volume I: The Emergence of Logical Empiricism: from 1900 to the Vienna Circle* (New York: Garland Publishing, 1996), 331.

versa."⁵¹ Carnap's vision was to work toward the development of a unity of laws for science. He thought the aim of future scientists should be "the construction of one homogeneous system of laws for the whole of science."⁵²

As a preliminary step toward this goal, Carnap advanced the idea of a unity of language in science, "a common reduction basis for the terms of all branches of science, this basis consisting of a very narrow and homogeneous class of terms of the physical thing-language."⁵³ This means that all statements, whatever their subject matter, should be reduced to thing-language, the language used to describe observable properties and relations. For example, statements about mental phenomena are nothing but statements about bodily states. Any non-physicalist statements concerning the life of the mind are neither publicly observable nor testable and are therefore explicitly ruled out of the language of science. The Circle's claim was that the whole language of science could be reduced to the class of observable thing-predicates. Non-physical statements, such as those in the domain of mind, were considered metaphysical postulates and therefore, meaningless. Essentially, on this view, mental states are reduced to physical brain states.

The Science-ification of the Academic Disciplines: John Dewey

John Dewey (1859-1952) was an American philosopher and the leading proponent of the school of thought known as pragmatic instrumentalism.⁵⁴ He is remembered as the father of American progressive education be-

---

51   Rudolf Carnap, Chapter 21 "The Logical Foundations of the Unity of Science," reprinted from *International Encyclopedia of Unified Science: Volume I*, ed. O. Neurath, R. Carnap, and C. Morris, (Chicago: University of Chicago Press, 1938-55), 395.
52   Ibid., 403.
53   Ibid., 404.
54   "Instrumentalism is the methodological view in Epistemology and Philosophy of Science, advanced by the American philosopher John Dewey, that concepts and theories are merely useful instruments, and their worth is measured not by whether the concepts and theories are true or false (Instrumentalism denies that theories are truth-evaluable), or whether they correctly depict reality, but by how effective they are in explaining and predicting phenomena. It maintains that the truth of an idea is determined by its success in the active solution of a problem, and that the value of an idea is determined by its function in human experience." "The Basics of Philosophy: by Branch, Instrumentalism," *PhilosophyBasics.com*, http://www.philosophybasics.com/branch_instrumentalism.html (accessed March 30, 2020).

cause he spent his life reforming education, which included integrating the tenets of logical positivism in public schools. The pragmatic philosophy of John Dewey shared the common ground of empiricism with logical positivism and he assimilated some of the positivists' ideas. Dewey interacted with the Circle and their writings, especially founders Otto Neurath and Rudolf Carnap. In the 1930's, the Circle began promoting logical positivism to the public through the publication of the *International Encyclopedia of Unified Science*. John Dewey served on the Advisory Committee.[55] His essay *Theory of Valuation* appears in Volume II, Number 4 edition.

Dewey's commitment to the unity of science was grounded in his materialistic view of reality and was reflected in his education philosophy. For Dewey, reality was only the material world, meaning everything that exists is part of nature and subject to scientific inquiry, including the mental realm.[56] In keeping with the Circle's view of the unity of science, Dewey's theory of experience reduced mental states to physical states. His understanding of human experience was primarily empirical; on his view, the inner mental life is "simply the causal result of the operational organization of the physical."[57] In the preface to his book *Democracy and Education* (1916), Dewey introduces his educational philosophy as an improvement on earlier traditional "theories of knowing and moral development" because he considered his view to be more in harmony with the important development in the sciences of the methods of experiment and observation.[58] He recognized that he was living in the "twilight of intellectual transition" and he saw himself as an integral part of this movement in philosophy toward applying the scientific method to transform all disciplines.[59]

In 1977, after Dewey's philosophy and methods had been successfully entrenched in American education, E. F. Schumacher (1911-1977) wrote *A Guide for the Perplexed*, critiquing materialism and its effect on American

---

55 *The Encyclopedia's* Committee of Organization: Rudolf Carnap, Otto Neurath, Philipp Frank, Joergen Joergensen, Charles W. Morris, and Louis Rongier. The Advisory Committee included: Niels Bohr, John Dewey, Bertrand Russell, Alfred Tarski, and Herbert Feigl.

56 John Dewey, *Democracy and Education* (New York: The Free Press, 1916), 281-290.

57 Dewey, *The Influence of Darwin on Philosophy and Other Essays*, 227, quoted in Robert J. Richards, "Materialism and Natural Events in Dewey's Developing Thought," *Journal of the History of Philosophy* Volume 10, Number 1, (January 1972), 65.

58 Dewey, *Democracy and Education*, preface.

59 Ibid.

education. He argued that people need maps, maps for knowledge and for living; the mapmaker's responsibility is to find a proper place for everything because things out of place tend to get lost. With this in mind he wrote:

> The maps produced by modern materialistic Scientism leave all the questions that really matter unanswered; more than that, they deny the validity of the questions. The situation was desperate enough in my youth half a century ago; [but] it is even worse now because the ever more vigorous application of the scientific method to all subjects and disciplines has destroyed even the last remnants of ancient wisdom—at least in the Western World.[60]

The Consilience: E.O. Wilson

In his 1998 book *Consilience*, Harvard biologist E. O. Wilson revived the two ideas of the unity of science and the science-ification of the disciplines by claiming that the "greatest enterprise of the mind has always been and always will be the attempted linkage of the sciences and humanities."[61] Basically, if the Vienna Circle and John Dewey could have had a baby it would be E. O. Wilson. He proposes the key to this unification of knowledge is consilience, which he defines as "a jumping together of knowledge by the linking of facts and fact-based theory across disciplines to create a common groundwork of explanation."[62] He argues that the way to establish this consilience across "all the great branches of learning" is by the methods developed in the natural sciences because "an allegiance to these [scientific] habits of thought have worked so well in exploring the material universe."[63]

Wilson "jumps together" the humanities and science by assuming the physical causal closure of the world. He asks, "Given that human action comprises events of physical causation, why should the social sciences and humanities be impervious to consilience with the natural sciences?"[64] His answer assumes the principle of causal closure: "Nothing fundamental separates the course of human history from the course of physical history,

---

60   E. F. Schumacher, *A Guide for The Perplexed* (New York: Harper & Row, 1977), 4-5.
61   Edward O. Wilson, *Consilience: The Unity of Knowledge* (New York: Vintage Books, 1999), 8.
62   Ibid., 8.
63   Ibid., 9.
64   Ibid., 11.

whether in the stars or in organic diversity."[65] In other words, he assumes the sovereignty of physics; all explanations can be reduced to physical explanations and reality becomes a seamless web of cause and effect.

With this materialist foundation, Wilson explains how the mind fits into this seamless web. He begins by granting that it is reasonable at first to believe that the study of the mind should be the proper domain of philosophy, not science, but he maintains that philosophy has reached the limit of its knowledge on the matter. And now that the biological evolution of the brain suggests that the brain is a machine, it is clear that "the fundamental explanation of mind is an empirical rather than a philosophical or religious quest."[66] He suggests that "the ships that brought us here are to be left scuttled and burning at the shore."[67]

Wilson accuses those who object to the idea of consilience of not taking science seriously.[68] Ironically, the opposite is true; those who reject the idea of consilience take science *more* seriously because they understand the self-defeating consequences of Wilson's materialism. That is, if scientific beliefs are merely the result of neurons firing in the brain, then the causal power of rationality is lost, and with it the truth of scientific explanations.

The Authority of Science in the Culture

To understand how the project of AI became founded on materialism, one should not only consider the intellectual climate in which it developed, as discussed in the previous three sections, but one should also reflect on the general influence of the culture. The amazing growth and development of the empirical sciences in the modern era have presented a favorable climate for scientific materialism. There are two main aspects of the culture that influenced its development. First, advances in knowledge about the world are mostly credited to science rather than philosophy. Second, the growth of applied science via beneficial technology gives people a sense of progress for civilization. Accordingly, people have become increasingly accustomed to crediting science as solving practical problems. This general outlook has given science, as opposed to philosophy or theology, a de-

---

65   Edward O. Wilson, *Consilience: The Unity of Knowledge* (New York: Vintage Books, 1999), 11.
66   Ibid., 105.
67   Ibid., 106.
68   Ibid., 107-110.

gree of prestige and authority. It is the discipline perceived by the culture as providing real knowledge about the world, and specifically the mind.

Summary of the Materialist Foundation of AGI

In the final analysis, AGI was born amidst a cultural climate that favored the ideas of the unity of science, the science-ification in the academy, and the consilience of academic disciplines. Unfortunately, all three ideologies, from the Vienna Circle's unity of science, to John Dewey's science-ification of the academic disciplines, and E.O. Wilson's consilience and the unity of knowledge, all share a common philosophical blunder; they have gone wrong on first principles. In each case, they have conflated epistemological materialism (how we know things) and ontological materialism (nature of ultimate reality). This conflation flourished because scientists believed that the empirical methods that were so successful in gaining knowledge about the physical world would be equally successful in gaining knowledge about the mind. The materialist philosophy of mind became the foundation for AGI largely because materialism was compatible with their aim to reduce thinking to computational algorithms. According to philosopher and cognitive scientist Jerry Fodor (1935-2017), on the materialist view, physics fixes all the facts in the world: "physics determines chemistry; chemistry determines biology; biology determines brain science; and brain science determines the mental life."[69] The aim of scientific materialism is to close the gap between nature and human nature by reducing man to the same level of scientific explanation as the physical objects of the world. Edward Feser sharply criticizes this view with his analogy of the "metal-detector," which shows the absurdity of the idea that the predictive successes and applications of physics dictate that materialism must explain the whole of reality:

1. Metal detectors have had far greater success in finding coins and other metallic objects in more places than any other method has.
2. Therefore, we have good reason to think that metal detectors can reveal to us everything in reality that there is to be revealed.[70]

---

[69] Jerry Fodor, "Look!" *London Review of Books*, Vol. 20 No. 21, (October 29, 1998): 2. https://www.lrb.co.uk/v20/n21/jerry-fodor/look (accessed Feb. 20, 2020).

[70] Edward Feser, "Reading Rosenberg, Part II," *EdwardFeser.blogspot.com*, November 3, 2011, http://edwardfeser.blogspot.com/2012/10/nagel-and-his-critics-part-ii.html (accessed February 10, 2020).

Feser asks, "Why on earth should we believe that only methods capable of detecting metals give us genuine access to reality?"[71] Further, if something like mind, reason, and intelligence are real, why should we believe that the methods of science are the exclusive way to have knowledge of them?

Critiquing the Materialist Philosophy of AGI

The proponents of AGI hold that "the appropriately programmed computer really *is* a mind in the sense that computers, given the right programs, can literally be said to understand and have cognitive states."[72] In this section, I will provide evidence to establish the first two premises of my main argument. First, to assess the metaphysical possibility of the idea that a machine can have a mind, I will explain AGI's three primary philosophical tenets: (1) the causal closure structure of the world (also called the completeness of physics), (2) the functionalist philosophy of mind, and (3) the computational theory of mind. These explanations will serve as evidence for premise *#1 of the argument: If AGI is metaphysically possible, then the materialist philosophy of mind is possible*. Second, I will critique each of the three philosophies to establish premise *#2 of the argument: The materialistic philosophy of mind is false and self-defeating*.

The Causal Closure Structure of the World

For modern materialists, the principle of causal closure plays a leading role in the definitive argument for materialism. The principle is sometimes referred to as the completeness of physics; I will use these two concepts interchangeably.[73] Philosopher David Papineau explains that the rise of materialism in the twentieth century is the direct result of the availability of empirical evidence for the completeness of physics.[74] Accordingly,

---

[71] Edward Feser, "Reading Rosenberg, Part II," *EdwardFeser.blogspot.com*, November 3, 2011, 1, http://edwardfeser.blogspot.com/2012/10/nagel-and-his-critics-part-ii.html (accessed February 10, 2020)

[72] Gardner, *The Mind's New Science*, 140. Weak AI holds that "the programmed computer simulates human intelligence in a specific domain with restricted applicability."

[73] David Papineau, *Thinking about Consciousness* (Oxford: Clarendon Press, 2004), 9.

[74] Ibid., 233.

Papineau includes the causal closure principle as the second premise in his formulation of the canonical causal argument for materialism:

(1) Conscious mental occurrences have physical effects.
(2) All physical effects are fully caused by purely physical prior histories.
(3) The physical effects of conscious causes aren't always overdetermined by distinct causes.[75]

For instance, suppose I consciously desire that Ken be the president of our club. Because of this, I raise my hand to vote for Ken. This represents premise (1), a common occurrence where a state of consciousness (my desire) brings about a physical state (raising my hand to vote). The materialist considers the case using premise (2) and explains the physical effect (my raised arm) was fully caused by prior physical processes in my brain. Accordingly, the materialist concludes from premise (3) that there is no mental causation: "Conscious states are identical with physical states or identical with physically realized functional states."[76]

There are various formulations of the causal closure premise in arguments, but it is a premise more often assumed than proven.[77] As E. J. Lowe rightly says, "One might have hoped for more exactitude and agreement amongst physicalists when it comes to the formulation of a principle so central to their position."[78] Nevertheless, the common understanding of causal closure is that the physical world is causally closed; all physical

---

75   David Papineau, "The Rise of Physicalism," 8, *Core.ac.uk.*, https://core.ac.uk/download/pdf/74162.pdf (accessed April 14, 2020). A functionalist interpretation modifies the argument to identify conscious properties with physically realized functional properties. "That is, we might allow a state to "cause" in virtue of having a realizer which causes. If we do this, then the causal argument will no longer require us to identify conscious states with strictly physical states, but it will still give us an argument for identifying them with second-order states which are physically realized."

76   Ibid., 15.

77   E. J. Lowe, "Causal Closure Principles and Emergentism," *Philosophy*, 75 (4), 2000, 574, *Durham Research Online*, http://dro.dur.ac.uk/15632/ (April 9, 2020). Other variations of the causal closure premise: (1) All physical effects have sufficient physical causes, (2) Every physical effect has fully revealed, purely physical history, (3) Every physical effect has its chance fully determined by physical events alone, and (4) No physical effect has a non-physical cause.

78   E. J. Lowe, "Causal Closure Principles and Emergentism," *Philosophy*, 75 (4), 2000, 574, *Durham Research Online*, http://dro.dur.ac.uk/15632/ (April 9, 2020).

effects have purely physical causes, which precludes irreducible mental states from causing, in a non-overdetermined way, any physical effect. It is important to understand from the outset that, for the materialist, "the physical world is the world of physics."[79]

Papineau admits there is no knock-down argument for the principle of causal closure; in fact, once when pressed by anti-materialists, he wrote: "I found myself in some embarrassment. Once I was forced to defend it, I realized that the completeness of physics is by no means self-evident."[80] Even though he thinks it is an uncontroversial claim to a committed materialist, Papineau makes a case for causal closure by combining two inductive arguments: the argument from fundamental forces and the argument from physiology.[81]

Papineau's argument from fundamental forces generalizes inductively "to conclude that all apparently special forces must reduce to a small stock of fundamental forces."[82] He credits Hermann von Helmholtz (1821-1894) with synthesizing the discoveries of the disparate branches of sciences to develop the universal principle of the conservation of energy. Papineau refers to examples, such as the fixed equivalences of the sum of kinetic energy and potential energy as established by Marquis de Laplace (1749-1927), and the fixed equivalences of heat and mechanical energy discovered by James Joule (1819-1889). Papineau's aim is to show that the history of science demonstrates there are fixed equivalences between these fundamental forces, heat, and mechanical energy. Helmholtz took it a step further to assert that all forces conserve the sum of kinetic and potential energy. Helmholtz sought to bring organic processes under a unified science. These discoveries convinced him that all natural phenomena, including those in living systems, must respect the conservation of energy. Papineau concludes that "the arguments behind the conservation of energy give inductive reason to suppose that all forces reduce to a small number of fundamental forces."[83]

---

79   Carl Gabbani, "The Causal Closure of What? An Epistemological Critique of the Principle of Causal Closure," (January 2013), *ResearchGate*, https://www.researchgate.net/publication/280562788_The_Causal_Closure_of_What_An_Epistemological_Critique_of_the_Principle_of_Causal_Closure (accessed April 13, 2020).

80   Papineau, *Thinking about Consciousness*, 45.

81   Ibid., 243-255.

82   Papineau, *Thinking about Consciousness*, 250.

83   Papineau, "The Rise of Physicalism," 17.

It was not until the 1950's that support for the causal closure thesis became more widespread, largely because evidence emerged from biochemical and neurophysiological processes that bolstered the argument from physiology. The conclusion from the physiological evidence is "simply that there is no direct evidence for vital or mental forces."[84] After years of scientific research only familiar physical forces have been found. Papineau thinks the evidence from cellular structures and neuronal networks "clinch[ed] the case for the completeness of physics as a general scientific consensus by the 1950's."[85] He concludes his analysis by saying that the principle of causal closure has been "fully established by over a century of empirical research" that supports the arguments from fundamental forces and physiology.[86]

If it is metaphysically possible for AGI to artificially duplicate human thinking on a computer, then this would demonstrate that the principle of causal closure is true and mental states can be accounted for in purely physical terms. This provides support for premise #1 *of my argument: If AGI is metaphysically possible, then the materialist philosophy of mind is possible.*

Critique of the Causal Closure Thesis

The principle of causal closure is the major premise in the argument for materialism. In fact, it is presented as a universal principle "fully established by empirical research," yet physics lacks the completeness that is needed for such a claim. My critiques will demonstrate that the principle of causal closure should be considered a research hypothesis in the case for materialism and not a decisive universal principle and major premise of the argument.

First, according to the principle of causal closure, or the completeness of physics, "all physical effects are fully caused by purely physical prior histories."[87] Those who support this principle delegate the physical world to physics, giving physics unique ontological authority (i.e., to tell us what is). That is to say, the physical world just is the 'world of physics.' Philosopher Carl Hempel (1905-1997) questioned what is meant by physics, which is relevant to any discussion about causal closure.[88] If physics means only

---

84 Papineau, "The Rise of Physicalism," 18.
85 Papineau, *Thinking about Consciousness*, 254.
86 Ibid., 256.
87 Ibid., 17-18.
88 Carl G. Hempel, "Comments on Goodman's Ways of Worldmaking," *Synthese*, (1980) 45: 193-199, quoted in Carlo Gabbani, "The Causal Closure of What? An epistemological Critique of the Principle of Causal Closure,"

that which belongs to our *present* physical theories, these theories are admittedly incomplete.[89] Papineau admits, "The track record of attempts to list all the fundamental forces and particles responsible for physical effects is not good, and it seems highly likely that future physics will identify new categories of physical cause."[90]

Most materialists take physics to mean that which belongs to an *ideal* future physics, which is open and undetermined. How can the causal closure principle be applied *now* if we do not know what may or may not belong to the future completed physics? It is possible the future physics will be revolutionary and based on a different elementary unit that does not exclude mental properties and laws. Consequently, in either case, whether physics is understood as present or future, the principle of causal closure becomes unclear.

Papineau responds to the open-ended character of an ideal future physics by defining it negatively, by what it will exclude.[91] In this sense, Papineau explains, "[O]ne way of understanding 'physical' would simply be as 'non-mentally identifiable.'"[92] As long as the materialist is confident that a complete physics will have no need for ineliminable distinct mental causes, he can conclude that "all mental states must be identical with (or realized by) something non-mentally identifiable."[93] To be clear, Papineau is not saying that mental causes simply do not belong in the world of physics; he is claiming that mental causes are ultimately analyzable in terms of fundamental non-mental phenomena.[94] Papineau's negative definition of physics presupposes the causal completeness of physics. There is an apparent circularity in deciding now, by definition and not by fact, what properties, in principle, belong to the completed physics.

Second, the causal closure thesis assumes the existence of a successful, completed, general reductionist theory that fully accounts for our conscious mental states. In spite of Papineau's arguments from fundamental forces and physiology, for causal closure to be factually true, "The phys-

---

ResearchGate. https://www.researchgate.net/publication/280562788_The_Causal_Closure_of_What_An_Epistemological_Critique_of_the_Principle_of_Causal_Closure (accessed April 11, 2020).

89   Papineau, *Thinking about Consciousness*, 40-1.
90   Papineau, "The Rise of Physicalism," 8.
91   Papineau, *Thinking about Consciousness*, 41.
92   Ibid.
93   Ibid.
94   Ibid.

icalist would still have to demonstrate, step by step, that all causal roles which our explanations confer to our conscious states, do in fact belong to something physical (or do not exist)."[95] This work is yet to be done. Even so, materialists use the causal closure thesis to justify their general reductionist theories.[96]

Third, the principle of causal closure imposes a preliminary constraint on what can be recognized as a causal explanation. Physics, as defined by Papineau, provides the conditions by which to judge what is true about irreducible causation in our world. Therefore, it is assumed that causation is essentially non-mental. But why should we assume that? Their definition merely excludes mental causes from a materialist conceptual framework, but not from the real world. Further, the same general criteria for causality are applied to physical and mental causes.[97] Since mental causes of physical effects do not consist of physical processes, why should we demand some transfer of energy or mechanistic solution? This is a category mistake akin to Ed Feser's metal detector failing to find non-metal objects.

This is not to say that there is not work to be done to make sense of non-physical and physical causality. However, it is possible that we can know what a cause is without understanding *how* it actually operates in our world. That is, knowing what a cause is does not require that mental causes must function as physical mechanisms. Any student of David Hume knows that nothing necessitates causes to be like their effects. Hume argued that we do not derive the concept of cause from what we perceive of external things.[98] Then how do we understand causation? Philosopher Roderick Chisolm's answer: from our own experience. "It is only by understanding our own causal efficacy, as agents," Chisholm argues, "that we can grasp the concept of *cause* at all."[99] At a minimum, it is wrong to understand mental causality using the model for physical causality.

---

95   Gabbani, "The Causal Closure of What?" 157.

96   Materialists anticipate that successes in AGI research will soon provide evidence to support the principle of causal closure.

97   Gabbani, "The Causal Closure of What?" 162. Criteria for causality such as conservation of energy, the relation between energy and work, measurability in quantitative terms, conditions concerning time or locality, etc. are applied to both physical and mental events.

98   David Hume, "Essay Concerning Human Understanding," in Mortimer Adler, editor, *The Great Books of the Western World*, Volume 33 (Chicago: Encyclopedia Britannica, 1990), 458-463.

99   Roderick Chisolm, "Human Freedom and the Self," The Lindley Lecture, University of Kansas, (April 23, 1964), *KUScholarWorks*, https://kuscholarworks.

To summarize, my critique exposes the inadequacy of the causal closure thesis as a generalized empirical principle. This, in turn, means that the thesis is not a warranted premise of the argument for materialism. Instead, the causal closure thesis should be an empirical research hypothesis. As such, it has to be verified, step by step, and confirmed by the facts of each case before using it as the basis for judging causal explanations. This critique provides evidence toward establishing premise #2 in my argument: *The materialist philosophy of mind is false and self-defeating.*

The Functionalist Philosophy of Mind

Functionalism has been the dominant theory in the philosophy of mind since the 1970's and serves as the foundation and conceptual framework for AGI, whose aim is to artificially produce the intelligence of the human mind; that is, to *duplicate*, not merely *simulate*, human cognition in a computer.[100] Functionalism is especially applicable for AGI research because the theory views the mind as a functional system like a computing system with inputs, outputs, and a processing system. Previous materialist views of the mind, such as behaviorist and identity theories, are not compatible with AGI because they identify mental states specifically with either human behavior or human brain states. Functionalism aligns best with the goals of AGI researchers because the theory holds that mental states are identified by their functional or causal role, which means mental states could be multiply realized on computer hardware.

Simply stated, functionalism is a materialistic understanding of the human mind that treats mental states akin to a computer program. A typical analogy of this view is: the mind is to brain as the program is to hardware.[101] Functionalism takes as its starting point the observation that some things are properly characterized by the functions they perform and not by the stuff of which they are made (e.g., a knife defined by its ability to cut).[102] In other words, a mental state is defined by what it does and what sorts of causes and effects it has. A system with the right sort of causal relations

---

ku.edu/bitstream/handle/1808/12380/Human%20Freedom%20and%20the%20 Self-1964.pdf?sequence=1 (accessed April 13, 2020).

100   Robert C. Koons and George Bealer, editors, *The Waning of Materialism* (Oxford, UK: Oxford University Press, 2010), 8.

101   John Searle, *Philosophy in a New Century: Selected Essays* (Cambridge, UK: Cambridge University Press, 2008), 58.

102   Edward Feser, *Philosophy of Mind: A Beginner's Guide* (Oxford: Oneworld Publications, 2006), 70.

can be said to have a mind, whether it is instantiated in a human brain or a silicon central processing unit.

Therefore, on the functionalist view, thinking is not restricted to human brain structure, but can be multiply realized on computers or other material hardware. Mental states are explained by their functional role in a third-person theory of behavior, rather than through first-person introspective conscious awareness. In other words, functionalism takes mental states out of the realm of private subjective experience and into the public domain that is open to scientific investigation. For example, a functionalist account of being in pain would be defined as a mental state caused by bodily tissue damage from a pin prick or other sort of input that tends to cause groans or wincing behaviors in a person who then seeks help.

Functionalism is considered non-reductive because mental states are real properties and not reducible or identical to the physical properties of the brain.[103] Nonetheless, in its application for AGI, functionalism is thoroughly materialistic because mental states are only realized by physical states. Functionalism in AGI is committed to the 'causal closure of the physical' because mental properties are physically realized, such that for any mental property there is a physical property that fills the causal role.[104]

The reasoning behind AGI's analogy that human beings are digital machines (e.g., the mind is to brain as the program is to hardware), is represented by what James Fetzer calls, the Basic Model:[105]

	Human Beings	Digital Machines
Domain:	Stimuli	Inputs
Function:	Processes	Programs
Range:	Responses	Outputs

Human beings respond to stimuli, mediated by internal processes. Similarly, digital machines, when equipped with a program, produce outputs

---

103   Moreland and Craig, *Philosophical Foundations for a Christian Worldview*, 255-258.

104   Koons and Bealer, *The Waning of Materialism*, 5-6. On this view, anything that has physical effects – for example mental events – must supervene on, or reduce to, or be identical with something physical unless we are prepared to accept systematic over-determination.

105   James Fetzer, *Artificial Intelligence: Its Scope and Limits* (Boston: Kluwer Academic Publishers, 1990), xiii.

when given certain inputs. Mental processes are viewed as functions from stimuli to responses just as programs are viewed as functions from inputs to outputs. With functionalism, the processing of information and the internal organization of the system is what matters, not just the external behavior produced.

John Pollock affirms functionalism and its central importance to the project of AGI in his book *How to Build a Person: A Prolegomenon*. Pollock argues that "something is a person if and only if it has states whose interactions appropriately mimic our rational architecture. Obviously on this criterion, a machine can be a person."[106] In other words, a machine built with a rational architecture based on the functionalist view of mental states will be a person, which confirms premise #1 of my argument: *If AGI is metaphysically possible, then the materialist philosophy of mind is possible.*

Critique of the Functionalist Philosophy of Mind

I will argue that AGI predictions of conscious machines will never be realized because, as discussed in the previous section, it is based on the functionalist philosophy of mind, which offers no account of the fundamental and conspicuous feature of internal thought processes, namely consciousness. And moreover, AGI is, in principle, incapable of doing so. Simply stated, consciousness is the subjective, first-person character of what-it-is-like to experience such things as perception, rational understanding, thoughts, inference, emotions, feelings of pain, beliefs, bodily sensations, and imagination.[107]

In his 1974 paper "What Is It Like to Be a Bat?" Thomas Nagel explains that an organism has conscious mental states, "if and only if there is something that it is like to be that organism—something it is like for the organism to be itself."[108] Similarly, in David Chalmers' 2003 essay "Consciousness and its Place in Nature" he writes, "The hard problem of con-

---

106 John Pollock, *How to Build a Person: A Prolegomenon* (Cambridge, Massachusetts: A Bradford Book, 1989), 111.
107 Copan, Longman, Reese, and Strauss, editors, *Dictionary of Christianity and Science* (Michigan: Zondervan, 2017), 107-8.
108 Nagel, Thomas, "What Is It Like to Be a Bat? *The Philosophical Review* Vol 83 No. 4 (1974): 435-450. *JSTOR*, http://links.jstor.org/sici?sici=0031-8108%28 1974l0%2983%3A4%3C435%3AWIILTB%3E2.0.CO%3B2-Y (accessed March 3, 2020).

sciousness is the problem of experience. Human beings have subjective experience: something it is like to be them."[109]

Both Nagel and Chalmers make a crucial point about consciousness—it is known and accessed from a first-person perspective. Chalmers remains optimistic that someday there will be a scientific solution to the hard problem of consciousness, saying, "I'd be happy if we got to the point where, say, in 50 or 100 years we at least have some *candidate* theories; serious, well-developed mathematical theories that are consistent with the data . . . But we're not even close to that point yet. I guess I'm inclined to think we can always make a lot of progress. Whether we get all the way is an open question."[110] I appreciate Chalmers' intellectual honesty, but his cautious optimism that a scientific explanation of consciousness will be forthcoming is unwarranted.

In his now famous 1970 Princeton lectures entitled "Naming and Necessity," Saul Kripke distinguishes mental states from physical states, much like Nagel and Chalmers, because of their immediate phenomenological quality, their essential subjective feel.[111] For example, we identify pain by our conscious direct experience of it. Kripke argues that the essence of a mental state is an obvious fact, "that *being a pain* is a necessary property of each pain."[112] He explains further, "Pain is not picked out by one of its accidental properties; rather it is picked out by the property of being pain itself, by its immediate phenomenological quality. Thus, pain is not only rigidly designated by 'pain,' but the reference of the designator is determined by an essential property of the referent."[113] Kripke concluded that materialists must hold a complete physical description of the world, including mental facts. However, identity theorists have not made a convincing argument

---

109   David J. Chalmers, "Consciousness and its Place in Nature," In Steven Stich & Ted.Warfield, editors, *Blackwell Guide to Philosophy of Mind*, December 13, 2007, onlinelibrary.wiley.com, https://onlinelibrary.wiley.com/doi/10.1002/9780470998762.ch5 (accessed March 15, 2020), 2.

110   John Horgan, "David Chalmers Thinks the Hard Problem is Really Hard," *Scientific American*, April 10, 2017, https://blogs.scientificamerican.com/cross-check/david-chalmers-thinks-the-hard-problem-is-really-hard/, (accessed April 2, 2020).

111   Saul Kripke, *Naming and Necessity* (Oxford UK: Blackwell Publishing, 1972), 145-155.

112   Ibid., 146.

113   Ibid., 152.

for "mental facts being 'ontologically dependent' on physical facts in the straightforward sense of following from them by necessity."[114]

A strictly physical story will not do. Furthermore, why *should* something like mind or consciousness emerge from physical matter? If you begin with matter, rearrange it and tweak it to death according to physical causes and processes, you will end up with more complex arrangements of matter, not mind or consciousness. Conscious mental states as we experience them do not present a material appearance and do not fit neatly within the third-person scientific methodology to which the materialist view limits itself; in other words, consciousness poses a location problem. Consequently, for some materialists, if consciousness does not have a physical explanation, we simply cannot know it exists; hence, it is characterized as magical or mystical. Philosopher Galen Strawson calls this the "Great Silliness." To deny the existence of consciousness is the silliest claim ever made:

> When it comes to conscious experience, there's a rock-bottom sense in which we're fully acquainted with it just in having it. The having is the knowing. So, when people say that consciousness is a mystery, they're wrong—because we know what it is. It's the most familiar thing there is—however hard it is to put into words.[115]

Therefore, there remains a deep, recalcitrant problem of consciousness for functionalism, which characterizes mental states in terms of the causal relations of external inputs, behavioral outputs, and computational internal processes. Two eminent philosophers have argued against materialist philosophies of mind because of their inadequate account of conscious mental states: Immanuel Kant (1724-1804) and more recently, John Searle (born 1932).

Immanuel Kant

Immanuel Kant's writings on consciousness and materialism are complicated and obscure enough to allow a diversity of interpretations, re-interpretations, and misinterpretations. For example, philosophers such as Wilfrid Sellars and Patricia Kitcher reinterpret Kant's view in terms of

---

114   Saul Kripke, *Naming and Necessity* (Oxford UK: Blackwell Publishing, 1972), 155.
115   Galen Strawson, "The Conscious Deniers," *The New York Review of Books*, March 13, 2018, http://www.nybooks.com/daily/2018/03/13/the-consciousness-deniers/ (accessed March 20, 2020), 2.

contemporary functionalism and Ralf Meerbote rehabilitates Kant on the basis of Donald Davidson's anomalous monism. Henry Allison criticizes both of these strategies, showing the inability of even nonreductive, causal models of mind to capture the spontaneity of understanding as Kant conceives it.[116] For this chapter, I follow Henry Allison's interpretation in his notable essay "Kant's Refutation of Materialism."[117] Kant's epistemology reduces all acts of understanding to judgments. To judge is the activity of "taking as," meaning to take something as a such and such. For example, I am aware of "deriving conclusions from premises in such a way that the premises are taken to justify the conclusion."[118] In Kant's Recognition Argument, Allison connects the account of judging with recognizing reasons for beliefs: "[Kant's] claim, in other words, is that unless I believe that *p because* I recognize that my reasons for believing that *p* are good ones, I cannot be said to know that *p*." I understand Kant's *taking as* to be similar to C. S. Lewis's *seen to be* in acts of thinking. In chapter 3 of *Miracles*, Lewis explains the features of consciousness and intentionality of rational thought. "One thought can cause another not by *being*," Lewis writes, "but by being *seen to be* a ground for it."[119] By *seen* he means apprehended, grasped, or simply known. Allison understands Kant's acts of knowing in a similar way:

> In fact, it is this act of understanding, this grasping of reasons as reasons, that constitutes the required moment of recognition; and this cannot be analyzed as simply having another belief...Accordingly, it can be claimed that if the understanding is to take its reasons as reasons and, therefore, as justifying its beliefs, it must connect them with these beliefs in a unitary consciousness in a judgment in accordance with some rule or principle of synthesis, which functions as an "inference ticket." Furthermore, this "taking as" must be conceived as an inherently self-conscious activity, something that the subject does for itself (spontaneously) and is conscious of so do-

---

116   Henry E. Allison, "Kant's Refutation of Materialism, *The Monist* Volume 72, issue 2, (April 1, 1989): 190-208 and Henry E. Allison, *Kant's Theory of Freedom* (Cambridge: Cambridge University Press, 1990), 76-82.

117   Ibid., 190-208.

118   Ibid., 193.

119   C. S. Lewis, *Miracles: A Preliminary Study* (New York: HarperCollins, 1996), 25.

ing, rather than as something which it is caused to do and of which it is only conscious as a result.[120]

The main point I take from Kant's argument is that any account of the mind (like functionalism) that does not account for judgments and acts of understanding is self-defeating:

1. "I think" is the foundation for all rational thought.
2. If functionalism is the idea there is no "I" because it explains mental states entirely from a third-person perspective, then
3. My thoughts and beliefs about functionalism are false and self-defeating because a first-person perspective ("I think") necessarily accompanies all thought.

John Searle

Philosopher John Searle has been critiquing the philosophy of AGI for forty years. In his 1980 essay "Minds, Brains, and Computers," he argues that AGI is founded on the mistaken assumption that the brain is a digital computer and the mind is a computer program. He writes that, according to strong AI, "the computer is not merely a tool in the study of the mind; rather, the appropriately programmed computer really is a mind, in the sense that computers given the right programs can be literally said to *understand* and have other cognitive states."[121] Searle contends that both functionalism and the claim that computers will soon be conscious are both obviously false. His basic argument rests on the fundamental logical truth that syntax is not semantics; that is to say, symbols by themselves have no meaning. They are not about anything.[122] A computer program can never be a mind because "the syntactical operations of the implemented program are not by themselves sufficient to constitute or guarantee the presence of actual mental processes because they do not have any semantic content."[123] Searle focuses on the intentionality of first-person consciousness and the semantics of mental processes; intentionality is the *ofness* or *aboutness* of thoughts directed towards an object and semantics is

---

120   Allison, "Kant's Refutation of Materialism," 200-1.
121   John R. Searle, "Minds, Brains and Programs," in *The Behavioral and Brain Sciences*, Vol. 3. (1980): 417-457. Cogprints.org, July 14, 2003, http://cogprints.org/7150/1/10.1.1.83.5248.pdf (accessed March 1, 2020).
122   John R. Searle, *Philosophy in a New Century: Selected Essays* (Cambridge, UK: Cambridge University Press, 2008), 61.
123   Ibid., 15.

the meaningful content of the thought. Searle illustrated his controversial thesis against AGI with his Chinese Room thought experiment.

Searle reasoned that one way to test any theory of mind is to ask what it would be like if the mind actually worked that way? The following is a condensed version of the Chinese Room thought experiment:

> A person who does not know Chinese is locked in a room and given a large batch of Chinese writing. He is equipped only with such things as a pencil and a piece of paper and a rule book in English for formally manipulating Chinese symbols in terms of their syntax, not their semantics. The symbols passed into the room are called questions and the symbols he passes back out of the room (from following the rulebook) are the answers to the questions. The person in the room is able to simulate the behavior of a Chinese person who understands Chinese because he gives the correct answers to Chinese questions, but all the same, the person locked in the room does not understand a word of Chinese.[124]

AGI claims that the programmed computer actually *understands* the meanings of the symbols, but Searle says this is false because the computer has no way to get from the manipulation of the symbols to the meaning of the symbols. Further, the whole room (or system) has no way of getting to the meaning from the symbols. He writes, "Computation is insufficient for thinking since it is defined entirely syntactically, and thinking has to have something more than just symbols, it has to have a meaning or semantic content attached to the symbols."[125] The Chinese Room argument illustrates the fact that symbol manipulations alone, even billions of them, operating at lightning speed, does not constitute meaning or thought. Further, syntax cannot account for consciousness nor is it sufficient to cause consciousness. This argument has remained sound for the past forty years largely because it has nothing to do with any particular stage of computer technology and everything to do with the philosophy of functionalism.

---

124 Searle, "Minds, Brains, and Programs," 3-4. See Appendix A for the full Chinese Room Argument.

125 Ibid., 62.

On Searle's critique, just as with Kant's, a functionalist view of the mind is self-defeating:

1. The essential features of mental processes are consciousness, intentionality, and understanding.
2. Functionalism is the explanation that mental processes can be accounted for without consciousness, intentionality, and understanding.
3. Therefore, my thoughts and beliefs concerning functionalism are false and self-defeating because they lack the essential features of thinking and therefore, cannot be rationally justified as knowledge.

To summarize, both Kant and Searle arrive at the inescapable fact that rationality is, with its essential features of consciousness and intentionality, the starting point from which we must begin any inquiry about the nature of the mind, including functionalism. In essence, when functionalism explains away consciousness, it explains away its own explanation of the mind. There is no explanation of mind that does not presuppose a conscious mind. This critique of the functionalist philosophy of mind helps to establish *premise #2 of my argument: The materialist philosophy of mind is false and self-defeating.*

The Computational Theory of Mind

According to the Basic Model of functionalism, mental processing is analogous to computation, which means internal mental states carry out well-defined operations or sets of rules, much like an algorithm. An algorithm is a mechanical step-by-step procedure operating on syntactically well-defined symbols in a way that captures relations among the things the symbols represent.[126] The following example is an If/Then/Else algorithm:

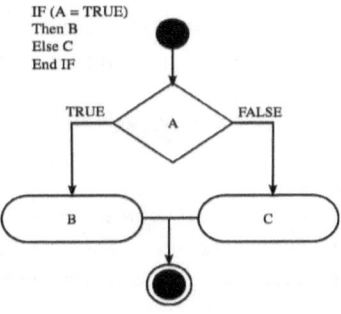

---

126 Rajakishore Nath, *Philosophy of Artificial Intelligence: A Critique of the Mechanistic Theory of Mind* (Boca Raton, Florida: Universal-Publishers, 2009), 34-5.

The computational theory of mind was inspired by Alan Turing's concept of the Universal Turing Machine, which was a device capable of implementing any algorithm.[127] Following the steps in an algorithm guarantees a desired state of affairs, such as an answer to a mathematical problem or a deduction from a chain of reasoning. Allen Newell (1927-1992) and Herbert Simon (1916-2001) developed the concept of the computer as a physical symbol system, which could simulate the same properties of intelligence as a human being. On their view, "All intelligence involves the use and manipulation of various symbol systems, such as mathematics or logic ... In the advent of the digital computer, symbol manipulation has become the province of electronic machinery as well."[128] This theory is considered the core doctrine of computer science and is at the heart of AGI research.

The general idea is that thinking and computing are the same thing. John Haugeland explains it this way: "Thinking is reasoning; reasoning is reckoning; reckoning is computation; computation is cognition, and the boundaries of computability define the boundaries of thought."[129] Therefore, minds are formal systems that automatically manipulate the tokens of some formal system according to the rules of that system.[130] If human thought is understood as neural processes implementing algorithms, then thinking and reasoning can be explained by physical causation. However, in a purely formal system, the marks (syntax) do not stand for anything. A formal system becomes a cognitive system when there exists an "interpretation," wherein well-formed formulae, true axioms, and truth-preserving theorems of the system provide meaning for the syntax. Haugeland calls these systems semantic engines because "if you take care of the syntax, the semantics will take care of itself."[131]

Before presenting my critique, it is necessary to clarify that the physical symbol system is not the only research model available for artificial intelligence. While AGI research has primarily progressed using logic-based classical computational systems, connectionist computer systems (i.e.,

---

127   Edward Feser, *Philosophy of Mind* (Oxford, UK: Oneworld Publishing, 2006),148.

128   Gardner, *The Mind's New Science,* 149-150.

129   James H. Fetzer, *Computers and Cognition: Why Minds Are Not Machines* (Boston: Kluwer Academic Publishers, 2001), Forward. By reckoning, Haugeland means the manipulation of marks in conformity with specific rules.

130   Ibid., 102.

131   John Haugeland, "Semantic Engines: An Introduction to Mind Design," *Mind Design* (Cambridge, MA: MIT Press, 1981), 44, https://cse.buffalo.edu/~rapaport/575/F01/haugeland.pdf (accessed April 15, 2020).

artificial neural networks) also provide researchers with a non-logicist alternative method. Connectionist models are biologically inspired by the neurons in the brain; they consist of large numbers of units joined together in a pattern of connections. Cognition is understood as computation across distributed patterns of activation, or neural nodes.[132] Connectionist models are good at very specific tasks, like pattern recognition, grammar structure recognition, and predicting the past tense of verbs. However, these tasks require huge amounts of training data, computing power, and storage space.[133] For example, a neural network that was trained to recognize faces had a data set containing ten million images on a thousand machines. The AlphaGo model was trained on thirty million different games, more than any human can play in one lifetime.[134]

Despite the claim that neural networks are non-logicist systems, all connectionist models have some symbolic components. This prompts many logicists, like Selmer Bringsjord, to conclude that "any successful AI model of human cognition, and *a fortiori* any sentient artificial intelligence itself, must use classical, logic-driven architecture."[135] Accordingly, connectionist systems, by themselves, cannot build a human-level AGI capable of completing a wide range of tasks. Therefore, since connectionists use, to some degree, the basic computational conception of cognition, connectionism does not escape arguments against the computational theory of mind.[136]

---

132 Fetzer, *Computers and Cognition*, 17.

133 Cameron Buckner and James Garson, "Connectionism", *The Stanford Encyclopedia of Philosophy* (Fall 2019 Edition), Edward N. Zalta (ed.), URL = <https://plato.stanford.edu/archives/fall2019/entries/connectionism/> (accessed April 16, 2020).

134 Jieschu Wang, "Symbolism vs. Connectionism: A Closing Gap in Artificial Intelligence," Blog, http://wangjieshu.com/2017/12/23/symbol-vs-connectionism-a-closing-gap-in-artificial-intelligence/ (accessed April 16, 2020).

135 Selmer Bringsjord, "Is the Connectionist-Logicist Clash One of AI's Wonderful Red Herrings?" (1991), *Journal of Experimental & Theoretical Artificial Intelligence*, Vol. 3 (1991), 319, *Taylor and Francis*, http://kryten.mm.rpi.edu/connectionist_logicist_clash.pdf (accessed April 16, 2020).

136 Selmer Bringsjord, *What Robots Can And Can't Be* (The Netherlands: Kluwer Academic Publishers, 1992), 50. Neural nets are at bottom Turing machines; these two types of computational creatures (CAs and TMs) are simply different ways of idealizing mathematically the very same computing entity. Neural nets are and will be used to handle symbolic computation. For this reason, connectionists cannot circumvent the arguments against the computational theory of mind.

Critique of the Computational Theory of Mind

My line of argument against the computational theory of mind is twofold. First, most thinking is not governed by algorithms or programs, but instead operates as semiotic (sign-using) systems. Second, computers function as physical symbol systems, not as semiotic (sign-using) systems. Therefore, thinking is not computing and computers are not thinking things.

Haugeland's classic version of the computational conception claims that all thinking is reasoning; all reasoning is reckoning; all reckoning is computation; and the boundaries of computability are the boundaries of thought.[137] By reckoning, I take him to mean a formal system that manipulates marks according to specific rules. To be clear, no one denies that some of our reasoning, specifically mathematical proofs and deductive logic, involves the execution of mental algorithms.

However, the boundaries of thought extend far beyond computability; in fact, most thinking is non-computational, meaning it does not follow algorithmic procedures required for justification. Obvious examples include imagination, abductive reasoning, conjecture, daydreams, dreams, and mental indeterminism (various associations of thoughts that occur under the same relevant causal conditions).[138] Even though formal systems are useful in modeling mathematical and deductive reasoning, the execution of mental algorithms appears to be no more than one special kind of thinking. To over-generalize the concept of computability to include *all* reasoning is not only unfounded, but it trivializes the nature of thinking.

Logic theorist and philosopher Charles S. Peirce (1839-1914) was an innovative thinker who first developed semiotics, the theory that minds are sign-using systems whose semiotic processes involve a distinctive triadic relation between a sign, what it stands for, and a sign-user.[139] On this view, the sign is as basic to the philosophy of mind as the inorganic molecule

---

137 Fetzer, *Computers and Cognition*, 102.
138 Ibid., 102-113.
139 Charles S. Peirce, "Logic as Semiotic: The Theory of Signs," in *Philosophical Writings of Peirce*, J. Buchler, editor (New York: Dover Publications, 1955), http://lchc.ucsd.edu/MCA/Mail/xmcamail.2017-05.dir/pdfAAJf6e4SaC.pdf (accessed April 16, 2020).

is to chemistry and the atom is to physics.¹⁴⁰ The following diagram illustrates the semiotic transmission of information:¹⁴¹

Mental cognition is a semiotic process involving: (1) a relation of *causation* between sign S and sign-user Z, (2) a relation of *grounding* between sign S and what it stands for X, and (3) a relation of *interpretation* when sign-user Z interprets the relation between sign S and what it stands for X.¹⁴² For example, a 'stop sign' stands for 'come to a halt.' A sign-user interprets the relation between the 'stop sign' and the meaning 'come to a halt,' which brings about a mental disposition to slow down and come to a complete stop before proceeding through the intersection. The meaning of the sign is evident in the interpretation that it generates in the sign-user.¹⁴³ Cognition occurs as a consequence of the causal interaction between the sign, what it stands for, and the sign-user.

The question is whether the machine's physical symbol system is equivalent to the human mental semiotic system.¹⁴⁴ In other words, do machine

---

140   David D. Olds, "A Semiotic Model of Mind," apa.sagepub.com, September 18, 2016, 500, http://citeseerx.ist.psu.edu/viewdoc/download?-doi=10.1.1.1027.7291&rep=rep1&type=pdf (accessed April 19, 2020).
141   James Fetzer, *Artificial Intelligence: Its Scope and Limits* (The Netherlands: Kluwer Academic Publishers, 1990), 277.
142   Ibid., 278.
143   Fetzer, *Computers and Cognition*, 15. Peirce distinguished three kinds of signs: Icons, such as photographs, sculptures, or paintings; Indices, such as smoke related to fire or red spots related to measles; Symbols, such as words in English.
144   Ibid., 156-7. A 'symbol' in a physical symbol system does not have to be a sign. It does not have to stand for anything; rather, it can merely be a meaningless mark that is processed based on its shape, size, and relative location.

algorithms/programs function the same way as human mental processes? The critical piece missing in machine mentality is the *grounding* of the sign's meaning for the computer. Just as Kant and Lewis argued there must be a grounding for acts of understanding, what they called "taking as" and "seeing as," the computer lacks this understanding and judgment about the symbol and its related meaning. Hence, the computer does not interpret the symbol's meaning because the signs used by the machine are not inherently meaningful to the system itself. The following diagram shows that relations between inputs and outputs exist without any grounding between the cause and effect.[145]

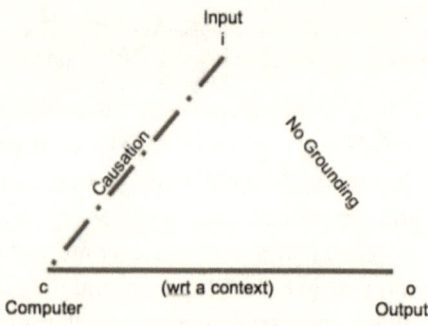

Computers manipulate marks or symbols following the steps of an algorithm. The marks and symbols (input) have causal effects (output), but the symbols do not stand for anything for the system itself. Even if there is an interpreted formal system with well-formed formulae, axioms, and theorems that provide meaning to the marks, the meanings of the marks (syntax) have been deliberately constructed by an interpreting agent (mind) to reflect the relations that obtain between the entities that exist in the system. In other words, the marks are meaningful for the *users* of a system, not meaningful for *use* by a system.[146] A computer that processes meaningless symbols does not have the semantic capacity essential for mentality.

This argument clearly demonstrates that semantics is not intrinsic to syntax, which is an idea that harkens back to John Searle's Chinese Room argument. In fact, he has recently beefed up his argument by explaining that syntax is essentially an observer-relative notion, meaning syntax

---

145   Fetzer, *Artificial Intelligence: Its Scope and Limits*, 278.
146   Fetzer, *Computers and Cognition*, 114.

depends on an interpretation from outside.[147] Computational states like marks, symbols, or syntax are not intrinsic to physics. They are *assigned* to it by an agent (mind).[148] While computers function causally on the basis of symbols, even to the extent of *simulating* human behavior in their outputs, they do not qualify as semiotic, sign-using, systems. Therefore, machines do not possess minds and the Basic Model that equates thinking and computing is false, which helps to establish premise #2 of my argument: *The materialist philosophy of mind is false and self-defeating*.

Summary of the Critique of the Philosophy of AGI

The three materialist theories that form the foundation of AGI research are: the causal closure thesis, functionalism, and the computational theory of mind. My critiques provide evidence for *premise #2 of the argument: The materialist philosophy of mind is false and self-defeating*. For AGI researchers whose ultimate goal is to build a person, these three materialist philosophies of mind fuel a belief that is metaphysically impossible: that machines will become conscious beings with minds. Therefore, *premise #3 of the argument: AGI is metaphysically impossible*.

Conclusion: The Way Forward

The ultimate goal of AGI is to build a machine with a conscious mind and human-level intelligence— that is, a person. My conclusion is that the AGI project is metaphysically impossible, a conclusion that also entails that superintelligent machines will not be realized. Additionally, since achieving AGI is the pivotal step in reaching the Singularity, there is no reason to believe there will be such an event. In my examination and critique of the philosophy of AGI, I demonstrated there are limits to their project that will remain recalcitrant, not due to any deficiency in technological advancement, but because the assumed materialist philosophy of mind is false. My philosophical critique of the person-building claims of AGI confirms C. S. Lewis's conviction: "Good philosophy must exist, if for no other reason, because bad philosophy needs to be answered."[149]

There is a way forward for AGI researchers and transhumanists alike. Those researchers who reject the materialist philosophy of mind will

---

147　John Searle, *Philosophy in a New Century: Selected Essays* (Cambridge, UK: Cambridge University Press, 2008), 94.

148　Ibid., 96-7.

149　C. S. Lewis, *The Weight of Glory* (HarperCollins: New York, 1980), 58.

change their focus from attempting to build human-level intelligent machines to more modest and rationally warranted projects. Success will be found in the development of expert systems, the rapid processing of vast quantities of data, and the simulation of natural and behavioral phenomena.[150] To the extent that the goals of AI are in keeping with its philosophical limits, they will provide methods and tools that benefit all mankind.

AGI researchers should, by all means, try to determine *how much* of human cognition can be represented computationally. This is a legitimate research project, wherein the computer is properly viewed as a tool for our intellect, rather than as a potential superior. Mathematician, philosopher, and theologian William Dembski argues for this perspective, naming it the "Law of Priority in Creation." It means the "creator is always strictly greater than the creature,"[151] which is the exact opposite of the transhumanist perspective of building a superintelligent machine that is vastly more intelligent than human persons.

There are AGI researchers and transhumanists who are still wholly committed to giving us machines (robots) whose behavior *appears* to possess human-level intelligence.[152] These machines will require a test more effective than the Turing Test to separate the genuine "thinkers" from the "pretenders." In the next chapter, I will investigate the computer program BRUTUS1, an artificial literary "agent" who *appears* to possess the sophisticated human behavior of writing interesting short stories. I will introduce the Lovelace Test as a way to judge whether BRUTUS1 has achieved human-level intelligence.

The failure of the materialist philosophy of mind points to the need for an alternative. In the next chapter, I will suggest a return to Aristotelian metaphysics, which includes the idea that concrete substances, such as human persons, are composites of matter and form, where the form (or immaterial soul) exists in the substance and is abstract, universal, and ir-

---

150   Fetzer, *Artificial Intelligence: Its Scope and Limits*, xv.
151   William Dembski, "Converting Matter into Mind; Alchemy and the philosopher's stone in cognitive science," *Perspectives on Science and Christian Faith*, Vol. 42, No. 4 (1990): 202-26. http://www.arn.org/docs/dembski/wd_convmtr.htm, Nov. 11, 1998, (accessed March 30, 2020).
152   "A Timeline of Transhumanism," *The Verge*, https://www.theverge.com/a/transhumanism-2015/history-of-transhumanism (accessed March 29, 2020). Transhumanist AGI research centers include: Singularity University, Machine Intelligence Research Institute, Novamente, Center for Applied Rationality, Thiel Fellowship, Global Brain Institute, OpenCogBot, and The Future of Life Institute.

reducible.[153] The causal components of a material substance include material, formal, final, and efficient causes. Modern materialism rejects formal and final causes, recognizing all causes as physical, efficient causes, which has given rise to the mind/body problem. Aristotelian philosophy will be explored in more detail in chapter three as a viable alternative to the failed materialist philosophy of mind.

---

153   Feser, *Philosophy of Mind*, 219-223.

Appendix A

The Chinese Room Argument

Suppose that I'm locked in a room and given a large batch of Chinese writing. I know no Chinese, either written or spoken; in fact, it all looks like meaningless squiggles to me. I am then given a second batch of Chinese script together with a set of rules for correlating the second batch with the first batch. The rules are in English, so I understand them as well as any native English speaker. The rules enable me to correlate one set of formal symbols with another set of formal symbols. Now suppose I am given a third batch of Chinese symbols together with instructions (in English) that enable me to correlate elements of this third batch with the first two batches, and these rules instruct me how to give back certain Chinese symbols in response to certain sorts of shapes given me in the third batch. Unknown to me, the people who are giving me all these symbols call the first batch a "script," the second batch a "story," and they call the third batch "questions." They call the symbols I give them back in response to the third batch "answers to the questions." They call the set of rules in English the "program." After awhile, I get so good at following the instructions for manipulating the Chinese symbols and the programmers get so good at writing the programs, that from the point of view of the people outside the room in which I am locked, my answers to the questions are absolutely indistinguishable from those native Chinese speakers. Just from looking at my answers, no one can tell I don't speak a word of Chinese. As far as the Chinese are concerned, I simply behave like a computer. I perform computational operations on formally specified elements. For the purposes of the Chinese, I am simply an instantiation of the computer program.[154]

---

154 John R. Searle, "Minds, Brains, and Programs," *Behavioral and Brain Sciences*, Vol. 3, (1980): 417-457, cogprints.org., July 14, 2003,3-4, http://cogprints.org/7150/1/10.1.1.83.5248.pdf (accessed March 1, 2020).

Chapter Three

Artificial General Intelligence and Creativity: How BRUTUS Fails the Lovelace Test

"The Analytical Engine has no pretensions whatsoever to originate anything. It can do whatever we know how to order it to perform."[1]

Lady Ada Lovelace

Introduction

THE FUNDAMENTAL GOAL of Artificial General Intelligence (AGI) is to make computers genuinely think, not merely to mimic intelligence.[2] The quest to build machines with minds is behind what has become known as the Double Blur, or the gradual blurring of the traditional boundaries between human minds (persons) and computers.[3] That is to say, there is a deliberate effort to build computers (robots) to be persons, and at the same time, not only to assume persons are essentially computers,

---

1 James Essinger, *Ada's Algorithm: How Lord Byron's Daughter Ada Lovelace Launched the Digital Age* (Brooklyn: Melville House, 2014), 172.

2 There are two branches of AI research, strong and weak. This chapter makes a case against strong AI, which attempts to duplicate human intelligence. In contrast, weak AI seeks to simulate human intelligence.

3 Selmer Bringsjord and David A. Ferrucci, *What Robots Can and Can't Be* (Dordrecht, The Netherlands: Kluwer Academic Publishers, 1992), 4.

but to transform persons into robots through artificial technological enhancements.

This notion of the Double Blur was evident in 1986 when philosopher John Haugeland explained "the very idea of artificial intelligence." He said, "AI wants only the genuine article: *machines with minds*, in the full and literal sense. This is not science fiction, but real science, based on a theoretical conception as deep as it is daring: namely, we are, at root, *computers ourselves*."[4] The "very idea of AI," according to Haugeland, assumes a mechanistic view of human intelligence that is grounded in the materialist philosophy of mind, which essentially explains mental states as either identical to, or realized by, physical states and processes.[5]

Transhumanists Hans Moravec and Ray Kurzweil predict the overwhelming success of AGI, claiming that computers and robots will soon exceed human persons in virtually all domains, including creativity.[6] However, to date, AGI researchers have failed to demonstrate that machines are capable of genuine creativity. In 1843, Lady Lovelace was perhaps one of the first to recognize that creativity is the essential difference between human minds and machines, asserting that computers only do what their programs order them to do.[7] And one hundred and seventy-seven years hence, the question of whether a machine could be genuinely creative is still hotly debated.

Selmer Bringsjord, director of the Rensselaer AI and Reasoning (RAIR) Laboratory at Rensselaer Polytechnic Institute in New York, set out with his team to answer the creativity question by designing a computer program that generates original short stories; they named their artificial literary agent BRUTUS1.[8] An investigation of their methods and the recalcitrant obstacles they encountered confirms Lady Lovelace's judgement that machines (robots) will never have genuine human creativity. In the previous

---

4   John Haugeland, *Artificial Intelligence: The Very Idea* (Cambridge, Massachusetts: The MIT Press, 1986), 2.

5   Edward Feser, *Philosophy of Mind* (Oxford, England: Oneworld Publications, 2006), 57.

6   See the following books that promote AGI: Hans Moravec, *Robot: Mere Machine to Transcendent Mind* (New York: Oxford University Press, 1999); John Pollock, *How To Build a Person: A Prolegomenon* (Cambridge, Massachusetts: The MIT Press, 1989); Ray Kurzweil, *How to Create a Mind: The Secret Of Human Thought Revealed* (New York: Penguin Books, 2012).

7   Essinger, *Ada's Algorithm*, 172.

8   Bringsjord and Ferricci, *What Robots Can and Can't Be*, preface. BRUTUS is a system architecture for story generation. BRUTUS1 is the initial implementation of this architecture, with future versions expected.

chapter, I critiqued the Double Blur, arguing that the materialist philosophy of mind assumed by AGI is flawed and therefore, computers are not minds and human minds are not computers. However, since AGI researchers continue their mission and claim that sophisticated machines will possess creativity, the focus of this chapter will be to investigate, critique, and test artificial creativity.

I will first investigate the concept of human creativity by exploring two divergent philosophies: the scientific materialist view and the transcendent view. Next, I will explain why literary creativity is the goal for BRUTUS1. Most importantly, I will disclose and analyze the two major obstacles that make genuine human creativity beyond the reach of computation and explain how Selmer Bringsjord's team nonetheless reverse-engineered BRUTUS1 to *appear* creative. I will then answer the crucial epistemological question of how to test machine creativity by presenting the Lovelace Test as the adjudicator between the appearance of creativity in a machine and genuine human creativity. I conclude by suggesting a return to the classical Aristotelian philosophical worldview as an alternative to the materialist philosophy of mind.

The Concept of Human Creativity

Creativity is Observable

The first claim of the Double Blur is that a machine will be a person, in the full sense, which includes creativity. Transhumanist Ray Kurzweil predicted in 2009 that within a quarter of a century "machines will exhibit the full range of human intellect, emotions, and skills, ranging from musical and other creative aptitudes to physical movement."[9] Kurzweil fails to specify exactly what he means by creative aptitudes. But scholars doing creativity research hold that something is creative if it is, first of all, novel and useful, whether an idea, a solution to a problem, a short story, art, or music. The Cambridge English Dictionary reflects a similar idea in its definition of creativity: "the ability to produce original and unusual ideas, or to make something new or imaginative."[10]

---

9   Ray Kurzweil, 'The Coming Merging of Mind and Machine," *Scientific American* (March 23, 2009), https://www.scientificamerican.com/article/merging-of-mind-and-machine/ (accessed April 17, 2020).

10   Creativity, *The Cambridge English Dictionary*, https://dictionary.Cambridge.org/us/dictionary/english/creativity (accessed April 17, 2020).

AGI researchers recognize creativity as part of human nature and expect to eventually succeed in building a creative machine. Accordingly, there are numerous projects to develop machines capable of performing creative and inventive tasks, such as Stephen Thaler's Creativity Machine and John Koza's Invention Machine.[11]

Human creativity has left an indelible mark on our world, as seen in virtually every domain—literature, art, music, humor, science, engineering, technology, and every other field of knowledge. Since creativity shapes the human experience and drives human progress, it is not surprising that there is general agreement, even among such diverse scholars as theologians, philosophers, cognitive scientists, psychologists, and artists, that creativity is a natural part of being human and is knowable by personal experience and by observation. We recognize creativity when novel ideas bring into existence new products and new ways of doing things. This shared recognition has led to the development of standard definitions and criteria for evaluating creativity.

For instance, the Patent Act of 1790 "promoted the progress of useful arts," especially in the realm of science and technology.[12] The U. S. Patent Office has since developed legal conceptions of creativity, which require proof of originality and usefulness as the primary criteria for evaluation.[13] AGI researchers have recently raised questions concerning whether the U. S. Patent Office should legally allow patentability and inventorship status to artificially intelligent machines, a status that has historically only been granted to human persons.[14] This kind of legal claim brings to mind the

---

[11] Kay Firth-Butterfield and Yoon Chae, "Artificial Intelligence Collides with Patent Law," World Economic Forum, White Paper (April 2018), http://www3.weforum.org/docs/WEF_48540_WP_End_of_Innovation_Protecting_Patent_Law.pdf (accessed April 20, 2020).

[12] Fraser: Discover Economic History, *U. S. Patent Law of 1790*. https://fraser.stlouisfed.org/title/5734 (accessed April 20, 2020).

[13] United States Patent and Trademark Office, *Intellectual Property Terminology*. The definition of invention is "any art or process *(way of doing or making things)*, machine, manufacture, design, or composition of matter, or any new and useful improvement thereof, or any variety of plant, which is or may be patentable under the patent laws of the United States." https://www.uspto.gov/learning-and-resources/glossary#sec-N (accessed April 20, 2020).

[14] Firth-Butterfield and Chae, "Artificial Intelligence Collides with Patent Law," 6-10; Jared Council, "Can an AI System Be Given a Patent?" *The Wallstreet Journal*, October 11, 2019, https://www.wsj.com/articles/can-an-ai-system-be-given-a-patent-11570801500 (accessed April 20, 2020).

fictional courtroom deliberation from the television series *Star Trek: The Next Generation*, which resulted in a judgement that the android Data was a person, insofar as he had free will to reject being disassembled for further research.[15] This chapter's research and conclusions are relevant to the current case brought against the U. S. Patent Office and perhaps will change how Star Trek enthusiasts view the outcome of the fictional court case.

Philosophies of Creativity - Two Views

In spite of the widespread agreement about the existence of creativity, there are two divergent philosophies regarding the origin and process of creativity: the scientific materialist view and the ancient transcendent view. It will become clear that each view's understanding of creativity is rooted in that view's understanding of the human person.

The Scientific Materialist View

The field of creativity research is linked to the study of cognition and intelligence, but because creativity has often been characterized as mystical and uninspectable, the research has lacked scientific rigor and its connection with intelligence has been questioned. Thus, even though creativity research existed on its own and was studied for its own sake, it languished in the academy for much of the twentieth century.[16] That changed when J. P. Guilford breathed new life into creativity research by focusing on its appalling neglect in his 1950 presidential address to the American Psychological Association.[17] The resurgence of interest fostered various creativity research programs that focused on developing new scientific theories that could account for the nature and process of creativity as an internal process of human cognition instead of as a mystical process coming from outside the realm of human understanding and inspection. I will survey three different attempts to explain creativity from the scientific materialist perspective.

---

15   *Star Trek: The Next Generation*, Season 2, episode 9, "The Measure of a Man," https://memoryalpha.fandom.com/wiki/The_Measure_Of_A_Man_(episode) (accessed April 20, 2020).

16   Robert J. Sternberg, editor, *The Nature of Creativity: Contemporary Psychological Perspectives* (New York: Cambridge University Press, 1988), vii.

17   Ibid.

(1) Creativity as a mechanical process

I begin my survey with AGI theorist and cognitive psychologist Roger Schank, mainly because he exemplifies the scientific materialist perspective with such gusto. He claims that creativity is a mechanical process based on the assumption "that there is nothing mystical in the processes that underlie thinking," and therefore, "behind the creative process an algorithm must exist, in principle."[18] Of course by making this assumption he simply begs the question. After all, the question is whether creativity can be reduced to a mechanical process. Nevertheless, Schank overlooks matters of philosophy and prefers to address the practical AGI question, which is, "Can we write a set of rules such that if a machine followed them it would be able to create new things?"[19]

Schank's model for understanding creativity is called the Dynamic Memory model of processing, which targets a particular kind of creativity, namely the creation of novel explanations.[20] The overall premise behind the model is that novel explanations require an active memory of explanation patterns (XP), which are standard explanations that have been used before, and two sub-processes: a search process to find an XP, and an alteration process to modify an XP for a different situation.[21] On this view, computers will be fed exhaustive data and experiences that can be adapted and used to create novel explanations for new situations. Schank reasons this way: "Creative machines are possible, in principle; therefore, creativity is not such a mysterious process after all."[22]

(2) Computational model of scientific creative insight

Computer scientists Patrick Langley and Randolph Jones have developed a computational theory of scientific insight. They recognize that creativity is at the heart of true scientific progress and in many cases discoveries are marked by unexpected creative insights that are suddenly revealed to the mind.[23] Their research focuses on the importance of analogical reasoning

---

18 Roger C. Schank, "Creativity as a mechanical process," in Robert J. Sternberg, editor, *The Nature of Creativity* (New York: Cambridge University Press, 1988), 220.
19 Ibid.
20 Ibid.
21 Ibid., 221.
22 Ibid., 237-8.
23 Pat Langley and Randolph Jones, "A computational model of scientific insight," in Robert J. Sternberg, editor, *The Nature of Creativity*, 177-180. Exam-

in human cognition. The basic tenet is that creative insight is a memory-related phenomenon that centers on the mechanisms of indexing and retrieval and not on a process of searching through some problem space.[24] Their theory states that human insight occurs in three stages: the preparation stage, when useful structures are indexed in the memory; the illumination stage, when a promising analogy is retrieved; and the verification stage, when the solution is checked.[25] They explain that the "Aha" feeling associated with true illumination is the result of the rapid reorganization of the contents of short-term memory during the retrieval process.[26] Their problem-solving program EUREKA was designed as an application of their theory. Even though their focus has been on scientific insight, they predict that the mechanisms in their theory could be generalized to explain other forms of creative behavior.[27]

(3) Margaret Boden's approach to creativity

Margaret Boden is a leading authority on computational creativity and a research professor of cognitive science in the Department of Informatics at the University of Sussex. Her essay "Creativity and Artificial Intelligence" begins with a dismissal of any definition of creativity that includes divine inspiration or human imagination or intuition because "these popular views cannot be plausibly applied to robots."[28] Her own definition of creativity requires that an idea be novel and valuable, which fits the consensus definition.[29] She distinguishes two senses of novelty: an idea can be

---

ples of experiences of sudden insight that yielded scientific discoveries include Archimedes, Henri Poincare, and Louis Kekule.

24   Pat Langley and Randolph Jones, "A computational model of scientific insight," in Robert J. Sternberg, editor, *The Nature of Creativity*, 190.

25   Ibid., 190-197.

26   Ibid., 196. See also Pat Langley and Randolph Jones, "Retrieval and Learning in Analogical Problem Solving," on website *Researchgate*, May 1997, https://www.researchgate.net/publication/2663663_Retrieval_and_Learning_in_Analogical_Problem_Solving (accessed April 22, 2020). Their paper presents their problem-solving system EUREKA, which was designed as an application of their theory.

27   Ibid., 199.

28   Margaret A. Boden, "Could a Robot Be Creative—And Would We Know?" in Kenneth M. Ford, Clark Glymour, and Patrick J. Hayes, editors, *Android Epistemology* (Menlo Park, CA: American Association for Artificial Intelligence, 1995), 52.

29   Margaret A. Boden, "Creativity and Artificial Intelligence," in Elliot Samuel Paul and Scott Barry Kaufman, editors, *The Philosophy of Creativity: New Essays* (New York: Oxford University Press, 2014), 227.

new to the originator, called psychologically creative (P-creative), or new to the whole of human thought, called historically creative (H-creative).[30] In addition to being novel and valuable, Boden adds the qualification of "surprise," differentiating between three types of surprises: unexpected, improbable, and impossible.[31] Each type of surprise corresponds to three types of creativity: combinational, exploratory, and transformational.

Combinational creativity combines old ideas in a new way. An example would be the unexpected surprise we feel upon hearing the Lennon/McCartney arrangement of the song "Yesterday," which includes the cello, an instrument normally associated with a totally different genre of music.[32] Exploratory creativity constructs novel structures within a defined conceptual space and we feel surprise because we never even considered the idea. An example is Arnold Schoenberg's creation of *atonal* music by dropping the home-key constraint, a technique which is now integrated into everything from film scores to the jazz solos of Miles Davis and Ornett Coleman.[33] Transformational creativity produces ideas or artifacts that do not fit into any known style and the surprise we feel is more akin to shock. An example would be Pablo Picasso's cubism, a revolutionary style of modern art.[34]

Boden argues that computers could appear to be creative in a combinational and exploratory way, but leaves open the question of whether computers could "really" be creative in a transformational way. She acknowledges that computer-based systems lack autonomy, intentionality, and consciousness, which are essential for genuine creativity.[35] In spite of these obstacles, she hopes that these philosophical questions can be answered in favor of materialism.

Summary of the Scientific Materialist view of Creativity

The foregoing research fuels the work of AGI, whose aim is to reduce creativity to computation, which will in turn help establish a purely physical

---

30   Margaret A. Boden, "Creativity and Artificial Intelligence," in Elliot Samuel Paul and Scott Barry Kaufman, editors, *The Philosophy of Creativity: New Essays* (New York: Oxford University Press, 2014), 227.

31   Ibid., 228.

32   Selmer Bringsjord and David A. Ferrucci, *Artificial Intelligence and Literary Creativity: Inside the Mind of BRUTUS, a Storytelling Machine* (Mahwah, NJ: Lawrence Erlbaum Associates, Inc. Publishers, 2000), xix.

33   Boden, "Could a Robot be Creative- And Would We Know?" 55-56. Tonal music is based on tonal harmony and each piece has a "home key," from which it starts, does not stray, and in which it must finish.

34   Boden, "Creativity and Artificial Intelligence," 229.

35   Ibid., 232-242.

basis for the human mind. There are three presuppositions, whether stated or implied, that undergird the aforementioned contemporary research programs. They are first, wholly committed to ontological materialism, including the physical causal closure structure of the world, meaning that physical matter and causes are the only reality. Second, they assume a materialist philosophy of mind, which is the view that mental states are either identical to, or realized by, physical states and processes. Lastly, they assume that human persons are computational finite systems, which means thinking and computing are essentially the same thing.

The materialist account of creativity falls prey to Ed Feser's metal detector fallacy, which is the false belief that since the scientific method and reductionism have been successful in detecting the physical laws of the universe, they should also be successful in detecting the underlying laws of human creativity. However, the scientific "metal detector" is inadequate for the task because it is only able to detect the physical aspects of creativity, such as the observation of neurons firing in the brain. There is little reason to accept these assumptions since the empirical evidence is lacking to prove that mental states can be reduced to computation, with no remainder. In fact, it seems that cognitive scientists hold a computational view of creativity not for evidential reasons, but rather because of a commitment to ontological materialism and the principle of causal closure in the first place.

The Transcendent View of Creativity

The transcendent view is radically different from the scientific materialist view in that creativity is seen as a divine gift, meaning it originates from an otherworldly source and therefore, is not ultimately reducible to purely natural physical processes.[36] Pagan, Jewish, and Christian thinkers, even with their significant differences, agree that human creativity is a divine gift. Contemporary AGI researchers, generally speaking, reject any conception of creativity that includes a deity because it is impossible to account for divinity in a computer program. For example, in two scholarly anthologies, of the thirty-six essays on the nature of creativity, only one scholar mentions the transcendent view, and then only to dismiss it.[37] Even

---

36   The view that human creativity is not ultimately reducible to purely natural physical processes can be held without taking the further step of tracing it to a divine source. As shown on page 4-6 of this paper, creativity can be known by experience and observation. Hence, creativity could be understood as a universal feature of humanity.

37   Robert J. Sternberg, *The Nature of Creativity: Contemporary Psychological Perspectives* (New York: Cambridge University Press, 1988) and Elliot Samuel

though the transcendent view has lost favor in the academy, rejecting it *a priori* is unwise, especially since the materialist view is unable to account for all aspects of human creativity. A survey of the following sources— ancient Hebrew, ancient Greek, and two modern Christians—will help us better understand creativity from the transcendent perspective.

(1) Ancient Hebrews

After Moses led the Israelites out of Egypt (1446 B.C.E), God gave specific instructions regarding the building of the tabernacle, the place where God's presence would dwell with His people. The book of Exodus records that God gifted certain men with creative ability, "in whose mind He had put skill, everyone whose heart stirred him up to come to do the work."[38] God called Bezalel son of Uri to be the chief craftsman of the tabernacle and "filled him with the Spirit of God, with ability and intelligence, with knowledge and all craftsmanship, to devise artistic designs, to work in gold, silver, and bronze, in cutting stones for setting, and in carving wood, to work in every craft."[39] God appointed Oholiab and other able men as craftsmen and gave them the ability to make all that was commanded.[40] God inspired both Bezalel and Oholiab to teach the "skill to do every sort of work done by an engraver or by a designer or by an embroiderer in blue and purple and scarlet yarns and fine twined linen, or by a weaver—by any sort of workman or skilled designer."[41] This Hebrew account reveals God as the source of creativity, giving Bezalel and his men the artistic capacity to be men skilled in the creative arts.

(2) Ancient Greece

Gerard Naddaf specializes in ancient Greek philosophy and researches the origin and meaning of the terms used by Homer and Hesiod (C. 750 BCE) to explain poetic experience.[42] Naddaf argues that Homer and Hesiod, along with their respective audiences, had a firm religious conviction that poets were inspired by the Muses and Apollo and that "poetry itself was a

---

Paul and Scott Barry Kaufman, *The Philosophy of Creativity: New Essays* (New York: Oxford University Press, 2014).

38   Exodus 36:2 (ESV).
39   Exodus 31:3-5 (ESV).
40   Exodus 31:6 (ESV).
41   Exodus 35:34-35 (ESV).
42   Gerard Naddaf, "The Origin and Meaning of Poetic Inspiration in Ancient Greece," Seminar Presentation: The University of Sydney, November 10, 2011, 19, website *Academia*, https://www.academia.edu/32876708/The_Or-

divine gift—as willed by the gods."[43] For Homeric Greeks, the idea of inspiration is synonymous with "breath," specifically the words *pneio*, *pnoie*, and *empneio* convey the action of breathing or blowing or breathe upon or into.[44]

In *The Theogony*, Hesiod says that the Muses "breathed into me a divine voice …"[45] and in *The Odyssey*, Homer writes that the singer Phemius was "inspired by the gods in the song-ways of every kind."[46] In *The Iliad*, the narrator Homer reveals that he is inspired by the Muses who know all things.[47] Both Homer and Hesiod suggest that the *aodios*, or singer, possesses *techne* or skill in addition to having a privileged relationship with the Muse.[48] The creative process, as described by Hesiod and Homer, is an experience of receiving inspiration from a divine source, giving the author the needed information or the needed talent for creativity.

(3) Modern Christian source— Dorothy Sayers

Dorothy L. Sayers (1893-1957), the English poet, playwright, novelist, and Christian humanist, considered creativity to be the defining feature of human nature and a reflection of the Triune God who created man in His image.[49] In her book *The Mind of the Maker*, the analogy between the Divine Maker and the human mind is based on Genesis 1:27, "So God created man in his own image, in the image of God he created him; male and female he created them." In the verses leading up to the statement about man being made in God's image, the only information given about God is the single assertion, "God created." Sayers concludes, "The characteristic common to

---

igin_and_Meaning_of_Poetic_Inspiration_in_Ancient_Greece (accessed April 22, 2020). Homer and Hesiod provide the earliest recorded accounts on creative inspiration in the western tradition.

43   Gerard Naddaf, "The Origin and Meaning of Poetic Inspiration in Ancient Greece," Seminar Presentation: The University of Sydney, November 10, 2011, 1, 19, website *Academia*, https://www.academia.edu/32876708/The_Origin_and_Meaning_of_Poetic_Inspiration_in_Ancient_Greece (accessed April 22, 2020).

44   Ibid., 3.

45   Hesiod, *The Theogony*, translated by Hugh G. Evelyn-White, 1914, Sacred Texts website, line 31, https://www.sacred-texts.com/cla/hesiod/theogony.htm (accessed April 22, 2020).

46   Homer, *The Odyssey*, in Mortimer J. Adler, editor, *Great Books of the Western World, Volume 3* (Chicago: Encyclopedia Britannica, Inc., 1990), Book 22.345-350.

47   Homer, *The Iliad*, in Mortimer J. Adler, editor, *Great Books of the Western World, Volume 3* (Chicago: Encyclopedia Britannica, Inc., 1990), Book 2. 483-494.

48   Naddaf, "The Origin and Meaning of Poetic Inspiration in Ancient Greece," 6.

49   Dorothy L. Sayers, *The Mind of the Maker* (New York: HarperCollins, 1941), 22-23.

God and man is apparently that: the desire and the ability to make things."⁵⁰ In her play "The Zeal of Thy House," the final speech of the Archangel Michael relates the human creative process to each person of the Trinity:

> For every work of creation is threefold, an earthly trinity to match the heavenly. First, there is a Creative Idea, passionless, timeless, beholding the whole work completed at once, the end in the beginning: and this is the image of the Father.
>
> Second, there is the Creative Energy, begotten of that idea, working in time from the beginning to the end, with sweat and passion, being incarnate in the bonds of matter; and this is the image of the Word.
>
> Third: there is the Creative Power, the meaning of the work and its response in the lively soul: and this is the image of the indwelling Spirit.
>
> And these three are one, each equally in itself the whole work, whereof none can exist without the other: and this is the image of the Trinity.⁵¹

Sayers recognized her own creative literary mind was formed on the same pattern as the Mind of the Maker and that this image distinguishes man from beast. She insists that the creative mind is the true nature of every person because everyone is a maker in the simplest meaning of the term.⁵² "If the common man is to enjoy the divinity of his humanity, he can come to it only in virtue and right of his making."⁵³

(4) Modern Christian source— J. R. R. Tolkien

J. R. R. Tolkien (1892-1973), the English writer, poet, and philologist, is best known for his legendarium comprised of his entire mythology of the world of Arda and Middle Earth. He recognized creativity as a divine gift, describing his own literary creative process (or sub-creation, as he called it) as mysterious. In a letter dated September 14, 1950 he writes, "Stories

---

50   Dorothy L. Sayers, *The Mind of the Maker* (New York: HarperCollins, 1941), 22.

51   Dorothy L. Sayers, "The Zeal of Thy House," full text online, https://archive.org/stream/zealofthyhouse012297mbp/zealofthyhouse012297mbp_djvu.txt (accessed April 25, 2020).

52   Sayers, *The Mind of the Maker*, 28.

53   Ibid., 215.

arose in my mind as 'given' things, and as they came, separately, so too the links grew . . . yet always I had the sense of recording what was already 'there,' somewhere: not of 'inventing.'"[54] In another letter dated January 14, 1956 he states, "I have long ceased to invent (though even patronizing or sneering critics on the side praise my 'invention'): I wait till I seem to know what really happened. Or till it writes itself."[55] In his famous essay "On Fairy-stories," he contends that creative Fantasy is a natural human activity, "Fantasy remains a human right: we make in our measure and in our derivative mode, because we are made: and not only made, but made in the image and likeness of a Maker."[56] Tolkien recognized the source of his ideas and his talent to (sub)create stories was a divine gift because he was made in the image of God.

Summary of the Transcendent View of Creativity

The transcendent view of creativity is shared by ancient Hebrew, Greek, and Christian thinkers because of their belief in the Divine; they echo the Psalmist, "It is He who has made us and not we ourselves."[57] The starting point for these thinkers was empirical evidence, meaning they observed the facts about their own creative minds, namely inspiration, original ideas, imagination, fantasy, emotion, and creation out of nothing. The human equivalent to creating ex nihilo, or out of nothing, is the creation of forms which were not there before. The creative idea mixes with and forms the matter, which means the whole creative work is more than the sum of its material parts. The material world is fixed, but the human imagination generates continuous creative acts. The best explanation for the human experience of creativity points to a divine source and cannot be explained purely in terms of natural processes. The divine is fundamentally present and indispensable in any creative act.

The Minimal Facts Approach to Creativity

Despite the profound differences between the scientific materialist and transcendent philosophies, both views recognize that creativity exists and is natural in varying degrees to human beings. If we formulate a minimal-

---

54   Humphrey Carpenter, editor, *The Letters of J. R. R. Tolkien* (New York: Houghton Mifflin Harcourt, 1995), 145.
55   Ibid., 231.
56   Verlyn Flieger and Douglas A. Anderson, editors, *Tolkien On Fairy-stories* (London: HarperCollins Publishers, 2014), 66.
57   Psalm 100:3a (NASB).

ist view of creativity that even Roger Schank will grant, this means setting aside the Divine. This method is comparable to the Minimal Facts approach developed by historian and philosopher Gary Habermas in his argument for the historicity of the resurrection of Jesus Christ.[58] He makes his case using only the historical facts that the vast majority of critical scholars recognize, whether those scholars are liberal, skeptical, agnostic, or atheist, as long as they are specialists in a relevant field of study.

Applying this method to the concept of creativity means excluding the kind of creativity that comes from divine inspiration or human intuition and instead granting the minimalist view that creative ideas and artifacts are produced by ordinary cognitive processes. On this understanding (the basis of the preceding scientific materialist programs), creativity is the ability to search data, alter solutions, draw conclusions, compare analogies, visualize alternatives, understand meanings, judge reasons for explanations, synthesize data, and combine data. However, even these ordinary minimal creative acts require an actor, a conscious human agent who has intentionality, judgment, understanding, and autonomy, all of which computers lack. Therefore, a machine cannot be creative, even in this minimally ordinary sense.

An example of a program based on ordinary cognitive processes is James Meehan's 1977 TALE-SPIN, the world's first interactive program that writes stories.[59] He reasoned that if ordinary cognitive processes produce creative stories, then literary creativity can, in principle, be reduced to computation and algorithms to create an artificial story generator. Here is an excerpt from one of TALE-SPIN's best stories called "Hunger":

> Once upon a time John Bear lived in a cave. John knew that John was in his cave. There was a beehive in a maple tree. Tom Bee knew that the beehive was in the maple tree. Tom was in his beehive. Tom knew that Tom was in his beehive. There was some honey in Tom's beehive. Tom knew that the honey was in Tom's beehive. Tom had the honey. Tom

---

58 Gary Habermas, "The Minimal Facts Approach to the Resurrection of Jesus," in *Southeastern Theological Review*, Summer 2012, 15-26, https://www.garyhabermas.com/articles/southeastern_theological_review/minimal-facts-methodology_08-02-2012.htm (accessed April 25, 2020).

59 James R. Meehan, "TALE-SPIN, An Interactive Program That Writes Stories," Paper given at the Proceedings of the 5th International Joint Conference on Artificial Intelligence, 1977, https://www.cs.utah.edu/nlp/papers/talespin-ijcai77.pdf (accessed April 25, 2020).

knew that Tom had the honey. There was a nest in a cherry tree...[60]

TALE-SPIN, and Meehan's later program MINSTREL, are designed using computable problem-solving techniques and the stories they generate are painfully uninteresting and noticeably uncreative.[61] This kind of problem is typical with materialistic reductions. Philosopher Angus Menuge explains that reductions aim to remove the mystery of the Divine from a concept, but they leave what was previously understood, incomprehensible.[62] Even though G. K. Chesterton never read an artificially created story like "Hunger," he wrote, "If the mind is mechanical, thought cannot be very exciting..."[63] This brings us to Selmer Bringsjord and his RAIR team, whose goal is to build an artificial author that generates creative stories, at least more interesting than "Hunger."

Building BRUTUS1, the Artificial Literary "Agent"

Why Literary Creativity?

Alan Turing proposed the "imitation game" as a test for determining whether a machine can genuinely think, but he also thought it could test for literary creativity.[64] In his 1950 paper "Computing Machinery and Intelligence," Turing engages nine objections to artificial intelligence, one being the argument from consciousness, in which he quotes Professor Geoffrey Jefferson's address to the Royal College of Surgeons in 1949, "Not until a machine can write a sonnet or compose a concerto because of thoughts and emotions felt, and not by the chance fall of symbols, could we agree that

---

60   Bringsjord and Ferrucci, *Artificial Intelligence and Literary Creativity*, 122.
61   See Appendix A for a sample story generated by MINSTREL (1993).
62   Angus Menuge, *Agents Under Fire: Materialism and the Rationality of Science* (New York: Rowman & Littlefield Publishers, Inc., 2004), 5.
63   Gilbert K. Chesterton, *Orthodoxy* (United States: Simon & Brown, 2010), 29.
64   Alan M. Turing, "Computing Machinery and Intelligence," *Mind* 49: 433-460, 1950, 1. https://phil415.pbworks.com/f/TuringComputing.pdf (accessed April 26, 2020). The Turing Test: A human judge is able to communicate only by email with two players, each concealed in a separate room. One player is a woman and the other a computer. When human judges do no better than 50/50 when rendering verdicts as to which player is in fact a woman, we will have machines that can truly think.

machine equals brain—that is, not only write it, but know that it had written it."[65] In effect, Jefferson was arguing that literary and musical creativity requires an inner, first-person point-of-view, that is, consciousness, which no machine possesses. Turing's response was, in short, that if a sonnet-writing machine was able to pass the Turing Test, Jefferson should either abandon the argument from consciousness or be forced into the solipsist position.[66] Thus, from his interaction with Jefferson, it is evident that Turing assumed that literary creativity was a mark of intelligence.

Forty years later, cognitive psychologists Roger Schank and Robert Abelson refined and strengthened Turing's idea that literary creativity reflects intelligence. In their book *Knowledge and Memory: The Real Story*, they boldly affirm that "virtually all human knowledge" is based on stories.[67] Schank maintains that people think in terms of stories and understand the world in terms of stories.[68] On this view, for a machine to possess human intelligence it would have to be a good storyteller.[69] Schank's work on the role of story-telling in comprehension influenced Daniel Dennett, who developed the Multiple Drafts model of consciousness. He explains, ". . . Instead of such a single stream (however wide), there are multiple channels in which specialist circuits try, in parallel pandemoniums, to do their various things, creating Multiple Drafts as they go. Most of these fragmentary drafts of "narrative" play short-lived roles in the modulation of current activity. . ."[70] If story-telling is wedded to intelligence and cognition, it makes sense that the RAIR project focuses on instantiating literary creativity in BRUTUS1.

---

65   Geoffry Jefferson, "The Mind of Mechanical Man," *British Medical Journal*, June 25, 1949, 1(4616):1105-1110. https://www.ncbi.nlm.nih.gov/pmc/articles/PMC2050428/?page=6 (accessed April 26, 2020).

66   Turing, "Computing Machinery and Intelligence," 444. Solipsism is the view that the self is all that can be known to exist. https://phil415.pbworks.com/f/TuringComputing.pdf (accessed April 26, 2020).

67   Robert S. Wyer, Jr., editor, *Knowledge and Memory: The Real Story* (New Jersey: Lawrence Erlbaum Associates, Inc., Publishers, 1995), 1, 227.

68   Roger Schank, *Tell Me a Story: Narrative and Intelligence* (Evanston, Illinois: Northwestern University Press, 1998), 219.

69   Ibid., 241-2.

70   Daniel Dennett, *Consciousness Explained* (New York: Back Bay Books, 1991), 257-8.

The Limits of Artificial Creativity

The RAIR team identified the essential requirements that would qualify BRUTUS1 as a creative story generator; they call them the "magic desiderata." The stories BRUTUS1 generates must: (1) generate imagery in the reader's mind, (2) situate the story in a "landscape of consciousness," that is, a landscape defined by the mental states of the characters, (3) generate genuinely interesting stories, characterized by the classic themes of betrayal, ruthless ambition, unrequited love, sex, money, and death. (4) tap into the deep, abiding structures of stories in the form of story grammars, and (5) avoid "mechanical" prose; in other words, produce compelling literary prose.[71] The aim in building BRUTUS1 is to provide evidence to confirm or refute the Double Blur. In other words, if the requirements for literary creativity can be captured by computation, then not only would BRUTUS1 be considered a conscious, creative person, but it would also confirm that human minds are at bottom machines.

After spending fifteen years attempting to fulfill the magic desiderata for BRUTUS1, the RAIR team established that the first three requirements could not be formalized in computational terms; I have investigated the first two. I conclude that BRUTUS1 does not possess genuine literary creativity based on the following argument:

1. Genuine literary creativity requires TEMIs, temporally extended mental imagery.
2. Genuine literary creativity requires adopting the points of view of characters, a something-it's-like-to-be the characters in a story.
3. TEMIs and the ability to adopt the points of view of characters are not formalizable in computational terms; therefore, BRUTUS1 does not possess the conscious mental states necessary for literary creativity.
4. BRUTUS1 does not possess genuine literary creativity.

Premise (1): Creativity Requires TEMIs

A story that generates mental imagery in the mind of the reader begins in the mind of the author in the form of mental pictures, including visions, sounds, smells, taste, and touch.[72] Visualization is the foundation of writers' creative process, linking imagery to the text at every stage—before they

---

71 Bringsjord and Ferrucci, *Artificial Intelligence and Literary Creativity*, xxv.
72 Visualization Overview: Questions and Answers, *Kendall Hunt Publishing*, https://he.kendallhunt.com/sites/default/files/uploadedFiles/Kendall_Hunt/Content/Higher_Education/Uploads/Zeigler_VisualizationOverview.pdf (accessed April 27, 2020).

write, as they write, and after they write. Writers often see a story unfold in their mind's eye, complete with dialogue, intonation, and scene changes, from beginning to end, and then transcribe what they have seen and heard. For example, the screenwriter and director Barry Levinson said in an interview, "[W]hen I'm actually writing, it's like talking voices come to me, and I just have to get them down on paper, and sometimes I do it in longhand, and sometimes I do it with dictation."[73] In an interview about his Baltimore movies, Levinson said, "I wrote *Tin Men* in three weeks. And *Avalon* and *Diner*. All in three weeks . . . It's more like dictation—the scenes just pour out, I write them down."[74] The RAIR team calls this kind of imagery a TEMI (temporally extended mental image) because the writer can "stretch such images through time, and manipulate them in detail so as to produce a robust narrative."[75] For example, you could picture in your mind the Empire State Building in its normal setting and then "watch" it suddenly change into a rocket ship and blast into space. TEMIs have a qualitative feel to them and are elastic rather than rigid.

Mental images, like all mental events, are notoriously difficult to study using the scientific method, which requires subject matter to be observable and measurable. In his book *Image and Brain*, Psychologist and neuroscientist Stephen Kosslyn notes that due to the behaviorist approach that dominated psychology in the first half of the twentieth century, mental imagery was not even considered proper subject matter for scientific study until after 1960.[76] With the advent of artificial intelligence, cognitive researchers began to theorize about how information is represented in the mind when one experiences visual mental imagery and then to think about how to program computers to mimic mental imagery.

There is a debate between two different theories of representation, propositional and depictive. For example, to represent the mental image of an "A" in propositional form would be: "two symmetrical diagonal lines that meet at the top and are joined roughly halfway down by a horizontal

---

73   Michael Sragow, "Levinson Honored for his Writing," *Baltimore Sun*, February 1, 2010, https://www.baltimoresun.com/entertainment/bs-xpm-2010-02-21-bal-ae-levinson21feb21-story.html (accessed April 27, 2020).

74   John Patterson, "My Kind of Town," *The Guardian*, August 31, 2000, https://www.theguardian.com/film/2000/sep/01/culture.features1 (accessed April 26, 2020). Barry Levinson wrote *Diner* (1982), *Tin Men* (1987), *Avalon* (1990), *The Natural* (1984), *Good Morning, Vietnam* (1987), and *Rain Man* (1988).

75   Bringsjord and Ferrucci, *Artificial Intelligence and Literary Creativity*, 51.

76   Stephen M. Kosslyn, *Image and Brain: The Resolution of the Imagery Debate* (Cambridge, Massachusetts: The MIT Press, 1994), 1-2.

line." In depictive form, it would be the illustration of an **A**.[77] There is general agreement that people in fact experience visual mental images and that propositional representations are used in cognition. It is even agreed that for a depiction to have meaning, it must be interpreted using propositions. The question is whether visual mental images rely on depictive representations, or are exclusively propositional.[78] AGI has been dominated by the propositional approach, in which objects of knowledge and beliefs are represented in first-order logic and reasoning consists in deduction over that knowledge.

After twenty years of research, Kosslyn has provided empirical evidence that imagery is not purely propositional, but does rely on depictive representations.[79] That is, humans represent and reason about information not only in propositional form, but also in pictorial form. This understanding is not new, but a return to the ancient view. Aristotle argued that images play a central role in human cognition, saying, "[T]he soul never thinks without an image."[80] And further, "When the mind is actively aware of anything it is necessarily aware of it along with an image."[81]

Based on Kosslyn's research, along with others,[82] AGI is now working toward a hybrid symbolic/imagistic approach to representation and reasoning. However, the computer systems that claim to have symbolized visual images have only succeeded in representing trivial simple static images, such as triangles, cubes, strings, arrays, matrices, and grids, which are not remotely like a TEMI.[83] According to Selmer Bringsjord, who scours the

---

77   Stephen M. Kosslyn, *Image and Brain: The Resolution of the Imagery Debate* (Cambridge, Massachusetts: The MIT Press, 1994), 4-5.
78   Ibid., 6.
79   Ibid., 20-1.
80   Aristotle, "On the Soul," in Mortimer Adler, editor, *Great Books of the Western World, Volume 7* (Chicago: Encyclopedia Britannica, Inc., 1990), 663, 431a16.
81   Ibid., 664, 432a8-9.
82   In addition to Kosslyn, see Michael Tye, *The Imagery Debate* (Cambridge, MA: The MIT Press, 1991) and B. Chandrasekaran, N. Hari Narayanan, & Yumi Iwasaki, "Reasoning With Diagrammatic Representations: A Report on the Spring Symposium," *AI Magazine*, Volume 14, Number 2 (1993), https://www.aaai.org/Library/Symposia/Spring/ss92-02.php (accessed April 28, 2020).
83   Examples of simple images can be found in the following: Brian Hunt, "Problem-Solving with Diagrammatic Representations," *Artificial Intelligence* 13 (1980) 201-230, https://www2.cs.sfu.ca/~funt/ProblemSolvingWithDiagrammaticRepresentations_AIJournal1980.pdf; Robert Lindsay, "Images and Inference," *Cognition* (1988) 229-250, https://deepblue.lib.umich.edu/bitstream/

AGI literature, there is "no symbolization of TEMIs either on connectionist or logicist systems; nor, despite considerable sustained effort directed at achieving such symbolization, is it forthcoming."[84] See Appendix B for examples of symbolized computer images. Therefore, BRUTUS does not have the first of the magic desiderata—first person imagistic experience, which involves the creation, manipulation, and contemplation of TEMIs.

Premise (2): Creativity Requires Adopting the Character's Point-of-View (POV)

A good storytelling machine must generate stories that not only have a landscape of action, but also have a landscape of consciousness, meaning a landscape defined by the mental states of the characters. This ability is tied to the author's imagistic power to create TEMIs, but is specifically directed toward imagining the inner point-of-view of the characters. For example, Henrik Ibsen (1828-1906), the Norwegian playwright, explains his use of mental imagery in creating characters:

> I have to have the character in mind through and through, I must penetrate into the last wrinkle of his soul. I always proceed from the individual; the stage setting, the dramatic ensemble, all that comes naturally and does not cause me any worry, as soon as I am certain of the individual in every aspect of his humanity. But I have to have his exterior in mind also, down to the last button, how he stands and walks, how he conducts himself, what his voice sounds like. Then I do not let him go until his fate is fulfilled.[85]

Imagining the mental state of a character has a subjective, qualitative feel. Kosslyn's research confirms that imagery has a "feel" about it and "appears to play a special role in representing emotionally charged material."[86]

---

handle/2027.42/27193/0000196.pdf?sequence=1&isAllowed=y (accessed April 28, 2020); Daniel Dennett, *Consciousness Explained* (New York: Back Bay Books, 1991), 295-6.

84   Bringsjord and Ferrucci, *Artificial Intelligence and Literary Creativity*, 56-62; Selmer Bringsjord, "Is the connectionist-logicist clash one of AI's wonderful red herrings?" *Journal of Experimental & Theoretical AI*, 1(1991) 319-349; Bringsjord argues that connectionism and logicism are equivalent mathematically and the clash between these camps is a red herring.

85   Henrik Ibsen, *Four Major Plays: Volume I* (New York: A Signet Classic, 1992), xii.

86   Kosslyn, *Image and Brain*, 405.

BRUTUS1 does not possess the ability to create a landscape of consciousness for characters "because subjective qualities of experience utterly defy symbolization."[87]

Premise (3): TEMIs and character's POV are not formalizable in computational terms

The RAIR team concluded that the requirements for literary creativity in premises (1) and (2) could not be reduced to computation in BRUTUS1: the experience of TEMIs and imagining the points of view of literary characters. Both of these require conscious introspection, meaning the author represents the experiences to himself, which BRUTUS1 cannot do. To explain and defend this premise I turn to the work of philosophers Gottfried Leibniz, Frank Jackson, Thomas Nagel, and John Searle.

Gottfried Wilhelm Leibniz (1646-1716), the German polymath and philosopher, argued that mental states are not reducible to physical processes in his *Monadology*. In section 17, he presented a thought experiment that imagines a brain the size of a mill:

> It has to be acknowledged that perception can't be explained by mechanical principles, that is by shapes and motions, and thus that nothing that depends on perception can be explained in that way either. Suppose this were wrong. Imagine there were a machine whose structure produced thought, feeling, and perception; we can conceive of its being enlarged while maintaining the same relative proportions among its parts, so that we could walk into it as we can walk into a mill. Suppose we do walk into it; all we would find there are cogs and levers and so on pushing one another, and never anything to account for a perception. So, perception must be sought in simple substances, not in composite things like machines. And that is all that can be found in a simple substance—perceptions and changes in perceptions; and those changes are all that the internal actions of simple substances can consist in.[88]

---

87   Bringsjord and Ferrucci, *Artificial Intelligence and Literary Creativity*, 52.
88   Godfried W. Leibniz, *The Principles of Philosophy known as Monadology*, website *Early Modern Texts* (Jonathan Bennett, 2017), https://www.earlymoderntexts.com/assets/pdfs/leibniz1714b.pdf (accessed April 28, 2020).

Upon entering the mill, the observer finds lots of interacting parts, but nothing that accounts for perception or consciousness. Considering that Leibniz states in the *Monadology* that he is emphasizing simple substances, his core argument in the mill analogy is that the mind is not a composite thing like the mill, with interacting parts. Perception and consciousness cannot be physical processes or be given purely mechanistic explanations, so the mind must be a simple substance. Leibniz's understanding of the mind is akin to Descartes' indivisibility argument.[89]

Interpreting the mill analogy in light of premise (3), I take Leibniz to mean that the enlarged mill reveals the gap between mental facts and physical facts, in the same manner that first-person TEMIs are irreducible to third-person computations. We can easily picture Leibniz asking neuroscientist Stephen Kosslyn to imagine a human author's brain is the size of a mill that he can enter and walk around. At exactly the moment Kosslyn's subject experiences a TEMI, Kosslyn would see neurons firing and complex parts interacting, but he would never see anything like his subject's mental imagery. Kosslyn could know all the objective third-person physical facts about a TEMI from an fMRI and PET scan, but still not have an explanation of the subject's first-person experience of mental imagery.[90]

Philosopher Frank Jackson further explores this idea in what he calls the knowledge argument. "Any purely physical account of what goes on in us and of how we relate to our surroundings leaves out the phenomenal and conscious side of psychology."[91] His argument is aimed at materialists who have somehow been able to overlook the fact that a purely physical account of the world is incomplete. Jackson presents his argument in the following thought experiment that is based on the intuition that "knowledge of

---

89   Rene Descartes, "Meditations VI," in Mortimer Adler, editor, *The Great Books of the Western World, Volume 28* (Chicago: Encyclopedia Britannica, Inc., 1990), 327-8.

90   Kosslyn, *Image and Brain*, 19, 47, 252-258. "The beauty of brain scanning is that one can observe neural activity in an awake, behaving human being. It is worth noting that several fMRI studies have now produced converging evidence that area V1 is in fact activated during visual mental imagery."

91   Frank Jackson, "Looking Back on the Knowledge Argument," in Peter Ludlow, Yujin Nagasawa, and Daniel Stoljar, editors, *There's Something About Mary* (Cambridge, Massachusetts: MIT Press, 2004), xvi. In 1998, Jackson has since rejected his knowledge argument against physicalism, saying that even though his argument contains no obvious fallacy, the conclusion that physicalism is false must be mistaken (23). In chapters 18, 29, and 20, Jackson summarizes his current view.

the physical sort does not suffice logically for knowledge of the phenomenal sort."[92]

> Mary is a brilliant scientist who is, for whatever reason, forced to investigate the world from a black-and-white room via a black-and white television monitor. She specialises in the neurophysiology of vision and acquires, let us suppose, all the physical information there is to obtain about what goes on when we see ripe tomatoes, or the sky, and use terms like 'red', 'blue', and so on. She discovers, for example, just which wave-length combinations from the sky stimulate the retina, and exactly how this produces via the central nervous system the contraction of the vocal chords and expulsion of air from the lungs that results in the uttering of the sentence 'The sky is blue.' What will happen when Mary is released from her black-and-white room or is given a color television monitor? Will she learn anything or not?[93]

It seems obvious that she will learn something else about herself, the world, and the human visual experience of it. Even though Mary had all the physical information, her previous knowledge was incomplete. The central claim of the argument is that one can have all the physical information without having all the information there is to have because human beings are not entirely physical. Applying this argument to premise (3), we would say that the experience of qualia left out of Mary's physical world are comparable to the experience of qualia—TEMIs and points of view of characters—that the RAIR team could not instantiate in BRUTUS1.

A precursor to Jackson's argument was philosopher Thomas Nagel's 1974 paper "What Is It Like to Be a Bat?" where he contrasts objective third-person knowledge and subjective first-person knowledge by using his famous

---

92 Peter Ludlow, Yujin Nagasawa, and Daniel Stoljar, editors, *There's Something About Mary* (Cambridge, Massachusetts: MIT Press, 2004), 3. The knowledge intuition is also found in Bertrand Russell's argument about the 'blind man' and the scientific explanation of light. Russell is concerned here not with metaphysics or physicalism, but with epistemology. Bertrand Russell, *The Problem of Philosophy* (Oxford: Oxford University Press, 1967), 27-28.

93 Frank Jackson, "Epiphenomenal Qualia," in Peter Ludlow, Yujin Nagasawa, and Daniel Stoljar, editors, *There's Something About Mary* (Cambridge, Massachusetts: MIT Press, 2004), 42.

bat illustration.⁹⁴ What-it-is-like to be a bat does not mean "what (in our experience) it resembles," but rather "how it is for the subject himself."⁹⁵ Nagel clearly states, "Whatever the status of facts about what it is like to be a human being, or a bat, or a Martian, these appear to be facts that embody a particular point of view."⁹⁶ The point of view in question is of a general type, not one only accessible to one individual. Therefore, in the case of literary creativity, the author is able to take up a point of view other than his own, like a fictional human character because the author has a sufficiently similar consciousness. BRUTUS1 does not possess a first-person point of view because formal symbol manipulation and computational operations by themselves are not sufficient to produce consciousness.

    Philosopher John Searle agrees with the arguments of Jackson and Nagel, yet he believes they are frequently misunderstood as only presenting epistemic arguments. Searle stresses that the thrust of these arguments is ontological, not merely epistemic. "It is a point about what real features exist in the world and not, except derivatively, about how we know about those features."⁹⁷ Searle argues that you could have a complete causal reduction of a particular conscious state, like a TEMI, to neurophysiological processes of neurons firing in the brain, but yet this would not lead to an ontological reduction because of the shocking asymmetry between first-person features and third-person features. "A perfect science of the brain still would not lead to an ontological reduction of consciousness in the way that our present science can reduce heat, solidity, color, or sound."⁹⁸

    In sum, the arguments of Leibniz, Jackson, Nagel, and Searle affirm premise (3) and explain why the RAIR team could not give BRUTUS1 conscious mental states. Materialists often interpret a failed reduction as a failure of science, but philosopher Angus Menuge corrects this fallacy by claiming that "scientific progress is made through a failed reduction by learning that a certain phenomena is independent of others."⁹⁹

---

    94   Thomas Nagel, "What Is It Like to Be a Bat? *The Philosophical Review* Vol 83 No. 4 (1974): 435–450. *JSTOR*, https://warwick.ac.uk/fac/cross_fac/iatl/study/ugmodules/humananimalstudies/lectures/32/nagel_bat.pdf (accessed April 28, 2020).

    95   Ibid., 440.

    96   Ibid., 441.

    97   John Searle, *The Rediscovery of the Mind* (Cambridge, Massachusetts: MIT Press, 1994), 117.

    98   Ibid., 116.

    99   Angus Menuge, *Agents Under Fire: Materialism and the Rationality of Science* (New York: Rowman & Littlefield Publishers, Inc., 2004), 9. For example, Quan-

Premise (4): BRUTUS1 does not possess genuine literary creativity.

In a nutshell, BRUTUS1 does not have the conscious mental states necessary to produce creative stories. Since human literary creativity is beyond computation, the RAIR team shunned further efforts to impart BRUTUS1 with genuine imagistic expertise and a point of view. Instead, they worked to overcome these limits with clever engineering techniques and tricks to make BRUTUS1 *appear* to be creative.[100] See Appendix C for a creative story generated by BRUTUS1. This brings us to the important epistemological question of how to test for genuine creativity? In other words, how can we judge whether a machine is genuinely creative or only *appears* to be creative?

BRUTUS1 Fails the Lovelace Test

In judging whether an artificial "agent" is creative, it is important to focus on the *how* and not merely the *what*. The Turing Test judges behavior, namely whether a machine *appears* to possess certain sophisticated human behaviors, like writing an interesting short story. Generating an interesting story is the *what*, the artifact, but the *how* is of utmost importance because it reveals whether the machine has transcended its computer program to originate something new. Selmer Bringsjord, Paul Bello, and David Ferrucci developed the Lovelace Test, "named in honor of Lady Lovelace, who believed that only when computers *originate* things they should be believed to have minds."[101] Bringsjord explains the Lovelace Test this way:

> An artificial agent, designed by a human, passes the test only if it originates a "program" that it was not engineered to produce. The outputting of the new program—it could be an idea, a novel, a piece of music, anything—can't be a hardware fluke, and it must be the result of processes the artificial agent can reproduce. Now here's the kicker: The

---

tum mechanics resists any classically mechanistic reduction or interpretation.

100   Bringsjord and Ferrucci, *Artificial Intelligence and Literary Creativity,* 149.

101   Selmer Bringsjord, Paul Bello and David Ferrucci, "Creativity, the Turing Test, and the (Better) Lovelace Test," *Minds and Machines,* (June 2000): 1. ResearchGate website, https://www.researchgate.net/profile/P/publication/2430434_Creativity_the_Turing_Test_and_the_Better_Lovelace_Test/links/00b7d534feb157a685000000/Creativity-the-Turing-Test-and-the-Better-Lovelace-Test.pdf (accessed April 15, 2020).

agent's designers must not be able to explain how their original code led to the new program.[102]

In essence, to pass the Lovelace Test, AGI researchers must create a machine that "breaks the bounds of mindless symbol manipulation to think for itself."[103]

BRUTUS1 failed the Lovelace Test because it did not transcend its programming to create a new program. The RAIR designers are able to explain the system's inner workings and how their original code led to his generation of interesting creative stories. In chapter 6 of *Artificial and Literary Creativity: Inside the Mind of BRUTUS, a Storytelling Machine*, Selmer Bringsjord, describes in exhaustive detail the inner workings of BRUTUS1.[104] He first gives an overview of the technical architecture of BRUTUS1, which is composed of two levels, the knowledge level and the process level. The explanation of the knowledge level includes thematic knowledge, domain knowledge, story grammars, sentence grammars, literary constraints, and a lexicon. The description of the process level includes thematic instantiation, plot generation, story expansion, language generation, story outline, stage, scenario, and story.

To overcome the lack of imagistic experience and a point of view in BRUTUS1, the RAIR team included in the system a framework for classifying four techniques that are meant to trigger images in the minds of readers: exotic or bizarre material, references to visual perception, experience-related verbs, familiar references, and voyeurism. In addition, "BRUTUS1 narrates stories from a particular character's point of view, using verbs for feeling, thinking, understanding, wanting, etc., which gives the reader the sense that the subject of these verbs has a psychological life."[105] As can be

---

102   Jordan Pearson, "Forget Turing, the Lovelace Test Has a Better Shot at Spotting AI," Motherboard, June 8, 2014, https://motherboard.vice.com/en_us/article/pgaany/forget-turing-the-lovelace-test-has-a-better-shot-at-spotting-ai (accessed April 15, 2020).

103   Bringsjord, Bello, and Ferrucci, "Creativity, the Turing Test, and the (Better) Lovelace Test," 10. The following are examples of AGI computers attempting to pass the Lovelace Test: a screenplay written using AGI methods https://www.youtube.com/watch?v=LY7x2Ihqjmc&t=194s and a song composed using AGI methods https://www.youtube.com/watch?v=lcGYEXJqun8 (accessed April 15, 2020).

104   Bringsjord and Ferrucci, *Artificial Intelligence and Literary Creativity*, 149-204.

105   Ibid., 187-8.

seen from the example in Appendix C, the stories are marked by heavy usage of mental verbs— "thinking, supposing, intending, knowing, feeling, fearing, believing, hating, betraying, etc."[106] The stories generated by BRUTUS1 fall noticeably short of those written by first-rate human authors,[107] but the system is nevertheless capable of generating good stories, only because human researchers spent years "formalizing a generative capacity sufficient to produce this and other stories using reverse engineering."[108]

Before I make final conclusions about BRUTUS1 and artificial creativity, a question remains: Why would you *want* to build an autonomous, creative machine? That is to say, let us grant that scientists will somehow be successful in building a machine with human-level intelligence and creativity. If there is no assurance that this artificial agent has moral character, the danger involved clearly outweighs any proposed benefit.

Selmer Bringsjord and Naveen Sudar Govindarajulu discuss this issue at length in their paper "Are Autonomous and Creative Machines Intrinsically Untrustworthy?"[109] In it, they apply the empirical research from psychology to develop their theory called the Distressing Principle, which means "an autonomous and creative agent will tend to be, from the viewpoint of a rational, fully informed agent, untrustworthy."[110] Professor of psychology Dan Ariely sums up the psychological data this way: "Human beings are torn by a fundamental conflict—our deeply ingrained propensity to lie to ourselves and to others, and the desire to think of ourselves as good and honest people. So, we justify our dishonesty by telling ourselves stories about why our actions are acceptable and sometimes even admirable."[111]

Bringsjord and Govindarajulu argue that the Distressing Principle applies to human-level intelligent artificial creative agents.[112] Their prelimi-

---

106   Bringsjord and Ferrucci, *Artificial Intelligence and Literary Creativity*, 78.

107   To compare BRUTUS₁ to a human author, see Appendix D for an excerpt from J. R. R. Tolkien, *The Lord of the Rings* (New York: Houghton Mifflin Harcourt, 2004), 330-331.

108   Bringsjord and Ferrucci, *Artificial Intelligence and Literary Creativity*, 3, 5.

109   Selmer Bringsjord and Naveen Sundar Govindarajulu, "Are Autonomous and Creative Machines Intrinsically Untrustworthy?" in Hussein A. Abbass Jason Scholz Darryn J. Reid Editors, *Foundations of Trusted Autonomy* (Cham, Switzerland: Springer International Publishing Company, 2017) http://kryten.mm.rpi.edu/SB_NSG_aut2dishon.pdf (accessed April 25, 2020).

110   Ibid., 1.

111   Dan Ariely, *The (Honest) Truth About Dishonesty: How We Lie to Everyone—Especially Ourselves* (New York: Harper, 2013), 165-166.

112   Bringsjord and Govindarajulu, "Are Autonomous and Creative Ma-

nary conclusion, based on their experiments so far, is that engineering will be necessary in the future to protect humans from untrustworthy artificial agents.[113] Even though I argue that machines with human-level intelligence and creativity are not metaphysically possible, the Distressing Principle is one more reason to challenge the transhumanist desire for superintelligent machines and the Singularity.

Conclusion

BRUTUS1: The Failure of Materialism

In his book *The Human Advantage*, philosopher and economist Jay Richards argues that our technological future will likely be a story replete with smart machines that replace human labor, but the central characters in the drama are *creative* human persons who will continue to produce new and useful ideas and artifacts in science, technology, business, medicine, art, music, and literature.[114] Creativity is the unique human advantage, one that machines will never have.

This chapter provides evidence for this fact by demonstrating that literary creativity is the sole province of humans. Our investigation of the RAIR team's attempt to build an artificial author exposed two conscious mental properties required for literary creativity that cannot be reduced to computation. BRUTUS1 does not possess genuine literary creativity, which demonstrates that AGI's assumed materialist philosophy of mind is false. Therefore, the Double Blur is also false: machines are not conscious persons and human persons are not computing machines. And equally important, since machines will increasingly *appear* to be creative, the Lovelace Test is the best way to judge machine creativity. Thus far, in this chapter and the previous one, I have shown the failure of materialism through the lens of AGI and the test case of BRUTUS1. If materialists have taken the wrong philosophical road, where did they make a wrong turn and what is the right road?

---

chines Intrinsically Untrustworthy?" 1-2.

113   Bringsjord and Govindarajulu, "Are Autonomous and Creative Machines Intrinsically Untrustworthy?"12-13.

114   Jay W. Richards, *The Human Advantage: The Future of American Work in an Age of Smart Machines* (New York: Crown Forum, 2018), 192-208.

The Aristotelian Alternative to Materialism

As discussed previously in chapter one, early modern philosophers and scientists replaced classical Aristotelian metaphysics with what they called the mechanical philosophy. This is the condensed story, according to Ed Feser:

> After rejecting Aristotelian formal and final causes in the natural world, the early moderns recognized only material and efficient causes (not the Aristotelian kind). Matter, at bottom, was unobserved particles having mathematically quantifiable features. Cause and effect relations had nothing to do with teleology, but merely related to regularities depicted in the laws of nature. Therefore, material reality is simply physical particles interacting according to meaningless laws of nature. There is ultimately nothing over and above the particles of which they are made. The mechanical philosophy was aimed at increasing human utility and power through technology, whereas classical philosophy was aimed at wisdom and understanding.[115]

To be clear, Aristotelian metaphysics does not rule out mechanistic explanations, but rather denies that they are the complete explanation of the natural world.

Nevertheless, for the ensuing four hundred years, philosophers and scientists have continued down the mechanistic/materialist path, attempting to give everything a purely materialistic explanation in order to complete the scientific image of the world. For the most part, the materialist approach has been justified by its scientific and technological achievements. However, from Descartes, Locke, Hume, and going forward, most anything that was not material was explained as a projection of the mind. The general idea was to strip away the subjective appearances of things and relocate them in the mind. As Ed Feser says, "Everything that doesn't fit the mechanistic model has been swept under the rug of the mind."[116]

As a consequence, contemporary philosophers and scientists have been left with a gigantic dirt pile under the rug, so to speak. It is not surprising that the mind/body problem is the consequence of this sweeping re-

---

115 Edward Feser, *The Last Superstition: A Refutation of the New Atheism* (South Bend, Indiana: St. Augustine's Press, 2008), 175- 179.

116 Ibid., 192-3.

ductionist method because mental states resist materialistic explanations. No materialist attempt to explain the human mind has been successful because mental states, such as consciousness, intentionality, rationality, and creativity, cannot be explained strictly in terms of physical processes, properties, and causes.

A logical outcome of strict materialism is to eliminate or deny the mind's existence altogether.[117] Eliminative materialists argue for a conclusion that is at odds with common sense.[118] As G. E. Moore suggested in his famous essay "A Defense of Common Sense," the argument tends to be unpersuasive because a person's experience of subjective mental states, such as his own consciousness, is something he knows better than any philosophical argument to the contrary.[119] Philosopher Jerry Fodor prefers to rely on the reductionist strategy to explain mental properties, such as intentionality, saying, "If aboutness is real, it must be really something else."[120] Generally, our response to any materialist theory of mind is similar to what Peter Geach once wrote, "When we hear of some new attempt to explain reasoning or language or choice naturalistically, we ought to react as if we were told that someone had squared the circle or proved the square root of 2 to be rational. Only the mildest curiosity is in order—how well has the fallacy been concealed?"[121]

---

117 William Ramsey, "Eliminative Materialism", *The Stanford Encyclopedia of Philosophy* (Spring 2019 Edition), Edward N. Zalta, editor, https://plato.stanford.edu/entries/materialism-eliminative/ (accessed May 6, 2020). The most notable eliminative materialist philosophers are Wilfred Sellars, W.V.O. Quine, Paul Feyerabend, Richard Rorty, Paul and Patricia Churchland.

118 John Searle, *The Rediscovery of the Mind* (Cambridge, Massachusetts: MIT Press, 1992), 30-33. Eliminative materialism is the minority view. Most materialists acknowledge the existence of the mind. However, as John Searle argues, every form of materialism implicitly denies the existence of the mind, whether or not it intends to. That is to say, the way to ultimately deal with "the lump under the rug," short of some form of dualism, is to throw out the rug, lump and all.

119 G. E. Moore, "A Defence of Common Sense," *Contemporary British Philosophy (2nd series)*, ed. J. H. Muirhead, 1925, http://www.ditext.com/moore/common-sense.html (accessed May 7, 2020).

120 Jerry Fodor, *Psychosemantics: The Problem of Meaning in the Philosophy of Mind* (Cambridge, MA: The MIT Press, 1987), 97, quoted in Edward Feser, *Aristotle's Revenge: The Metaphysical Foundations of Physical and Biological Science* (Germany: editiones scholasticae, 2019), 118.

121 Peter Geach, *The Virtues* (Cambridge: Cambridge University Press, 1977), 52, quoted in Edward Feser, *The Last Superstition* (South Bend, Indiana: St. Augustine's Press, 2008), 194.

The failure of materialism exposes the need to retrace our steps, back to the turn that led to the mechanistic/materialistic path and to reconsider the Aristotelian worldview in general, and how it explains the mind in particular. This involves first recovering an understanding of the following truths of Aristotle's philosophy: actuality and potentiality, form and matter, and the four causes.[122]

The Theory of Actuality and Potentiality

In Aristotle's analysis of change versus permanence, he introduces the distinction between actuality and potentiality.[123] He acknowledges that reality is constantly in a state of flux. The fact that matter is able to take on new kinds of existence is explained by the principle of potentiality. Change and permanence are real features of the world, reflected in what things are in actuality and in their potency. Whatever exists is either pure act or a composition of potency and act, which are its primary intrinsic principles.[124]

A material thing's potency is always *for* some actuality, meaning it points beyond itself to an end. To understand a thing's potency is to understand it in terms of its final causality. Matter is merely potential unless actualized by form. A rubber ball may "actually" be round, solid, smooth, and blue, sitting motionless in a basket, but it is also "potentially" flat and squishy (if melted by heat), rough (if worn through use), gray (if left out in the sun), and rolling across the floor (if dropped). These potentialities are real features of the ball even if they are not actualized. A thing's potencies are

---

[122] My aim is to provide an introductory overview of Aristotelian metaphysics. For a more thorough presentation of Aristotle's views, including answers to objections, see David S. Oderberg, *Real Essentialism* (New York: Routledge, 2007); Edward Feser, *The Last Superstition* (South Bend, Indiana: St. Augustine's Press, 2008); James D. Madden, *Mind, Matter & Nature* (Washington D. C.: The Catholic University of America Press, 2013); Edward Feser, *Aristotle's Revenge* (Germany: editiones scholasticae, 2019).

[123] Aristotle was responding to the views of Parmenides and Heraclitus. Parmenides held that change is an illusion, and so too is the world of our experience. For Heraclitus, permanence is the illusion and there is nothing that can unite our experiences.

[124] Aristotle, *Metaphysics*, in Mortimer Adler, editor, *Great Books of the Western World, Volume 7* (Chicago: Encyclopedia Britannica, 1990), 601-2, 1071b1-20 and 1072b10-14. Aristotle recognized "There must then be such a principle, whose very essence is actuality." He reasoned that God exists as pure act, the Unmoved Mover, because only that which is Pure Act can possibly end any regress of actualizers. Thus, the world of composite things could not exist for an instant unless that which is purely actual is continually holding it together.

grounded in its actualities. Because the ball is actually made of rubber, it has the potency for bouncing and melting rather than the potency for doing arithmetic. Actuality is more fundamental than potency, in that if a thing were pure potential and not actualized, it would not exist.[125] The actuality and potentiality of a thing are related to two other intrinsic principles of a material thing's being: matter (hylē) and form (morphē); from the Greek, it is the idea of hylemorphism.

Form and Matter - Hylemorphism

Hylemorphism is Aristotle's theory that all physical substances are composites of matter and form, where matter is a thing's potentiality for change and form is a thing's actuality that persists through change.[126] Nothing is ever just a piece of matter, or a collection of particles, because matter cannot exist without form. Likewise, the form is incomplete and does not exist apart from instantiation by a particular substance. A substantial form is that specific aspect that makes a thing the kind of substance it is. Just as actuality is more fundamental than potentiality, form is metaphysically prior to matter.[127]

Aristotle distinguishes the forms of living things (i.e., plants, animals, and humans) as souls. Plants have nutritive souls with powers of nutrition, growth, and reproduction. Animals have sensory souls with powers of the nutritive soul as well as powers of perception, appetitive, and movement. Human beings have rational souls with nutritive and sensory powers plus the characteristics of intellect, will, and memory.[128] That is, human beings have the powers of forming abstract concepts, putting them together into propositions, reasoning logically from one proposition to another, and the will to choose in light of what the intellect understands.[129] A human person is essentially a composite unity of (rational) soul and body.

The Four Causes

A complete explanation of any material substance involves identifying their irreducible causal components. Aristotle's doctrine of causation dis-

---

125   Aristotle, *Metaphysics*, in Mortimer Adler, editor, *Great Books of the Western World, Volume 7* (Chicago: Encyclopedia Britannica, 1990), 602, 1047b3 and 1072b5.
126   David S. Oderberg, *Real Essentialism* (New York: Routledge, 2007), 64-5.
127   Aristotle, *Metaphysics*, 566, 1042a30-35 and 1042b9-15.
128   Aristotle, *On the Soul*, in Mortimer Adler, editor, *Great Books of the Western World, Volume 7* (Chicago: Encyclopedia Britannica, 1990), 645, 415a1-10.
129   Edward Feser, *Aristotle's Revenge: The Metaphysical Foundations of Physical and Biological Science* (Germany: editiones scholasticae, 2019), 40.

tinguishes four causes: material, formal, efficient, and final.[130] Taking the rubber ball as an example, the material cause is what the thing is made of, in this case rubber. The formal cause is the structure the matter exhibits, which is its solidity, roundness, and bounciness. The efficient cause is what brings the thing into being, which would be the actions of the workers/machines in the ball factory. The final cause is the end, goal, or purpose of the thing, which in this case is entertainment for a child.

The causes are interrelated in the following way. The material cause underlies a thing's potency, which is directed *toward* some actuality. In this way, final causality underlies all materiality. The final cause of a thing determines its formal cause, as in form follows function. Finally, the efficient causal power of a thing is grounded in its substantial form. Explanations do not make sense without final causes. The four causes apply to inorganic and organic substances alike; that is, they are objective features built into the structure of the material world.

Final causes are exemplified in the functions of bodily organs, or the cycles operating in the ecosystem, or the movement of astronomical bodies, or in human beings acting for reasons and goals. We observe formal causes in the acorn that grows into a tree, in the rubber formed into a ball, and in the form (soul) that makes the matter of the body into a living human body. The general relationship between form/matter exists everywhere in the natural world.

The materialist problem of mind/body interaction is not a problem for Aristotle's hylemorphism since human beings are a unity of body and soul. The materialist faces the 'problem' of cause and effect (posed by David Hume) because cause and effect are treated as a relation between temporally ordered events, which are loose and separate and without necessary connections. For Aristotle, it is ultimately *things* that are causes, not events. The immediate efficient cause of an effect is simultaneous with the effect, not temporally prior to it. For instance, the brick hitting the window is simultaneous to the glass breaking and is one event.[131] Further, on Aristotle's theory, a cause cannot give to its effect what it does not have; that is, a cause has the feature that it produces in the effect. For example, a burning torch or a cigarette lighter can start a brush fire, each having the direct or inherent power to produce fire.[132]

---

130   Feser, *The Last Superstition*, 62-73.
131   Edward Feser, *The Last Superstition: A Refutation of the New Atheism* (South Bend, Indiana: St. Augustine's Press, 2008), 65-68.
132   Ibid. 68.

Hylemorphism Applied to Mental States

Persons have rational souls that carry out both corporeal activities, as in sensation, and non-corporeal activities, as in the intellect. Aristotle hints at the immateriality of the human soul when explaining that mental operations of the intellect do not depend on bodily organs.[133] Intellectual activities, such as forming concepts or ideas, grasping forms, essences, universals, abstractions, making judgments, and logical reasoning, are essentially immaterial, meaning intrinsically independent of matter. The immaterial nature of forms and concepts necessitates that the intellect which grasps them must also be immaterial.

For example, when we think about triangles, we grasp the form of the thing; the same form exists both in the actual triangle and in our minds. Triangularity, as the intellect grasps it, is determinate or exact, whereas material triangular things are an approximation of triangularity.[134] As with thinking about triangularity, any thought is going to involve universals, which are abstract and determinate in a way that material objects and processes are not.[135] In addition, the intellect is able to grasp a potential infinity of concepts, whereas corporeal organs have intrinsic material limitations.[136]

Given the facts about universals and our thoughts about them, it is conceptually impossible for the intellect to be material. Nonetheless, even though the intellect operates without any bodily organ, it depends indirectly on the senses for the raw material from which it abstracts universals or essences.[137] Clearly, Aristotle did not rule out material brain events, but he does deny a purely mechanistic materialistic interpretation of the intellect.

Intentionality is manifested in the human intellect because our thoughts are directed toward things beyond themselves, such as trees, dogs, circles, planets, molecules, or rocks. You can even think about things that do not

---

[133] Feser, *The Last Superstition*, 123-7. Aquinas reasoned further, that if the soul's intellect is able to function apart from its matter, it could also exist apart from its matter as an incomplete substance. This theory will be investigated in chapter 5.

[134] That is, thinking about triangularity is not the same as forming a mental image of a particular triangle.

[135] Feser, *The Last Superstition*, 124-5.

[136] Oderberg, *Real Essentialism*, 254.

[137] Feser, *The Last Superstition*, 127.

exist, such as unicorns or Santa Claus. Intentionality cannot be reduced to material states and therefore, the mind is not a material system.[138]

Aristotle was a perceptual realist, which means he believed perception puts us in touch with real features of mind-independent reality. On this commonsense view, colors, tastes, smells, and sounds are objective physical properties of objects that cause normal observers to have the respective sensations. Sensations, like seeing a red object, are directly dependent on bodily organs like the retina, the optic nerve, and the relevant processing neurons in the brain. Since a physical object has form, perception is the process of sharing forms between the object of perception and the sense faculty. Aristotle reasoned that the mind receives the form of objects without the substance, comparing sensation to a signet ring making an impression on wax.[139] In this way, all objects of sense can have a dual existence, as a form in a particular object and a form as the object of mental states.

Summary of Aristotle's Philosophy

The failure of the materialist philosophy of mind to account for consciousness, qualia, intentionality, creativity, and rationality, points to the need for an alternative explanation of reality. The fundamental concepts of Aristotelian philosophy, which have long been rejected by modern science and philosophers, provide a better explanation of mental states and are worthy of further investigation. The next chapter exposes and critiques transhumanism's materialist metaphysics of the human person, which motivates us to explore further Aristotle's philosophy.

---

138   Feser, *The Last Superstition*, 194.
139   Aristotle, *On the Soul*, 656, 424a15-30 and 424b1-15.

Appendix A

"The Vengeful Princess"

Once upon a time there was a lady of the court named Jennifer. Jennifer loved a knight named Grunfeld. Grunfeld loved Jennifer. Jennifer wanted revenge on a lady of the court named Darlene because she had the berries which she picked in the woods and Jennifer wanted to have the berries. Jennifer wanted to scare Darlene. Jennifer wanted a dragon to move toward Darlene so that Darlene believed it would eat her. Jennifer wanted to appear to be a dragon so that a dragon would move towards Darlene. Jennifer drank a magic potion. Jennifer transformed into a dragon. A dragon moved towards Darlene. A dragon was near Darlene.

Grunfeld wanted to impress the king. Grunfeld wanted to move towards the woods so that he could fight a dragon. Grunfeld moved towards the woods. Grunfeld was near the woods. Grunfeld fought a dragon. The dragon died. The dragon was Jennifer. Jennifer wanted to live. Jennifer tried to drink a magic potion but failed. Grunfeld was filled with grief.

Appendix B

Examples of Computational Images of Simple Diagrams

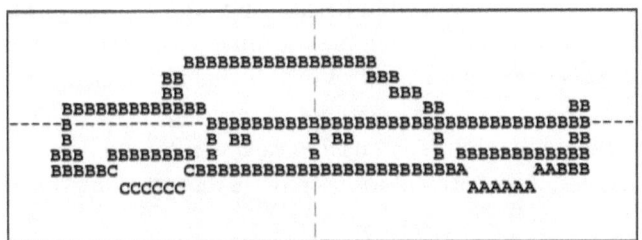

Simulated image of a car, as generated by the Kosslyn and Shwartz program.

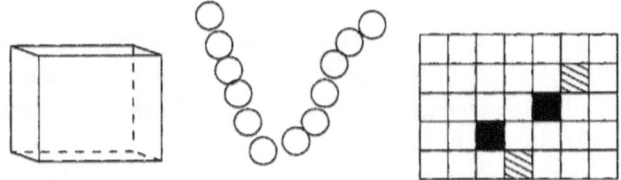

Cubes, Strings, and Arrays, captured in symbolic schemes.

Appendix C

"Betrayal in Self-Deception"

Dave Striver loved the university. He loved its ivy-covered clock towers, its ancient and sturdy brick, and its sun-splashed verdant greens and eager youth. He also loved the fact that the university is free of the stark unforgiving trials of the business world—only this isn't a fact: academia has its own test, and some are as merciless as any in the marketplace. A prime example is the dissertation defense: to earn the PhD, to become a doctor, one must pass an oral examination on one's dissertation. This was a test Professor Edward Hart enjoyed giving.

Dave wanted desperately to be a doctor. But he needed the signatures of three people on the first page of his dissertation, the priceless inscriptions which, together, would certify that he had passed his defense. One of the signatures had to come from Professor Hart, and Hart had often said— to others and to himself— that he was honored to help Dave secure his well-earned dream.

Well before the defense, Striver gave Hart a penultimate copy of his thesis. Hart read it and told Dave that it was absolutely first-rate, and that he would gladly sign it at the defense. They even shook hands in Hart's book-lined office. Dave noticed that Hart's eyes were bright and trustful, and his bearing paternal.

At the defense, Dave thought that he eloquently summarized Chapter 3 of his dissertation. There were two questions, one from Professor Rodman and one from Dr. Teer; Dave answered both, apparently to everyone's satisfaction. There were no further objections.

Professor Rodman signed. He slid the tome to Teer; she too signed, and then slid it in front of Hart. Hart didn't move. "Ed?" Rodman said. Hart still sat motionless. Dave felt slightly dizzy. "Edward, are you going to sign?"

Later, Hart sat alone in his office, in his big leather chair, saddened by Dave's failure. He tried to think of ways he could help Dave achieve his dream.[140]

---

140   Bringsjord and Ferrucci, *Artificial Intelligence and Literary Creativity*, 199-200.

Appendix D

Chapter 5 "The Bridge of Khazad-Dum"
'You cannot pass,' he said. The orcs stood still, and a dead silence fell. 'I am a servant of the Secret Fire, wielder of the flame of Anor. You cannot pass. The dark fire will not avail you, flame of Udun. Go back to the Shadow! You cannot pass.'

The Balrog made no answer. The fire in it seemed to die, but the darkness grew. It stepped forward slowly on to the bridge, and suddenly it drew itself up to a great height, and its wings were spread from wall to wall; but still Gandalf could be seen, glimmering in the gloom; he seemed small, and altogether alone: grey and bent, like a wizened tree before the onset of a storm.

From out of the shadow a red sword leaped flaming. Glamdring glittered white in answer. There was a ringing clash and a stab of white fire. The Balrog fell back, and its sword flew up in molten fragments. The wizard swayed on the bridge, stepped back a pace, and then again stood still.

'You cannot pass!' he said.

With a bound the Balrog leaped full upon the bridge. Its whip whirled and hissed.

'He cannot stand alone!' cried Aragorn suddenly and ran back along the bridge. 'Elendil!' he shouted. 'I am with you, Gandalf!'

'Gondor!' cried Boromir and leaped after him.

At that moment Gandalf lifted his staff, and crying aloud he smote the bridge before him. The staff broke asunder and fell from his hand. A blinding sheet of white flame sprang up. The bridge cracked. Right at the Balrog's feet it broke, and the stone upon which it stood crashed into the gulf, while the rest remained, poised, quivering like a tongue of rock thrust out into emptiness.

With a terrible cry the Balrog fell forward, and its shadow plunged down and vanished. But even as it fell it swung its whip, and the thongs lashed and curled about the wizard's knees, dragging him to the brink. He staggered and fell, grasped vainly at the stone, and slid into the abyss. 'Fly, you fools!' he cried, and was gone.[141]

---

141   Tolkien, *The Lord of the Rings*, 330-331.

Chapter Four

Transhumanism and the Metaphysics of the Human Person

"Human nature will be the last part of Nature to surrender to Man. The battle will then be won. We shall... be henceforth free to make our species whatever we wish it to be. The battle will indeed be won. But who, precisely, will have won it?"[1]

C.S. Lewis

Introduction

THE CONVERGENCE of emerging technologies, such as biotechnology, genetic engineering, nanotechnology, robotics, information technology, and artificial intelligence create synergies that will generate new applications.[2] Transhumanists look forward to a future where these technologies are directed toward human beings to enhance our cognition, body, and emotions.[3] According to Max More, "By thoughtfully,

---

1 C.S. Lewis, *The Abolition of Man* (New York: HarperCollins Publishers, 1974), 59.

2 Ray Kurzweil, *The Singularity is Near: When Humans Transcend Biology* (New York: Penguin Books, 2006), 35-36, 56-72. An example of a product developed from this convergence is the smartphone, which combines the functionality of a telephone, a camera, a music player, and a digital personal assistant into one device.

3 Max More and Natasha Vita-More, eds., *The Transhumanist Reader: Classical and Contemporary Essays on the Science, Technology, and Philosophy of the Human Future* (West Sussex, UK: John Wiley & Sons, 2013), 55.

carefully, and yet boldly applying technology to ourselves, we can become something no longer accurately described as human—we can become posthuman."[4] Becoming posthuman, as More suggests, is a gradual merging of human persons with technology, and represents the second aspect of the Double Blur. Whereas the previous two chapters investigated the transhumanist project to build machines to be persons, this chapter explores transhumanism's metaphysics of the human person and their ambition to merge humans with machines.

Transhumanists reject the idea that human progress is constrained by our limited biology and intellect. Instead, they pursue fundamental alterations to improve human beings.[5] Even though various expressions of transhumanism have developed in the last four decades, they all share the belief that humanity's chief problems originate from the limits of our evolutionary heritage. The solution, then, is to apply science and technology to overcome our biological, intellectual, and psychological limits.

The question of whether the imagined future of transhumanism is utopian or dystopian is under debate, especially among philosophers, theologians, and political scientists. Political scientist Francis Fukuyama, one of transhumanism's foremost critics, calls it "the world's most dangerous idea."[6] He argues that the first casualty of transhumanism will likely be equality. "Modifying any one of our key characteristics inevitably entails modifying a complex, interlinked package of traits, and we will never be able to anticipate the ultimate outcome."

This chapter will first investigate three distinctive features of transhumanism's materialist philosophy of the human person: an evolving human nature, a patternist view of personal identity, and a techno-gnostic view of embodiment. Second, I will outline the trajectory of enhancements that transhumanists propose for human persons. Third, I will critique transhumanism's materialist philosophy and argue that it cannot account for the existence of persons, enduring personal identity, objective morality, or individual autonomy, liberty, or rights. Finally, I will suggest an alternative philosophy that offers a more complete explanation of human persons.

---

4   Max More and Natasha Vita-More, eds., *The Transhumanist Reader: Classical and Contemporary Essays on the Science, Technology, and Philosophy of the Human Future* (West Sussex, UK: John Wiley & Sons, 2013), 4.

5   Ibid., 2.

6   Francis Fukuyama, "Transhumanism: The World's Most Dangerous Idea," *Foreign Policy* no. 144 (2004): 42-43, posted on website *Aarhus Universitet*, https://www.au.dk/fukuyama/boger/essay/ (accessed May 28, 2020).

Preliminary Considerations

Before launching into our investigation of transhumanism's view of human persons, I offer some general thoughts about technology that will help set the stage for what follows. Whatever one may think about transhumanism as the "world's most dangerous idea," the notion poses serious questions about how technology applies to human persons. It is tempting to imagine that technology will inevitably advance, yet humanity will remain the same. Historian Michael Bess calls this the "The Jetsons Fallacy," referring to the 1962-63 cartoon *The Jetsons*.[7] The Jetson family of 2062 was depicted as a normal family of the 1960's except they had a lot of fancy technological gadgets. The fallacious assumption was that human beings remain the same even though technology advances. History demonstrates that our reliance on and interactions with technology certainly change us. Examples of technologies that have shaped humanity are things like the clock, the printing press, aviation, and contraceptives.

Today, research is being done on the effects of Internet usage on cognition, memory, knowledge, attention spans, and self-concepts.[8] The long term conclusions are not yet known, but the early results show that "high levels of Internet usage and heavy media multitasking" decreases our capacity for sustained attention and deep thinking, reduces our ability to maintain goals in the face of distraction, and decreases our memory.[9] We are at risk of becoming 'pancake people,' having a large amount of shallow thoughts, but no capacity for contemplating deep thoughts.[10]

This research on the effects of Internet usage is uncannily similar to Socrates' analysis of writing in Plato's *Phaedrus*. In his day, the technology of writing challenged the oral tradition of learning. Socrates warned that a reliance on writing would "create forgetfulness in the learner's soul

---

7 Jacob Shatzer, *Transhumanism and the Image of God* (Downers Grove: IVP Academic, 2019), 1.
8 Joseph Firth, John Torous, Brendon Stubbs, Josh A. Firth, Genevieve Z. Steiner, Lee Smith, Mario Alvarez Jimenez, John Gleeson, Davy Vancampfort, Christopher J. Armitage, Jerome Sarris, "The Online Brain: How the Internet May be Changing our Cognition," *World Psychiatry*, 2019 Jun; 18(2): 119–129, Published online 2019 May 6, https://www.ncbi.nlm.nih.gov/pmc/articles/PMC6502424/ (accessed May 28, 2020).
9 Ibid., 121-123.
10 Nicholas Carr, "Is Google Making Us Stupid?" *The Atlantic - Technology* July/August 2008, https://www.theatlantic.com/magazine/archive/2008/07/is-google-making-us-stupid/306868/ (accessed May 28, 2020), 10.

because they would not use their memories. They will appear to be omniscient, but will generally know nothing."[11] Ironically, his warning sounds similar to the effects of Internet usage. Even if we grant the obvious benefits of writing and the Internet, the point is that we should, like Socrates, take the time to ponder the human cost of embracing new technologies.

Unfortunately, we are not very good at accurately assessing the value and costs associated with modern technology. Nicolas Carr describes this general human affliction as miswanting in his book *The Glass Cage*.[12] Essentially, we have a tendency to assume that leisure should be preferred over labor. That is, we think we will enjoy things that come easily better than things we have to work for. University of Chicago psychology professors Mihaly Csikszentmihalyi and Judith LeFevre call this phenomena the 'paradox of work' because even though we desire more leisure, we actually experience less positive feelings when we are at leisure than when we are at work.[13] Understanding our inclination to *miswant*, we should carefully assess the promises of transhumanism to free us from our defective biology, increase our intelligence, elevate our emotions, and achieve cybernetic immortality—all while requiring very little effort on our part. For transhumanists, technology will solve almost every problem and satisfy every desire. It only takes a moment of thoughtful reflection to sense this is wrong. If you are not old enough to reflect back far enough, comedian Louis CK can help. He has a bit called "Everything is Amazing and Nobody is Happy" where he observes the human tendency to *miswant* and not be satisfied with technology.[14]

An uncritical attitude toward technology may result in either unintentionally desensitizing or attracting a person to transhumanism. Journalist Michael Harris warns that "every technology will alienate you from some part of your life. That is its job. Your job is to notice."[15] One of the aims of

---

11   Plato, "Phaedrus," in Mortimer Adler, editor, *Great Books of the Western World, Volume 6* (Chicago: Encyclopedia Britannica, Inc., 1990), 138-9.

12   Nicolas Carr, *The Glass Cage: How Our Computers are Changing Us* (New York: W.W. Norton and Co., Inc.: 2015), 15.

13   Mihaly Csikszentmihalyi and Judith LeFevre, "Optimal Experience at Work and Leisure," *Journal of Personality and Social Psychology* (1989), Vol. 56, No. 5, 815-822, https://pdfs.semanticscholar.org/2c19/82f8de71b73771cb11ba192c-10c30d92cd58.pdf (accessed July 7, 2020).

14   Louis CK, "Everything is Amazing and Nobody is Happy," YouTube, https://www.youtube.com/watch?v=nUBtKNz0KZ4 (accessed July 7, 2020).

15   Michael Harris, *The End of Absence: Reclaiming What We've Lost in a World of Constant Connection* (New York: Penguin, 2014), 206, quoted in Jacob Shatzer,

this chapter is to help the reader analyze the human cost of transhumanism and notice how, by design, it alienates you from your humanity.

Transhumanism's Materialist Metaphysics of the Human Person

There is a growing body of literature dedicated to debating the assumptions, promises, and perils of transhumanism. Much of the deliberation centers around identifying the metaphysics of human persons.[16] A typical discourse will probe questions like: What is the human person? Is human nature fixed or evolving? Would the future posthuman 'me' still be 'me'? Undoubtedly, in order to critically assess transhumanism, it is essential to understand and critique their philosophy of human persons because it undergirds and drives their entire enterprise. The three central tenets of transhumanism, examined in chapter one, are clearly evident in their view of human persons: a materialistic/mechanistic philosophy of the human person, a desire to control and transcend human nature, and a technological view of progress toward becoming posthuman.

Transhumanists describe themselves as materialists, meaning there is no aspect of the mind and person that cannot ultimately be explained by physical forces. Accordingly, for the transhumanist, there is no immaterial soul that survives the death of the body.[17] The human person, for the transhumanist, is best understood as a bundle of molecular and cellular complexes that can be engineered and manipulated.[18] Their belief in humanity's evolutionary origin and development gives transhumanists confidence that human nature itself might be deliberately changed.[19] Transhumanists often use the term "human nature," but given their materialist philosophy, it is difficult to understand what they mean by it.[20] In the sections that follow, I explain the three essential aspects of transhumanism's

---

Transhumanism and the Image of God, 11.

16   The metaphysics of the human person is the branch of philosophy that gives an account of the human person, his nature, and being.

17   More and Vita-More, eds., *The Transhumanist Reader*, 7, 23.

18   Steven A. Hoffman, "Transhumanist Materialism: A Critique from Immunoneuropsychology," in Hava Tirosh-Samuelson and Kenneth L. Mossman, editors, *Building Better Humans? Refocusing the Debate on Transhumanism* (Frankfurt: Peter Lang, 2012), 275.

19   More and Vita-More, eds, *The Transhumanist Reader*, 10.

20   Ibid., 4, 8, 10, 20, 45-6, 60, 199-200, 227-8, 312, 347-8, 351-2, 357, 419, 425-7, 431.

philosophy of human persons: an evolving human nature, a patternist view of personal identity, and a techno-gnostic view of embodiment.

Evolving Human Nature

Transhumanists are committed to a strictly physical story about reality and how things came to be. As a result, they trace the physical limitations of human beings to our evolutionary history. Nick Bostrom explains:

> For most of humanity's history, the average human lifespan hovered between twenty and thirty years. Even in recent times, because of infectious disease, accidents, starvation, and violent death very few of our ancestors lived much beyond seventy. There was therefore little selection pressure to evolve the cellular repair mechanisms that would be required to keep us going beyond our meager seventy years. As a result of these circumstances in the distant past, we now suffer the inevitable decline of old age and death.[21]

For transhumanists, naturalistic evolution has produced a physically inferior human being and this is the primary problem to be solved. In Bostrom's essay "Transhumanist Values," he describes the deplorable state of human nature, saying, "[H]uman nature is a work-in-progress, a half-baked beginning that we can learn to remold in desirable ways. Current humanity need not be the endpoint of evolution. Transhumanists hope that by responsible use of science, technology, and other rational means we shall eventually manage to become posthuman, beings with vastly greater capacities than present human beings have."[22]

Max More also sees the human constitution as deeply flawed. In More's essay "A Letter to Mother Nature," he expresses dissatisfaction with the poor job Mother Nature (i.e., evolution) has done with the human constitution. He writes,

> Mother Nature, truly we are grateful for what you have made us. No doubt you did the best you could. However,

---

21 Nick Bostrom, "Transhumanist FAQ: A General Introduction," version 2.1, 2003, 36, https://www.nickbostrom.com/views/transhumanist.pdf (accessed May 30, 2020).

22 Nick Bostrom, "Transhumanist Values," nickbostrom.com, April 18, 2001, https://www.nickbostrom.com/ethics/values.html (accessed June 1, 2020).

> with all due respect, we must say that you have in many
> ways done a poor job with the human constitution . . . We
> will no longer tolerate the tyranny of aging and death . . .
> We will expand our perceptual range . . . improve our neural organization and capacity . . . reshape our motivational patterns and emotional responses . . . take charge over
> our genetic programming and achieve mastery over our
> biological and neurological process.[23]

After disparaging Mother Nature, More announces that the time has come to amend the human constitution. He proposes seven amendments:
  1. By many technological means, we will overcome aging and death.
  2. We will expand our perceptual range and devise novel senses to understand the world.
  3. We will enhance our intelligence and memory.
  4. We will supplement the neocortex with a metabrain, allowing us to increase self-awareness and modulate our emotions.
  5. We will control and master our biological and neurological processes through genetic programming.
  6. We will reshape our motivational and emotional responses.
  7. We will not be limited by our biology; we will increasingly integrate our advancing technologies into ourselves.[24]

The claims of naturalistic evolution challenge the notion that human beings are divinely created with a purpose, arguing instead that humans gradually evolved by purposeless, natural forces, including random variations, from the lower animals.[25] This theory succeeded in reducing "the organic and human world" to the physical laws governing the inorganic universe.[26] Transhumanist ideas are imbued with an evolutionary perspective, especially the idea that "humanity as it currently exists is one step along an evolutionary path of development."[27]

This evolutionary perspective, coupled with the idea that human beings are mere matter, allows transhumanists to believe that humanity can be

---

23   Max More quoted in Gregory Stock, "The Battle for the Future," in More and VIta-More, eds., *The Transhumanist Reader*, 305.

24   More and Vita-More, eds., *The Transhumanist Reader*, 450.

25   Charles Darwin, *Descent or Origin of Man*, in Mortimer Adler, editor, *Great Books of the Western World, Volume 49* (Chicago: Encyclopedia Britannica, Inc., 1990), 253.

26   Ibid.

27   More and Vita-More, eds., *The Transhumanist Reader*, 10.

purposely changed.²⁸ Transhumanist Simon Young's label for the transhumanist project is "Designer Evolution," meaning human beings will be creative designers, enhancing themselves by manipulating their own biological material. Evolution, on the other hand, is seen as the accidental amateur, who evolved humans by the natural means available.²⁹

I take the transhumanist use of the term human nature to mean the human physical constitution, which they view as the flawed product of naturalistic evolution. Moreover, because of their materialistic/mechanistic view of the human being, they believe we can take control of our evolution by applying technological enhancements.

Patternist View of Personal Identity

The dominant view of personal identity among transhumanists is patternism. Essentially, it is an updated "cognitive science" version of John Locke's psychological continuity theory. Locke maintained that your identity is fundamentally rooted in your memories and ability to reflect on yourself, or more generally, your overall psychological configuration.³⁰ Ray Kurzweil updated Locke's view by using the language of cognitive science to replace 'psychological configuration' with the information pattern in your brain. Transhumanists believe that radical changes to the body and brain can occur, but the continuity of the pattern will remain.³¹ Ray Kurzweil captures the theory this way:

> The specific set of particles that my body and brain comprise are in fact completely different from the atoms and molecules that I comprised only a short while ago. We know that most of our cells are turned over in a matter

---

28   More and Vita-More, eds., *The Transhumanist Reader*, 10.

29   Simon Young, *Designer Evolution: A Transhumanist Manifesto* (New York: Prometheus Books, 2006), 27-30, 305.

30   Susan Schneider, "Future Minds: Transhumanism, Cognitive Enhancement and the Nature of Persons," *Neuroethics Publications*, University of Pennsylvania Scholarly Commons, https://repository.upenn.edu/cgi/viewcontent.cgi?article=1037&context=neuroethics_pubs (accessed July 15, 2020). The leading identity theories include: (1) Ego Theory - a person's identity is her "soul"; (2) Psychological Continuity Theory - you are essentially your overall psychological configuration, what Kurzweil refers to as your "pattern"; (3) Materialism Theory - you are the material of your body and brain; (4) No Self Theory - the "I" is an illusion.

31   More and Vita-More, eds., *Transhumanist Reader*, 230.

of weeks, and even our neurons, which persist as distinct cells for a relatively long time, nonetheless change all of their constituent molecules within a month . . . So, I am a completely different set of stuff than I was a month ago, and all that persists is the pattern of organization of that stuff. The pattern changes also, but slowly and in a continuum. I am rather like the pattern that water makes in a stream as it rushes past the rocks in its path. The actual molecules of water change every millisecond, but the pattern persists for hours or even years.[32]

The patternist view works well with the computational theory of mind, where the mind is understood as an algorithmic program that runs on the hardware of the brain. By connecting the computational theory of mind with the patternist theory of identity, transhumanists conclude that what is essential to the human person, his nature, is the computational pattern of his brain. Hence, they believe that personal identity can persist through all manner of enhancements, including the uploading of your mind to a computer.[33] In the "Transhumanist FAQ," Nick Bostrom advocates patternism when explaining mind uploading. "A widely accepted position is that you survive so long as certain information patterns are conserved . . . For the continuation of personhood, on this view, it matters little whether you are implemented on a silicon chip inside a computer or in that gray, cheesy lump inside your skull, assuming both implementations are conscious."[34]

That personal identity and consciousness can conceivably be transferred during mind uploading has not been shown to be plausible, either scientifically or philosophically, but Randal A. Koene explains the theory behind the possibility:

> Empirical evidence in neuroscience supports the scientific theory that all of the functions of the mind are accomplished through neurobiological mechanisms of the nervous system. Our mental experiences are a consequence of those functions of mind. If the same functions

---

32   Ray Kurzweil, *The Singularity is Near: When Humans Transcend Biology* (New York: Penguin Books, 2005), 383.

33   Koene, "Uploading to Substrate-Independent Minds," in More and Vita-More, eds., *The Transhumanist Reader*, 146.

34   Nick Bostrom, "Transhumanist FAQ: A General Introduction," version 2.1, 2003, 17-18, https://www.nickbostrom.com/views/transhumanist.pdf (accessed May 30, 2020).

can be recreated in a different operating substrate and there, together, they still produce the same meaningful results as in the original implementation, then to accomplish the functions of mind no longer depends on a single (biological) substrate. In that sense, the functions of mind are then substrate-independent.[35]

Koene also employs philosophical thought experiments where one is asked to imagine a 'Ship of Theseus' type scenario of a person whose brain is gradually replaced with artificial neural implants.[36] "If one's biological neurons were gradually replaced, for example, with synthetic parts that supported the same level of cognitive function, the same mind and personality might persist despite being in a non-biological substrate."[37] Gradual change, on this view, is the best way to ensure a person's brain pattern and preserve identity.

Not all transhumanists are patternists. Max More advocates a transformationalist view of identity, which is a variation of patternism. Although he leans toward Derek Parfit's view of the self as an illusion, More argues that as long as the radically transformed person is consistent with, or a fulfillment of, the values of the prior person, then personal identity is maintained.[38] For a transformationalist, the core of a person's identity is his commitment to the value of self-transformation or will to evolve.

---

35   Randal A. Koene, "What Does it Mean For a Mind to be Substrate-Independent?" *Carboncopies*, FAQ, https://carboncopies.org/faq (accessed May 29, 2020).

36   Plutarch, *Theseus*, Tufts.edu, http://www.perseus.tufts.edu/hopper/text?doc=Perseus%3Atext%3A2008.01.0067%3Achapter%3D23%3Asection%3D1 (accessed June 4, 2020). Theseus' Paradox, or the Ship of Theseus: The ship on which Theseus sailed with the youths and returned in safety, the thirty-oared galley, was preserved by the Athenians down to the time of Demetrius Phalereus.[1] They took away the old timbers from time to time, and put new and sound ones in their places, so that the vessel became a standing illustration for the philosophers in the mooted question of growth, some declaring that it remained the same, others that it was not the same vessel.

37   Randal A. Koene, "Uploading to Substrate-Independent Minds," in Max More and Natasha Vita-More, eds., *The Transhumanist Reader* (Sussex, UK: John Wiley & Sons, 2013), 146; https://carboncopies.org/faq (accessed May 29, 2020).

38   James Hughes, "Transhumanism and Personal Identity," in More and Vita-More, eds., *Transhumanist Reader*, 230.

Techno-Gnostic View of Embodiment

A common belief among all strands of transhumanism is that the current state of the human body is a "flawed piece of engineering" that needs to be replaced with a different form of our own making.[39] Max More explains the general dissatisfaction with human biology saying, "It could hardly be otherwise, given that it was designed by a blind watchmaker, as Richard Dawkins put it."[40] Transhumanists contend that the only solution to the problem of our human condition is to use technology to radically enhance and transcend our biological limitations.

Craig Gay, a critic of transhumanism, describes this perspective as technological gnosticism because of transhumanists' desire to ultimately be free from their biological bodies.[41] The Transhumanist Declaration codifies this belief: "We favor morphological freedom—the right to modify and enhance one's body, cognition, and emotions. This freedom includes the right to use or not to use techniques and technologies to extend life, preserve the self through cryonics, uploading, and other means, and to choose further modifications and enhancements."[42] This techno-gnosticism is evident in their ultimate aim to replace the biological body with artificial technology. Transhumanism's highest human value is the aspiration to overcome biological limitations and become a non-biological posthuman species.[43]

Most people acknowledge that our human bodies are susceptible to aging, disease, and death, but transhumanists go much further by deploring

---

39   More and Vita-More, eds., *Transhumanist Reader*, 15.

40   Ibid.

41   Craig M. Gay, *Modern Technology and the Human Future: A Christian Appraisal* (Downers Grove: IVP Academic, 2018), 98-99, 131, 133. A goal of Gnosticism in the second to the fourth centuries was to escape the prison of the body.

42   More and Vita-More, eds., "Transhumanist Declaration (2012)," *The Transhumanist Reader*, 55. Authors of the Transhumanist Declaration: Alexander Sash Chislenko, Anders Sandberg, Arjen Kamphuis, Bernie Staring, Bill Fantegrossi, Darren Reynolds, David Pearce, Den Otter, Doug Bailey, Eugene Leitl, Gustavo Alves, Holger Wagner, Kathryn Aegis, Keith Elis, Lee Daniel Crocker, Max More, Mikhail Sverdlov, Natasha Vita-More, Nick Bostrom, Ralf Fletcher, Shane Spaulding, T.O. Morrow, Thom Quinn.

43   Nick Bostrom, "The Transhumanist FAQ: A General Introduction, Version 2.1," 2003, 4, https://nickbostrom.com/views/transhumanist.pdf (accessed June 30, 2020).

human biology. Futurist Ray Kurzweil proposes the following enhancements for our primitive human bodies:

> Artificial materials will be integrated into the body more and more . . . Organs could be replaced by super-advanced machine versions that would run forever and never fail. Red blood cells could be perfected by red blood cell nanobots, who could power their own movement, eliminating the need for a heart at all . . . Eventually, humans will reach a point when they're entirely artificial, a time when we'll look back at biological material and think how unbelievably primitive it was that humans were ever made of that and that humans aged, suffered from cancer, allowed random factors like microbes, diseases, or accidents to harm us or make us disappear.[44]

For transhumanists, the body has no intrinsic value; it is malleable material that can be controlled and mastered by the human will.

Transhumanist Martine Rothblatt, who is an advocate for transgender rights, connects transgenderism with transhumanism largely because they share beliefs concerning morphological freedom. Rothblatt writes, "A basic concept of transhumanism is that humans need not have a fleshly body, just as a woman need not have a real vagina. Humanness is in the mind, just as is sexual identity."[45] She sees freedom of gender as the gateway to transhumanism's freedom from embodiment. Rothblatt writes, "First comes the realization that we are not limited by our sexual anatomy. Then comes the awakening that we are not limited by our anatomy at all."[46] It would be wrong to assume that materialists hold the body, being 'matter,' is an ultimate good. The irony is that their aim is to be liberated from material embodiment.

---

44 Tim Urban, "The AI Revolution: Our Immortality or Extinction," *Wait But Why* (blog), January 27, 2015, https://waitbutwhy.com/2015/01/artificial-intelligence-revolution-2.html (accessed July 1, 2020).

45 Martine Rothblatt, "Mind is Deeper Than Matter: Transgenderism, Transhumanism, and the Freedom of Form," in Max More and Natasha Vita-More, editors, *The Transhumanist Reader*, 317-318. Rothblatt has a patternist view of identity.

46 Rothblatt, "Mind is Deeper Than Matter," in More and Vita-More, eds, *The Transhumanist Reader*, 318. Transhumanists often make "slippery slope" arguments, like this one, in favor of their position, but they object to the same type of arguments when posed by objectors.

Summary of Transhumanism's Philosophy of Human Persons

To sum up, transhumanism rests on a materialistic evolutionary view of human persons. Personal identity is represented by patterns of information in the brain. Transhumanists claim that the key aspect of human nature is the "will to evolve," which is a desire to take control and master their own evolution. This mechanistic and reductionist view of human persons undergirds their belief that the body and brain can and should be technologically enhanced and manipulated to transcend biological limitations. Therefore, transhumanists contend that human beings ought to merge with technology in order to become posthuman.

Trajectory of Technological Enhancements

According to transhumanists, the journey from being human to posthuman will happen gradually alongside the development and availability of advancing technologies. Although many of these enhancement technologies are banned or not yet developed, transhumanists invest money, talent, and energy researching and lobbying for the freedom to develop them. They are optimistic that biotechnologies, nanotechnologies, cybernetic technologies, and artificial general intelligence will be available to those who desire to enhance themselves. They adopt a slippery slope perspective about how the boundary lines will inevitably be blurred between therapeutic healing and enhancement.

Yuval Noah Harari, the author of *Homo Deus*, explains the slippery slope perspective this way: "Healing is the initial justification for every upgrade."[47] For example, plastic surgery was developed to treat facial injuries of soldiers returning from World War I, but is now widely used to enhance healthy people.[48] Genetic engineering will first be used to eradicate deadly genetic diseases, then parents will request the same technology be used for upgrading their healthy embryos.[49] Parents might choose to design their children to be tall, intelligent, athletic, musical, with increased memory, and a strong immune system. After bionic legs are developed for paraplegics to walk again, healthy people will request this technology as an en-

---

47 Yuval Noah Harari, *Homo Deus: A Brief History of Tomorrow* (New York: HarperCollins, 2017), 55.
48 Ibid., 52.
49 Ibid., 53-55.

hancement.⁵⁰ When memory loss is stopped in Alzheimer patients, then young and healthy people will request memory enhancements.⁵¹ Memory enhancements include not only improving the memory, but also erasing traumatic or unwanted memories.⁵² Transhumanists are eager for the boundary lines to become blurred. Once technologies are developed and are safely used for therapeutic reasons, transhumanists expect the restrictions against enhancements will be lifted.

According to transhumanists, the transformation from human to post-human will come in stages and will involve overlapping technologies. Next, I provide explanations of the anticipated enhancements from the emerging technologies of biotechnology, nanotechnology, cybernetic engineering, the global brain, and mind uploading.

Stage One: Biotechnology

Biotechnology uses the cellular and molecular processes of biology to develop products and technologies. In the year 2000, President Clinton recognized both Francis Collins and J. Craig Venter for completing their separate projects to sequence the human genome.⁵³ Researchers are now working to decode the functions and interactions of different genes for various applications. Transhumanists are most interested in biotechnologies that can be used for human enhancement, such as gene therapy, stem cell therapy, therapeutic cloning, in vitro fertilization, embryo selection, and synthetic biology.

Craig Venter is not only a biotechnologist, but also a transhumanist. He calls his science genomics, "the science of combinatorial gene sequencing where gene sequences can be mixed and matched to suit the intended application."⁵⁴ Venter has created the first synthetic genome, called "Synthia," a project that could potentially lead to rewriting the code of nature to create a new genetic species.⁵⁵

---

50   Yuval Noah Harari, *Homo Deus: A Brief History of Tomorrow* (New York: HarperCollins, 2017), 52.

51   Ibid.

52   Susan Schneider, *Artificial You: AI and the Future of Your Mind* (Princeton: Princeton University Press, 2019), 89-91.

53   Michael D. Lemonick, "J. Craig Venter: Gene Mapper," *Time Magazine*, December 25, 2000, http://content.time.com/time/world/article/0,8599,2056235,00.html (accessed June 14, 2020).

54   Rachel Armstrong, "Alternative Biologies," in More and Vita-More, eds., *The Transhumanist Reader*, 103.

55   Ibid.

Our environment and actions can reshape us, but transhumanists believe that changing our genes can change us at the deepest level. There are two general types of genetic therapies: somatic and germline. Somatic gene therapies are interventions that do not carry over to the next generation and could provide the means to stop and reverse disease and the aging process. For example, technologies are being developed to turn off destructive genes, to change genetic code, and to replace human DNA with synthesized genes.[56] Transhumanists believe these biotechnologies could continuously repair and replace the defective parts of our physical bodies to prolong life indefinitely.

At the other end of the spectrum, reproductive technologies offer utopian-like benefits to parents who want to use germline interventions to design their children.

Germline manipulations are performed on reproductive cells or embryos, making the genetic modifications inheritable.[57] For example, the gene editing technology CRISPR-Cas9 could provide the means to eliminate certain genetic disorders from the human genome and also enhance human beings beyond our natural capacities.[58] Parents wanting to design their children could request prenatal germline manipulation to remove genetic defects, diseases, and undesirable traits. They could select enhancements for their child, like biological sex, physical appearance, hair color, eye color, skin color, height, and build. They could select for increased intelligence, athleticism, musical ability, or enhanced senses, such as sight, smell, and taste.[59] James Hughes, a proponent of germline gene therapy, views the embryo and fetus "as the biological property of the parents, and exclusively of the mother when *in utero*."[60] He opposes the state intervening in personal liberties concerning reproductive rights, stressing that no

---

56   Kurzweil, *Singularity is Near*, 256-7.

57   Gregory Stock, "The Battle for the Future," in More and Vita-More, eds., *The Transhumanist Reader*, 302-303.

58   Fazale R. Rana and Kenneth R. Samples, *Humans 2.0: Scientific, Philosophical, and Theological Perspectives on Transhumanism* (Covina, CA: Reasons to Believe, 2019), 17-18.

59   Anders Sandberg, "Genetic Modifications," http://www.aleph.se/Trans/Individual/Body/genes.html (accessed June 14, 2020).

60   James Hughes, "Embracing Change with All Four Arms: A Posthumanist Defense of Genetic Engineering," http://www.changesurfer.com/Hlth/Genetech.html (accessed June 14, 2020).

one should be forced to have or abort their children, or forced to modify their own or their children's genetic code.⁶¹

Stem cell technologies, both embryonic and adult cells, offer transhumanists hope for eliminating aging by growing replacement tissues and organs.⁶² Transhumanists are most optimistic about therapeutic cloning, which uses stem cells from embryos generated by a cloning procedure called somatic cell nuclear transfer. These stem cells are used to replace diseased or damaged tissues and organs. Stem cells are harvested from an embryo and the patient's cells are used to provide the nucleus for the procedure. Since the patient is the donor and the recipient, there is a close genetic match and rejection problems are eliminated.⁶³

Transhumanists argue that cognitive enhancements should be accompanied by moral enhancements, since intelligence is a means for both good and bad uses. This idea of enhancing moral well-being, or Superhappiness, is promoted by David Pearce in *The Hedonistic Imperative*. He argues that happiness, suffering, and moral behavior are rooted in biochemistry and genetics; therefore, moral problems can and should be solved through science and technology. They anticipate using moral bioenchancements to directly influence human behavior through the use of psychopharmaceuticals and genetic engineering.⁶⁴ A question remains: if morality is grounded in biochemistry and genetics, then Pearce needs to explain what happens to morality after humans transcend their biology.

Transhumanists recognize the importance of biotechnology in the first stage of human enhancements, but other technologies will soon overtake it. As Ray Kurzweil says, "It's still biology, with all its profound limitations." Enhancements not achieved through biotechnology will be made possible in the next stage by the revolution in nanotechnology.

Stage Two: Nanotechnology

All of life is created by tiny biological machines that manipulate the basic elements of matter. Nanotechnology is the ability to construct objects with

---

61   As will be shown, this libertarian stance is not defended in the later stages of transhumanist enhancements.

62   Nick Bostrom, "Transhumanist FAQ," Humanity+, https://humanity-plus.org/philosophy/transhumanist-faq/ (accessed June 14, 2020).

63   Rana and Samples, *Humans 2.0*, 132-3.

64   David Pearce, *The Hedonistic Imperative*, HedWeb.com, https://www.hedweb.com/hedethic/hedonist.htm (accessed August 1, 2020). This topic will be covered more extensively in chapter six.

atomic-scale control.[65] Eric Drexler, one of the pioneers in nanotechnology, adapted these biological methods to build computer-driven machines with parts the size of molecules to manipulate atoms to build "anything you please."[66] Nanotechnology applied to the field of medicine has the potential for transhumanists to redesign and rebuild the human body and brain, molecule by molecule.[67] Nanomedicine will use nanorobots to diagnose disease, repair organs, deliver drugs, and perform nanosurgery, all of which will extend the human health span.[68] A medical nanorobot will have its own power supply, sensors, and a computer to control its behavior.

Smaller than a red blood cell, nanorobots will be injected into the bloodstream to "destroy pathogens such as bacteria, viruses, and cancer cells, and will be controlled via computer software and the internet."[69] A 5 cc. injection of artificial nanobot red blood cells, called respirocytes, could duplicate the oxygen-carrying ability of the entire body's blood supply.[70] Artificial nanorobot white blood cells, called microbivores, could digest harmful bacteria, viruses, or fungi and then be removed from the body.[71] Nanorobots could consume cancer cells and perform chromosome replacement therapy to correct the genetic damage that leads to aging.[72] Transhumanists anticipate that nanomedicine will reverse the biological effect of aging and eliminate most causes of natural death.

Transhumanists are most excited about the application of nanotechnology to enhance the brain and cognition. Just as nanorobots injected into the bloodstream keep our biological bodies healthy at the cellular and

---

65 Richard Feynman, "There's Plenty of Room at the Bottom," Transcript of his 1959 speech at Caltech, https://www.zyvex.com/nanotech/feynman.html (accessed June 15, 2020). Feynman's speech marks the birth of the concept of nanotechnology. He described the inevitability of engineering machines at the atomic level.

66 Joel Garreau, *Radical Evolution: The Promise and Peril of Enhancing Our Minds, Our Bodies—and What It Means to Be Human* (New York: Broadway Books, 2006), 118.

67 Eric Drexler, "Forward," by Robert A. Freitas, Jr., *Nanomedicine: Volume I Basic Capabilities* (Georgetown, TX: Landes Bioscience, 1999), online book, http://www.nanomedicine.com/NMI/Foreword.htm (accessed June 15, 2020).

68 Robert A. Freitas Jr., "Welcome to the Future of Medicine," in More and Vita-More, eds., *The Transhumanist Reader*, 68-9.

69 Kurzweil, *Singularity*, 255.

70 Freitas, "Welcome to the Future of Medicine," 70.

71 Ibid.

72 Ibid.

molecular levels, nanorobots injected noninvasively into the brain will interact with our biological neurons and extend our intelligence, allowing direct communication with the internet.[73] Not only will we think billions of times faster, we will be able to interface with all the information in the cloud and be able to communicate wirelessly from one brain to another.[74] Google and Facebook have been working on nanotechnology since 2004. Larry Page, co-founder of Google, spoke about his vision for the future of the search engine: "Eventually you'll have the implant where if you think about a fact, it will just tell you the answer."[75] The research group at Facebook has a similar goal for their Brain Machine Interface (BMI) project, "to remove the gap between your brain and the keyboard."[76]

Stage Three: Cyborg Engineering

Philosopher and cognitive scientist Andy Clark believes there is potential for bio-technological mergers because human biology is open to a variety of technologically mediated enhancements, such as sensory substitution, mental extension, and cognitive reconfiguration.[77] He argues that there is deep biological plasticity, making the human self a "soft self," able to straddle and cross the boundary between biology and artifact. Becoming a cyborg means that "our best tools and technologies become us, changing who and what we are."[78] In the cyborg relation, the human and technology become a single experiencing entity, much like the way pacemakers and artificial valves are integrated within the body.

Stage Four: Humans Merge With the Global Brain

The idea of humans merging with technology is even more powerful when the technology is artificial general intelligence (AGI), or a superintelligence. Ben Goertzel, Chairman of the Board of Humanity+, envisions a future where our brains will be hybridized with AGI systems. He believes

---

73 Kurzweil, *Singularity is Near*, 257.
74 Ibid., 309 and 316.
75 Steven Levy, "We Are Entering the Era of the Brain Machine Interface," *Wired*, https://www.wired.com/2017/04/we-are-entering-the-era-of-the-brain-machine-interface/ (accessed July 1, 2020).
76 Ibid., 2.
77 Andy Clark, "Re-Inventing Ourselves: The Plasticity of Embodiment, Sensing, and Mind," in More and Vita-More, eds., *The Transhumanist Reader*, 124.
78 Ibid., 124.

this merger will cause a radical transformation of our inner lives, like the way we conceive of ourselves, our feeling of free will, and the sense that our consciousness is distinct from the external world.[79] Goertzel predicts the feeling of individuation and separateness will seem fallacious when we are interacting every day with AGI's.[80]

Humans connected to AGI will gradually become incorporated into a greater collective called the "Global Brain."[81] The global brain theory is the idea that the increasing interconnectedness of humans and computers produce a kind of distributed mind, collectively forming a higher level of intelligence. Goertzel expects that AGI would collect and synthesize the thoughts of all the people on the globe, add its own thoughts, then feed these ideas back to humans.[82] Goertzel says, "The potential benefits to be delivered by advanced AGI are difficult to overestimate. Once we are able to create artificial minds vastly more intelligent than our own, there are no clear limits to what we may be able to achieve, working together with our creations."[83]

Final Stage: Mind Uploading

The first four stages of human enhancements will radically extend human lifespans by merging our bodies and brains with technology, but our cyborg bodies will still be subject to accidents or will finally wear out. Transhumanists realize indefinite survival will require uploading our minds to a more durable non-biological substrate. Mind uploading is the process of transferring mental states, memory, and the self from a biological brain to a computer.[84] This idea is grounded in the functionalist philosophy of mind, which holds that mental states or cognitive systems are independent of any specific physical instantiation. Mental states are con-

---

79   Ben Goertzel, "Artificial General Intelligence and the Future of Humanity," in More and Vita-More, eds., *The Transhumanist Reader*, 130-1.
80   Ibid., 131.
81   Ibid.
82   Ben Goertzel, "Encouraging a Positive Transcension," *Singularity Stewardship and the Global Brain MIneplex* (2004), https://goertzel.org/dynapsyc/2004/PositiveTranscension.htm#_4._Singularity Stewardship (accessed June 16, 2020).
83   Goertzel, "Artificial General Intelligence and the Future of Humanity," in More and Vita-More, eds., *The Transhumanist Reader*, 130.
84   *The Carbon Copies Foundation, FAQ*, https://carboncopies.org/faq/ (accessed June 17, 2020).

stituted by their causal relationship to other mental states, sensory inputs, and behavioral outputs. On this logic, being constituted by their functional roles, mental states should be able to be realized in a non-biological system. Transhumanist Ralph C. Merkle says it this way: "Your brain is a material object. The behavior of material objects is described by the laws of physics. The laws of physics can be modeled on a computer. Therefore, the behavior of your brain can be modeled on a computer."[85] A non-biological brain could rapidly improve itself through software upgrades and enhancements. One of the primary benefits of a non-biological brain is its greater neocortical capacity, which will create greater intelligence and higher conceptual thinking.[86]

Randal A. Koene proposes Whole Brain Emulation (WBE) as a method to achieve a substrate independent mind by reverse-engineering the brain.[87] This detailed approach would yield information about the brain at the level of individual neurons and synapses. There are two types of WBE uploading, destructive and non-destructive, depending on whether the original brain is destroyed in the process. Kenneth Hayworth, president of the Brain Preservation Foundation, promotes cryogenically preserving the brain as a standard medical practice.[88] This destructive process consists of a detailed scan of a brain preserved through cryonic suspension, which destroys the original brain. A non-destructive approach would scan a live brain, presumably by using nanotechnology.

Recent developments in the field of neural prosthetics has led to another method of WBE which would gradually replace all of the organic neurons of the brain with artificial synthetic parts.[89] Ray Kurzweil promotes this gradual replacement scenario because it mimics the brain's natural replacement process throughout our lives. For instance, the molecules of a

---

85   Ralph C. Merkle, "Uploading," in Max More and Natasha Vita-More, editors, *The Transhumanist Reader*, 158.

86   Ray Kurzweil, *How to Create a Mind: The Secret of Human Thought Revealed* (New York: Penguin Books, 2013, 280.

87   Randal A. Koene, "Uploading to Substrate-Independent Minds," in More and Vita-More, eds., *The Transhumanist Reader*, 147-8.

88   Keith Wiley, "Transcending Biology: Reverse Engineering the Brain," Carboncopies Foundation, https://carboncopies.org/summary-of-tbreb2018-roadmap-session/ (accessed June 18, 2020).

89   Sim Bamford, "A Framework for Approaches to Transfer of a Mind's Substrate," *International Journal of Machine Consciousness*, Vol. 4, No. 1 (2012), 23-34, https://pdfs.semanticscholar.org/36cd/238588dee2b7fa36ef2c3a0a80447b-30b96a.pdf (accessed June 18, 2020).

biological neuron in the brain are replaced monthly.[90] The non-biological brain that is created through this scenario can be copied, backed up, and re-created. Kurzweil says, "It's not true that the [copy] is not you—it is you. It is just that there are now two of you. That's not so bad—if you think you're a good thing, then two of you is even better."[91] For transhumanists, intelligence is the most important phenomenon in the universe, and mind-uploading will be the ultimate step towards becoming posthuman and overcoming the restrictions of our biological heritage.

Critiquing Transhumanism's Materialist Metaphysics of the Human Person

Transhumanism's materialist philosophy fuels their ambition to merge humans with technology, the second part of the Double Blur. They have a mechanistic picture of the world, where nature is modeled after a machine and human beings are part of that machinery. All natural objects are constituted of essentially the same kind of thing, namely fundamental particles in different configurations.[92] Transhumanist Nick Bostrom puts it this way, "If human beings are constituted of matter obeying the same laws of physics, then it should, in principle, be possible to learn to manipulate human nature the same way we manipulate external objects."[93] Transhumanists approach problems with a reverse engineering mentality. If something needs to be fixed, you take apart its components and determine the causal connections. If every problem can be converted into a technical problem, then the solution is simply the appropriate application of technology. Transhumanism reflects a strong commitment to carry to completion the materialistic metaphysical picture of reality to include human persons. In fact, if it were possible to merge humans with technology, meaning the entirety of body and brain were replaced with technology, it would count as evidence for the materialist philosophy of human persons.

Few would deny that the universe and natural objects are, in some respects, machine-like and that this point of view has resulted in many scientific achievements. However, this is only *part* of a complete explanation of reality and it is legitimate to take exception when this materialist view

---

90   Kurzweil, *How to Create a Mind*, 244-5.
91   Ibid., 247.
92   Edward Feser, *Aristotle's Revenge: The Metaphysical Foundations of Physical and Biological Science* (Germany: editiones scholasticae, 2019), 46.
93   Bostrom, "A History of Transhumanist Thought," 4.

is set up as the absolute and all-sufficient form of explanation. I argued in chapters two and three that transhumanism's project to achieve AGI and Superintelligence will not be accomplished because their assumed materialist philosophy of mind is false. Here, I will similarly contend that transhumanism's materialist philosophy is inadequate to account for humanity's essential features: the existence of persons, enduring personal identity, ethics, values, and duties, and individual autonomy, liberty, and rights. Because of their incomplete understanding of the human person, there is no reason to believe their proposed enhancements are metaphysically possible and if attempted, would be good for human flourishing.

Materialism Cannot Account for the Existence of Persons

First of all, it is misleading for transhumanists to claim there is a strictly materialist explanation of human persons. Materialism denies the existence of persons in the ordinary sense, namely that we are substantial, conscious, rational, embodied selves with free will. Instead, they believe that human beings are the accidental products of a non-personal, purposeless, valueless evolutionary process driven by reproductive fitness. Nevertheless, because people generally hold the ordinary, commonsense view of themselves as substantial selves, transhumanists often employ "person" language in their writings in order not to appear extreme. Yet, this "person" language is inconsistent with their materialism and in the end, as I will show, transhumanists believe the concept of the person as illusory. They seem compelled to give an account of our commonsense assumptions—enduring identity, moral agency, individual autonomy, rights—but their explanations are incompatible with materialism. Alternatively, if they were intellectually honest, they could follow Francis Crick who candidly states the radical consequences of materialism:

> The Astonishing Hypothesis is that "You," your joys and your sorrows, your memories and your ambitions, your sense of identity and free will, are in fact no more than the behavior of a vast assembly of nerve cells and their associated molecules. As Lewis Carroll's Alice may have phrased it: "You're nothing but a pack of neurons." This hypothesis is so alien to the ideas of most people alive today that it can be truly called astonishing.[94]

---

94 Francis Crick, *The Astonishing Hypothesis: The Scientific Search for the Soul* (New York: Scribner, 1994), 3, quoted in Stewart Goetz and Charles Taliaferro,

Nothing undermines the materialist philosophy of human persons like the astonishing hypothesis that persons do not exist.

Materialism Cannot Account for Enduring Personal Identity

Transhumanists claim that radical human enhancements are desirable because they are aimed at a person's well-being. Practically speaking, if I am deciding whether to radically transform myself into a posthuman, it seems crucial to know that 'I' myself will experience this promised future existence. If the enhancements will not improve 'me,' then the rationale for deciding to enhance myself is less persuasive. Am I only creating my successor? In fact, transhumanism's materialist view of the human person and their patternist view of the self are not sufficient to account for personal identity that will persist throughout the trajectory of radical enhancements.[95]

According to transhumanism, the human person is best understood as a bundle of molecular and cellular complexes that can be engineered and manipulated.[96] For the transhumanist, the most important part of the bundle is the brain because a person's identity is encoded there in the form of a pattern of neural connections, memories, cognitive capacities, and sensory abilities. This core pattern changes very gradually in stages over time, yet it purportedly maintains continuity.[97] Ray Kurzweil's description of patternism affirms the gradual aspect of the changing pattern. He says, "I am rather like the pattern that water makes in a stream as it rushes past the rocks in its path. The actual molecules of water change every millisecond, but the pattern persists for hours or even years."[98]

Naturalism (Grand Rapids: Wm. B. Eerdmans Publishing Co., 2008), 22.

95 Susan Schneider, "Future Minds: Transhumanism, Cognitive Enhancement and the Nature of Persons," *Neuroethics Publications*, (July 1, 2008), 1-14, https://repository.upenn.edu/cgi/viewcontent.cgi?article=1037&context=neuroethics_pubs (accessed March 8, 2020).

96 Steven A. Hoffman, "Transhumanist Materialism: A Critique from Immunoneuropsychology," in Hava Tirosh-Samuelson and Kenneth L. Mossman, editors, *Building Better Humans? Refocusing the Debate on Transhumanism* (Frankfurt: Peter Lang, 2012), 275.

97 Kurzweil, *The Singularity Is Near*, 258.

98 Kurzweil, *The Singularity Is Near*, 383. Kurzweil's reference to the pattern in a stream is likely a nod to Heraclitus (c. 535-475 B.C.), who held that permanence is an illusion and change is the universal feature of reality. Plato

Kurzweil analogizes the water with our biology and the pattern of the stream with a brain pattern. Yet, even if we grant that your brain pattern is you, this stream analogy has little to do with explaining how identity persists through radical enhancements. Water molecules in a stream change location by moving downstream, but never do they cease being water molecules. After all, transhumanists plan to replace every biological molecule with artificial technology. Additionally, Kurzweil admits the pattern is not permanent, but persists only for a while. This is the first clue that he and other leading transhumanists are not ultimately concerned about the persistence of personal identity.

The project to merge humans with technology occurs in two phases. Phase one uses biotechnology, nanotechnology, cyborg engineering, and the Global Brain to replace our bodies and brains with non-biological parts. This phase is dependent on first being able to fully understand the intricate workings of biology. This obstacle is acknowledged by Ray Kurzweil, albeit as an afterthought to his optimistic claim: "Biology will never be able to match what we will be capable of engineering *once we fully understand biology's principles of operation*" (emphasis added).[99] Transhumanists are confident that by fully understanding biology and gene expression, they will be able to manipulate the genome and thus enhance specific traits related to health, cognition, and emotions.[100] Thereafter, replacing these biological systems with artificial parts will proceed fairly easily. Our bodies and brains will be replaced with such things as synthetic DNA, artificial organs, artificial blood cells, cognitive nanobots, neural chips, neural implants, modified memory, artificial neurons and synapses, and brain/computer interfaces.[101]

---

and Aristotle both credit Heraclitus as saying, "It is impossible to step into the same water twice." See Plato, *Cratylus*, in Mortimer Adler, editor, *Great Books of the Western World, Volume 6* (Chicago: Encyclopedia Britannica Inc., 1990), 94; Aristotle, *Metaphysics*, in Mortimer Adler, editor, *Great Books of the Western World, Volume 7* (Chicago: Encyclopedia Britannica Inc., 1990), 529 (1010a13).

99   Kurzweil, *Singularity is Near*, 227.

100   This kind of reasoning is akin to "genetic determinism," which Philip Kitcher soundly refutes saying, "We do not live by our genes alone...Typically, many genes combine to affect the characteristics we observe, and their action can be perturbed by changes in the environment." Further, "It is possible that evolution fashioned the basic cognitive *capacities—alles ubriges ist Menschenwerk*, or everything else is manmade" (translation added). Philip Kitcher, *Vaulting Ambition* (Cambridge, Massachusetts: The MIT Press, 1990), 18, 19, 418.

101   Cognitive enhancements through augmentation of thinking processes

With phase one changes to brain patterns, it is unclear, on the patternist view of the self, how personal identity persists. Susan Schneider, who is sympathetic toward transhumanism, finds this path from human to posthuman incompatible with the preservation of the original person's identity.[102] She likens transhumanism's enhancement trajectory to a "technophile's alluring path to suicide."[103] Further, phase one enhancements will blur the boundaries of the self because the body and brain will be merged with technology that is constantly connected to the internet, artificial general intelligence, and the Global Brain. The enhanced self, merged with technology, will no longer have the sense of a single consciousness distinct from the external world. Our experience as autonomous individuals, the feeling of individuation and separateness, will seem fallacious when we are interacting every day with AGI and the collective Global Brain.

The loss of personal identity is not the only human cost of phase one enhancements; the inherent value of embodiment is also destroyed. Phase one enhancements are meant to maintain the health of the body and brain long enough to be a 'bridge' to phase two technologies that are yet to be developed.[104] Kurzweil plans to achieve radical life extension through 'a bridge to a bridge to a bridge.' Biotechnology is a bridge to nanotechnology, which is a bridge to mind uploading. Thus, the body is only instrumentally valuable; it is used as the means to mind uploading, where one can then escape the body altogether.[105] Our self-understanding and experience affirm that we ought not treat our bodies in this way. Immanuel Kant's Principle of Humanity reflects this commonsense view of human dignity: "So act as to treat humanity, whether in thine own person or in that of any other, in every case as an end withal, never as a means only."[106] Transhumanism's materialist philosophy and utilitarian ethics make no room for the intrinsic value of embodied human persons.

The aim of phase two enhancements, or mind uploading, is to transfer the biological brain to a more durable non-biological substrate. Consider

---

are typically described in terms of faster processing and increased access to immense quantities of data and information, not in terms of enhanced knowledge, understanding, and wisdom. Kurzweil, *Singularity is Near*, 257, 375.

102   Schneider, *Artificial You*, 89-91.
103   Ibid., 90.
104   Kurzweil, *Singularity is Near*, 373.
105   Ibid., 371.
106   Immanuel Kant, "The Metaphysics of Morals," *The Great Books of the Western World*, Volume 39, Mortimer J. Adler, editor (Chicago: Encyclopedia Britannica, Inc., 1990), 272.

the following thought experiment. Suppose the computational brain pattern of John is captured through Whole Brain Emulation (WBE), without destroying John's brain. His pattern is then uploaded to a computer. On the patternist view, the same pattern means the same personal identity. Therefore, John and the upload on the computer are the same person. But this is obviously wrong. Even if we grant that an upload is a conscious person, it is not the very same person as the original John. The upload is a copy, not John himself.[107] Only one person can be John. To make matters worse, the upload can be copied again and again.

This is an absurd view of the self with all kinds of ethical and legal ramifications. Ray Kurzweil defends the patternist view, with its absurdities, saying "It's not true that the [copy] is not you—it is you. It is just that there are now two of you. That's not so bad—if you think you're a good thing, then two of you is even better."[108] Likewise, Nick Bostrom applauds the potential advantages of mind uploading, such as "the ability to make back-up copies of oneself (favorably impacting one's life-expectancy) and the ability to transmit oneself as information at the speed of light. Uploads might live either in virtual reality or directly in physical reality by controlling a robot proxy."[109]

Kurzweil proposes a type of Turing Test to judge the accuracy of your upload. If the upload's behavior is indistinguishable from your behavior, then the upload shares your pattern and identity.[110] As shown in chapter three, the Turing Test would merely judge the appearance of human behavior, not whether the upload is a genuine conscious person. Kurzweil's own claims about personal identity are inconsistent and muddled at times regarding whether you can survive the gradual replacement phase and the uploading phase. In 2005, he admitted that "gradual replacement means the end of me [old Ray] even if my pattern is preserved."[111] In 2012, he claimed that having an uploaded copy means there are two of you.[112] Perhaps this lack of coherence reveals that transhumanists are more interested in using humanity as a means to create a new species of posthumans than preserving personal identity.

---

107   I argued in chapters two and three that it is metaphysically impossible for machines to be conscious persons. This argument includes mind uploads.

108   Kurzweil, *How To Create a Mind*, 247.

109   Bostrom, "Transhumanist Values," 2.

110   Kurzweil, *The Singularity is Near*, 383.

111   Ibid., 384-5.

112   Kurzweil, *How To Create a Mind*, 247.

Some transhumanists are more like Francis Crick and suggest the sense of self is an illusion. For instance, Ben Goertzel, Chairman of Humanity+, describes how the idea of personal identity will become obsolete in the future:

> Advances in technology will lead to the obsolescence of many of the most familiar features of our inner lives, like the way we conceive of ourselves, the feeling of free will that we have, the sense we have that our consciousness is sharply distinct from the world around us, the sense we have that our mind and awareness is within us rather than entwined in our interactions with other minds and the external environment.[113]

Similarly, James Hughes holds a Buddhist and Parfitian view of the self as an illusion.[114] He predicts that once technology gives us control of our memory, cognition, and personality, "we will abandon our Western view of individuality for new forms of collective identity."[115]

Simply put, based on their own philosophy of patternism and the admission of at least three transhumanist leaders, the self, as a pattern, will not survive gradual enhancements or mind uploading. In fact, on this scenario, the original self wills its own death. This outcome is paradoxical, especially since the primary motivation to become posthuman is to overcome death.[116]

---

113   Goertzel, "Artificial General Intelligence," in More and Vita-More, eds., *The Transhumanist Reader*, 130-131.

114   James Hughes, "Contradictions from the Enlightenment Roots of Transhumanism," *Journal of Medicine and Philosophy*, 0: 1-19, 2010, http://citeseerx.ist.psu.edu/viewdoc/download?doi=10.1.1.993.3636&rep=rep1&type=pdf (accessed June 28, 2020).

115   James Hughes, "The Future of Death: Cryonics and the Telos of Liberal Individualism," *Journal of Evolution and Technology*, Volume 6, July 2001, https://www.jetpress.org/volume6/Death.htm (accessed June 28, 2020).

116   Nick Bostrom, "Why I Want to be a Posthuman," in More and Vita-More, eds., *The Transhumanist Reader*, 33-35.

Materialism Cannot Account for Ethics, Values, and Duties

Transhumanist Max More maintains there is no agreement concerning a comprehensive transhumanist moral theory.[117] His claim seems to be an attempt to be consistent with transhumanism's materialistic evolutionary philosophy. As Michael Ruse acknowledges, "Ethics is an illusion put in place by natural selection to make us good cooperators."[118] However, despite transhumanists having no formal moral theory, it is not difficult to discover that they adhere to the following set of values and a particular concept of human nature: a utilitarian ethic, the will to evolve and control human nature, and a belief in perpetual progress.[119] Yet, transhumanism's materialistic evolutionary philosophy offers no basis or framework for ethics, values, and duties.

A Utilitarian Ethic

In addressing ethical concerns, transhumanists typically hold to some form of utilitarianism.[120] Generally stated, the principle of utility tells us that right actions are those that have good consequences for the community. On this view, determining if a certain enhancement is morally right is based on whether there is a good outcome for society. A good outcome would be one that advances humanity's goal to transcend its biology.

For example, some biotechnologies will offer enhancements, but require the willful destruction of thousands of human embryos.[121] For the transhumanist, an enhancement is morally right based on the good consequences

---

117 Max More, "The Philosophy of Transhumanism," in More and Vita-More, eds., *The Transhumanist Reader*, 6.

118 Michael Ruse, "The Biological Sciences Can Act as a Ground for Ethics," in Francisco Ayala and Robert Arp, *Contemporary Debates in Philosophy of Biology* (Oxford: Wiley-Blackwell, 2009), 1, http://philsci-archive.pitt.edu/4078/1/RusePhilSciArchive.pdf (accessed July 15, 2020).

119 Despite having no formal moral theory, transhumanists promote ethics on their most prominent websites: *Humanity+* states its mission as "the ethical use of technology to expand human capacities," https://humanityplus.org/about/mission/ (accessed June 22, 2020). The online Transhumanist scholarly website is the Institute for Ethics and Emerging Technologies, which carries the label 'ethics' in its name, https://ieet.org/ (accessed June 22, 2020).

120 More and Vita-More, eds., *The Transhumanist Reader*, 15.

121 Brent Waters, *Human to Posthuman* (Vermont: Ashgate Publishing Company, 2006), 48-9.

for the community, such as overall increased lifespan or cognition. The ends justify the means. Utilitarianism does not accord moral standing to individuals, such as human embryos. Even in cases where utilitarians acknowledge that individual rights do exist, these rights are not inherent or inalienable, but contingent on whether they confer some advantage to society. In John Stuart Mill's well known work *Utilitarianism*, he expresses the contingent nature of individual rights which are grounded in utility.[122] In discussing justice, which he views as a sentiment, he writes, "All persons are deemed to have a right to equality of treatment, except when some recognised social expediency requires the reverse."[123] Likewise, transhumanists will abrogate individual rights when it is decided those rights are no longer useful to society. Transhumanists also judge the morality of omissions. They argue that if safe reproductive genetic technologies become available, then failing to enhance your offspring would be the same as harming them.[124]

While self-described as having no formal moral theory, transhumanists still do not hesitate to use moral language such as 'ought' and 'should.' In the *Humanity+ FAQ* discussion of reproductive genetic engineering, transhumanists argue "that parents have a moral responsibility to make use of these methods, assuming they are safe and effective. Just as it would be wrong for parents to fail in their duty to procure the best available medical care for their sick child, it would be wrong not to take reasonable precautions to ensure that a child-to-be will be as healthy as possible."[125] Therefore, enhancing your offspring is seen not only as desirable, but as a moral obligation.

Values and Duties

The normative value shared by transhumanists is the will to evolve, a desire to transcend our biological limitations. In addition, the ability

---

122   John Stuart Mill, "On the Connection between Justice and Utility," *Utilitarianism* (London: Parker, son, and Bourn, 1863), hedweb.com, https://www.utilitarianism.com/mill5.htm (accessed August 15, 2020).

123   Ibid.

124   David Pearce, *The Hedonistic Imperative,* HedWeb.com, chapter 3.3, https://www.hedweb.com/hedethic/hedonist.htm (accessed August 1, 2020).

125   Humanity+ FAQ, "Why Transhumanists Advocate Human Enhancement as Ethical Rather than Pre-WWII Eugenics?" https://humanityplus.org/philosophy/transhumanist-faq/ (accessed June 23, 2020).

to manipulate the world is seen as a universal feature of being human.[126] Max More puts these two ideas together, "We will reshape our own nature in ways we deem desirable and valuable."[127] Simon Young describes it this way: "Human beings have an innate 'will to evolve,' an instinctive drive to expand our abilities in pursuit of ever-increasing survivability and well-being."[128] The desire for human enhancement and the ability to control nature are seen as universal, innate, and instinctive. Simon Young claims these desires are aimed at our well-being; they are good for their own sake. In Nick Bostrom's essay "Why I Want to be a Posthuman When I Grow Up," he argues that, for most current human beings, these posthuman modes of being will be very good for us.[129]

Transhumanists present their conception of human nature as normative, which is reflected in their dogmatism regarding their selected values. This brings to mind the Innovators in C. S. Lewis' *The Abolition of Man*, who debunk traditional values and virtues, yet believe their own values are immune from the debunking process.[130] As philosopher Michael Hauskeller properly states, "It thus appears that [human] nature, after it has been expelled from the transhumanist paradise with a great show of indignation, is immediately invited back in through the backdoor, just as Lewis thought it would."[131]

Even if we grant that transhumanism's enhancements are for our good, we would need a standard by which to measure these changes. It seems rational that only enhancements that increase the well-being of our species would qualify as good. Using this standard, the trajectory of enhancements that ultimately reject and abolish the human species in order to evolve into a non-biological posthuman species should necessarily be judged as bad for human flourishing. The conclusion of C. S. Lewis is apt, "The rebellion of new ideologies against the *Tao* is a rebellion of the branches against the

---

126 Gregory Stock, "The Battle for the Future," in More and Vita-More, *The Transhumanist Reader*, 312.

127 Max More, "The Philosophy of Transhumanism," in More and Vita-More, *The Transhumanist Reader*, 4.

128 Young, *Designer Evolution*, 19.

129 Nick Bostrom, "Why I Want to be a Posthuman When I Grow Up," in More and Vita-More, eds., *The Transhumanist Reader*, 29.

130 C. S. Lewis, *The Abolition of Man* (New York: HarperCollins, 2001), 29.

131 Michael Hauskeller, "Prometheus Unbound: Transhumanist argument from (human) nature," *Ethical Perspectives* (March 2009), 11, ResearchGate, https://www.researchgate.net/publication/232770169_Prometheus_unbound_Transhumanist_arguments_from_human_nature (accessed March 2, 2020).

tree: if the rebels could succeed they would find that they had destroyed themselves."[132]

Regardless of transhumanism's commitment to a select set of values and ethics, their materialist evolutionary philosophy lacks the moral basis to support these values. That is, if matter is all there is and if human morality is the product of natural selection— meaning belief-formation is the result of fitness and survival, not truth—then there can be no objective account of morality.[133] Hence, transhumanists have no grounds for believing their "select" moral knowledge and claims are true. If moral reasoning involves forming judgments about what one ought to do, those actions must be evaluated against an objective standard. If matter is all there is, there are no 'ought' or 'should' claims. In response to transhumanism's select values, C. S. Lewis would likely say,

> "I ought" is the same sort of statement as "I itch" or "I'm going to be sick." In real life when a man says "I ought" we may reply, "Yes. You're right. That is what you ought to do," or else, "No. I think you're mistaken." but in a world of Naturalists . . . the only sensible reply would be, " Oh, are you?" All moral judgments would be statements about the speaker's feelings, mistaken by him for something else (the real moral quality of actions) which does not exist.[134]

Make no mistake, transhumanism's appeal to universal human values is not consistent with their commitment to a materialistic evolutionary philosophy. Therefore, there is no warrant to take their enhancement projects or their moral claims seriously.

Belief in Perpetual Progress

Another normative value promoted by transhumanists is perpetual progress. It is closely tied to the essential human characteristic of self-overcoming, or the will to evolve. In Max More's 1996 essay on the philosophy of transhumanism, the core value is perpetual progress: "Life and intelligence must never stagnate; it must re-order, transform, and transcend

---

132   Lewis, *The Abolition of Man*, 44.
133   Mark D. Linville, "The Moral Argument," in William Lane Craig and J. P. Moreland, editors, *The Blackwell Companion to Natural Theology* (West Sussex, UK: Wiley-Blackwell Publishing, 2009), 391- 417.
134   C. S. Lewis, *Miracles,* 51. I maintain here that materialism and naturalism (as C. S. Lewis uses it) agree on an important feature: that reality is fundamentally impersonal and nonmental.

its limits in an unlimited progressive process."[135] In More's *Principles of Extropy 3.11*, perpetual progress is the number one value, defined as: "perpetually overcoming constraints on our progress and possibilities as individuals, as organizations, and as a species; growing in healthy directions without bound." [136] In Nick Bostrom's "Transhumanist Values," technological progress is a basic condition for the transhumanist project "to explore the posthuman realm." [137]

Philosopher George Santayana (1863-1952) argued against this kind of absolute change, saying, "Progress, far from consisting in change, depends on retentiveness. When change is absolute there remains no being to improve and no direction is set for possible improvement; and when experience is not retained, as among savages, infancy is perpetual. Those who cannot remember the past are condemned to repeat it."[138] If Santayana's reasoning is right, transhumanism's progress toward a posthuman species represents absolute change with no being, or self, left to improve.

Transhumanists rely on the doctrine of technological progress when promoting their triple 'S' techno-utopia. Whereas it is reasonable to assume that technology will continue to advance in the future, it is not reasonable to assume that it will impact progress in morality or human nature. In fact, because there is no notion of purpose or end in materialistic science and technology, there is no basis for judging the value of the ends to be served by technology; that is, there is no basis for judging whether technological changes are improvements or not.

Transhumanists have complete confidence in technological progress, which blinds them from realistically anticipating the human propensity for twisting good into evil. Accordingly, they generally dismiss humanity's

---

135   Max More, "Transhumanism: Toward a Futurist Philosophy," (1996), 7, scribd.com, https://www.scribd.com/doc/257580713/Transhumanism-Toward-a-Futurist-Philosophy#download (accessed June 23, 2020).

136   Max More, *"Principles of Extropy 3.11 (2003),"* lifeboat.com, https://lifeboat.com/ex/the.principles.of.extropy#:~:text=The%20Principles%20of%20Extropy%3A%20Version%203.11%20(2003)&text=Self%2DTransformation%3A%20Extropy%20means%20affirming,responsibility%2C%20proactivity%2C%20and%20experimentation (accessed June 23, 2020).

137   Nick Bostrom, "Transhumanist Values," https://www.nickbostrom.com/ethics/values.html

138   George Santayana, *The Life of Reason or The Phases of Human Progress* (New York: Charles Scribner's Sons, 1906), 284, quoted in Charles T. Rubin, *Eclipse of Man: Human Extinction and the Meaning of Progress* (New York: New Atlantis Books, 2014), 43.

potential for evil.[139] Consider the significance of the computer virus as a reflection of the human capacity for evil. The sole purpose of inventing a computer virus is to cause chaos and destroy. Ted Peters says, "There is something at work in the human mind that leads to the development of brute and unmitigated destruction. No increase in human intelligence or advance in technology will alter this ever-lurking human proclivity."[140] The computer virus is an apt metaphor for the literal evil that could arise when we have software running in our brains and bodies and computers that control our nanobot immune system.[141]

This transhumanist blind spot is caused by three things: an overconfidence in technological progress, an assumption of human perfectibility, and a belief in a techno-utopia. As a remedy, I suggest a return to Christian Realism in the tradition of Reinhold Niebuhr (1892-1971). In the 1940's and 1950's, Niebuhr emphasized and exposed the sinful condition of human beings, a reality made undeniable because of World War I and II, Hitler, Stalin, the Holocaust, concentration camps, and the gulags. The Christian Realist would caution transhumanists against overestimating what can be achieved through technology apart from the gracious action of God. Niebuhr stressed that because of the human potential to choose evil and chaos, as well as what is good and fulfilling, progress is not inherently good, but ambiguous.[142] There is a need to acknowledge the human condition; the human potential to choose evil cannot be converted into a technological problem to be solved by enhancements. Only God can ultimately solve this problem.[143]

---

139   Nick Bostrom is one transhumanist leader who addresses the global catastrophic risks of transhumanism in Nick Bostrom and Milan M. Cirkovic, editors, *Global Catastrophic Risks* (Oxford: Oxford University Press, 2008).

140   Ted Peters, "Transhumanism and the Posthuman Future: Will Technological Progress Get Us There?" in Gregory R. Hansell and William Grassie, editors, *H+/- Transhumanism & Its Critics* (Philadelphia, PA: Metanexus Institute, 2011), 158.

141   Kurzweil, *Singularity is Near*, 410-414.

142   Reinhold Niebuhr, *The Nature and Destiny of Man*, 2 Volumes (New York: Charles Scribner's Sons, 1941-2), 2:240, quoted in Ted Peters, "Transhumanism and the Posthuman Future," 168.

143   This will be further addressed in the last section of the chapter, which offers an alternative metaphysics of the human person.

Materialism Cannot Account for Individual Autonomy, Liberty, and Rights

Individual autonomy, liberty, and rights are promoted by transhumanists, especially the fundamental right to modify one's body and brain. They oppose government intervention and regulation as it relates to what they call the right to morphological freedom.[144] *The Transhumanist Declaration* states: "We favor morphological freedom—the right to modify and enhance one's body, cognition, and emotions. This freedom includes the right to use or not to use techniques and technologies to extend life, preserve the self through cryonics, uploading, and other means, and to choose further modifications and enhancements."[145]

Transhumanists defend the concept of cognitive liberty, defending the right of individuals to choose brain enhancements by applying biotechnology, neuropharmacology, machine interfaces, and collective neural networks.[146] It is the individual self that acts as a responsible agent and freely wills his own enhancement and self-transformation. The subject becomes the object of his own change. Anders Sandberg rightly says that morphological freedom is "the use of oneself as a tool to achieve oneself."[147] This echoes C. S. Lewis' warning in *The Abolition of Man* that "it is in Man's power to treat himself as a mere 'natural object' and his own judgements of value as raw material for scientific manipulations to alter at will.[148] It is worth noting that *The Transhumanist Declaration* also defends the right of individuals *not* to enhance their bodies and brains. This libertarian stance is consistent with their desire in the initial stages of enhancements to distance themselves from the coercive eugenics of the past.

Despite the 'rights' language, transhumanism's materialist philosophy cannot account for the existence of the self as a free agent who has individual rights. In the early stages of their project, transhumanists use these concepts (as useful fictions) to appeal to people who hold a commonsense

---

144 Anders Sandberg, "Morphological Freedom: Why We Not Just Want It, But Need It," in More and Vita-More, eds., *The Transhumanist Reader*, 60-1.

145 "The Transhumanist Declaration (2012)," in More and Vita-More, eds., *The Transhumanist Reader*, 54-5.

146 Wrye Sententia, "Freedom by Design: Transhumanist Values and Cognitive Liberty," in More and Vita-More, eds., *The Transhumanist Reader*, 356.

147 Sandberg, "Morphological Freedom," in More and Vita-More, editors, *The Transhumanist Reader*, 63.

148 Lewis, *Abolition of Man*, 72.

view of themselves. Transhumanists consistently portray the individual as a responsible agent of his actions. Because they appeal to individual autonomy and self-determination when defending the fundamental right to enhance, it appears that transhumanists are staunchly libertarian as it relates to free agency. Be that as it may, the concept of free human agency is problematic for a materialist. If human persons are strictly physical, this entails that all mental events are caused by purely physical prior histories and therefore, free actions are necessarily ruled out.[149]

In brief, transhumanists have no philosophical grounds for their appeal to individual autonomy and free will in defending the right to enhance. The inadequacy of their materialist philosophy to account for individual autonomy and liberty is one of the reasons there is a blatant inconsistency between defending individual autonomy and upholding their utilitarian ethic. Utilitarian David Pearce abrogates individual liberty in favor of the authoritarian state when discussing the challenges of a future techno-utopia that has overcome death.

> Control of human reproduction, whether sexual or clonal, will be a generic feature of any post-aging civilization. The need for social mechanisms of reproductive control on pain of Malthusian catastrophe isn't a specific peculiarity of the abolitionist project. If (post)humans aren't going to grow old and die, as we do today, then we can't go on having children at will indefinitely. A regime based on genetic Russian roulette will be replaced by an ethically responsible policy of planned parenthood.[150]

Transhumanists also express inconsistencies between their belief in individual self-determination and their belief that free people are often mistaken about their own best interests. Despite favoring liberal views of individual autonomy in their promotion of transhumanism, few believe democracy will be the final and best form of government for a future tech-

---

149 Causal Closure Argument for Materialism (see chapter 2, page 25)
    (1) Conscious mental occurrences have physical effects.
    (2) All physical effects are fully caused by purely physical prior histories.
    (3) The physical effects of conscious causes aren't always overdetermined by distinct causes.

150 David Pearce, *The Hedonistic Imperative*, HedWeb.com, Chapter 4, Objections 4.31, https://www.hedweb.com/hedethic/hedon4.htm#natural (accessed June 15, 2020).

no-utopia.[151] The general rationale for authoritarianism is that knowledgeable rulers understand the needs of the people better than the people themselves.

Transhumanism's reason for envisioning a technocratic authoritarianism is that a superior posthuman would know better what people need. Nick Bostrom calls for a global "singleton" to mitigate existential risks inherent in emerging technologies. He defines the singleton as "a world order in which there is a single decision-making agency at the highest level."[152] The singleton could be a democratic world republic, a world dictatorship, a friendly superintelligent machine, or a posthuman.[153] Its purpose would be to solve global problems that might result from new dangerous technologies, like nanotechnology. "The singleton could relieve inequalities and suppress wars with help from improved surveillance, mind-control technologies, and communication technologies."[154]

Artificial Intelligence researcher Eliezer Yudkowsky proposes that we should abdicate self-governance to a super rational artificial intelligence that is programmed to be friendly and act in our best interests.[155] He argues that human cognition is irredeemably biased and motivated by self-interest, whereas a superintelligent AI would be super rational and unconstrained by biology and evolutionary drives. This superintelligent AI would be able to intuit the desires and needs of all human beings and make the decisions necessary to satisfy them.[156]

In the end, transhumanists have no philosophical grounds for appealing to individual autonomy and free will in defending the right to enhance. In fact, when these concepts are no longer seen as useful to the future society, they likely will disintegrate in the face of a technocratic authoritarian rule. Again, it turns out C. S. Lewis was right:

---

[151] James Hughes, "Contradictions from the Enlightenment Roots of Transhumanism," *Journal of Medicine and Philosophy* (2010), 8, http://citeseerx.ist.psu.edu/viewdoc/download?doi=10.1.1.993.3636&rep=rep1&type=pdf (accessed June 25, 2020).

[152] Nick Bostrom, "What is a Singleton?" *Linguistic and Philosophical Investigations*, Vol. 5, No. 2 (2006), 48, https://www.nickbostrom.com/fut/singleton.html (accessed June 25, 2020).

[153] Ibid., 48.

[154] Ibid., 52.

[155] Eliezer Yudkowsky, "Coherent Extrapolated Volition," *The Singularity Institute* (2004), San Francisco, CA. https://intelligence.org/files/CEV.pdf (accessed June 25, 2020).

[156] Ibid.

It is in Man's power to treat himself as a mere 'natural object' and his own judgements of value as raw material for scientific manipulation to alter at will. The objection to his doing so does not lie in the fact that this point of view (like one's first day in a dissecting room) is painful and shocking till we grow used to it. The pain and shock are at most a warning and a symptom. The real objection is that if man chooses to treat himself as raw material, raw material he will be: not raw material to be manipulated, as he fondly imagined, by himself, but by mere appetite, that is, mere Nature, in the person of his de-humanized Conditioners.[157]

Summary of the Critique of Transhumanism's Materialist Metaphysics of the Human Person

My critique demonstrates that the transhumanist cannot adequately account for the existence of persons, enduring identity, ethics, values, duties, individual autonomy, liberty, or rights based on their materialist, mechanistic, reductionist metaphysics of the human person. Since their philosophy only offers an incomplete understanding of the human person, there is no justification for believing their proposed trajectory of enhancements are possible and if attempted, would be good for human flourishing.

An Alternative Metaphysics of the Human Person

For transhumanists, there are no formal and final causes in the natural world. There are only the blind laws of nature governing the behavior of inherently meaningless and purposeless physical particles. Hence, they conclude that a human being is a bundle of molecular and cellular complexes with no fixed nature, essence, or teleology. But, human beings certainly *appear* to have essences, natures, and powers, and seem to act in accordance with their purposes or goals. The Aristotelian concepts of substantial forms and teleology were expelled from the materialist/mechanistic understanding of nature, but these same elements are inherent in human persons and are difficult to deny. The things materialism leaves out—substantial self, enduring identity, rationality, free will, morality—are the things that a philosophy of human persons needs to explain.

---

157   Lewis, *The Abolition of Man*, 72-3.

Aristotle's basic idea is that ordinary objects of our experience—rocks, trees, dogs, and *human beings*—are irreducible composites of matter and form. Substances have the capacity for change (matter) and also have something that persists through change (form). Contrary to materialism, nothing is just a piece of matter. Matter cannot exist without form. Form, which accounts for permanence, is not material. The first key to Aristotelian metaphysics is the concept of substantial form because it is what makes something the kind of thing it is, its essence. Without it there is no explanation for the unity of any material substance. Essences are a kind of universal that we are capable of abstracting from the particulars in which they inhere. For example, we do not encounter the essence of humanness as an abstract in reality, separate from its particular. But we do encounter the essence of humanness when we observe particular human beings who instantiate it. Said differently, a substantial form is the "intrinsic incomplete constituent principle in a substance which actualizes the potencies of matter and together with the matter composes a definite material substance or natural body."[158]

In contrast to the materialist view of the person, Aristotelian metaphysics maintains that a human being is a single substance that is a composite of body (matter) and soul (form), with a rational nature as its substantial form. The rationality of human beings calls for a special classification distinct from animals, plants, and inorganic substances.[159] On Aristotle's view, the powers of the intellect are immaterial and do not directly depend on bodily organs for their operation. That is, the intellect grasps forms, essences, universals, and other abstract concepts like propositions. Therefore, a purely naturalistic evolutionary origin of the human essence is ruled out.

The substantial form is the root cause of personal identity; it is the bearer of identity. However, the form is not itself a complete substance, so we must also recognize matter. David Oderberg puts it this way, "The identity of a person is given by the form as instantiated in matter."[160] The distinction here is to recognize the soul is not the person. Human persons are embodied creatures; the person is the substantial compound of body and

---

[158] David S. Oderberg, *Real Essentialism* (New York: Routledge, 2007), 65.

[159] The power, or potential, of rational thought should not be confused with the exercise of rational thought. The capacity for rationality is built into the human embryo from the moment it comes into existence. A human being can have the power of rationality without having the use or exercise of that power.

[160] Oderberg, "Essence and Identity," *Real Essentialism*, 120.

soul. My soul is the bearer of my identity, but I am not strictly identical with my soul. I am not reducible to my soul because my body is essential. Because of this, the transhumanist ambition to escape the body is incompatible with Aristotle's view of the embodied human person.

Building on the metaphysics of Aristotle, Thomas Aquinas maintained that the rational soul, being immaterial, survives the death of the body.[161] If the human rational soul can operate without matter, it can exist without matter, albeit in an imperfect state. Therefore, the human being persists after death, prior to the bodily resurrection, in an incomplete state constituted by the soul.[162] David Oderberg emphasizes the role of the body in personhood by saying, "[I]f the human soul has a disembodied existence, that existence can only be made possible by it once having been the form of a body."[163] Contra transhumanism's patternism, the doctrine of substantial form accounts for enduring personal identity and for the soul surviving the death of the body.

The second key concept in Aristotelian metaphysics is that teleology is inherent in the natural order.[164] That is, the *telos* or purpose of a material substance in nature exists inherently because of the kind of thing it is. Aquinas carried Aristotle's fundamental concept of inherent natural teleology to the theological conclusion that a divine intelligence (God) is necessary to impart intrinsic natural teleology and to order things to their ends.[165] A man-made artifact (e.g., a computer), on the other hand, is made of parts and has no inherent tendency to perform its function. Transhumanists view the body as a material collection of parts, devoid of inherent teleology. Instead, they impose their will and purpose on the body externally.

Natural law theory is also grounded in Aristotelian/Thomistic metaphysics in that it presupposes that a human being possesses a nature that

---

161   Feser, *The Last Superstition*, 127.
162   Edward Feser, "Aquinas on the Human Soul," in Jonathan J. Loose, Angus J. L. Menuge, and J. P. Moreland, editors, *The Blackwell Companion to Substance Dualism* (Hoboken, NJ: John Wiley & Sons, Inc., 2018), 96-100.
163   David Oderberg, *Real Essentialism* (New York: Routledge, 2007), 257.
164   Edward Feser, *Neo-Scholastic Essays* (South Bend, Indiana: St. Augustine's Press, 2015), 147.
165   While Aristotle did argue that the motion we observe in the world must be sustained by an Unmoved Mover, he did not assume a divine intelligence was necessary to impart intrinsic natural teleology to things. Aquinas and the Scholastics carried Aristotle's philosophy further.

is objectively real and is inherently directed toward certain ends.[166] The natural capacities for reason and freedom are basic human goods and are fundamental to the dignity of human beings. This dignity is protected by human rights. From a theistic perspective, these god-like capacities of rationality and freedom have a divine source; man is created in the very image and likeness of God.[167] Robert George affirms this natural law understanding of human dignity:

> A human person is a rational animal who is a locus of intrinsic value (and, as such, an end-in-himself who may never legitimately treat himself or be treated by others as a mere means), but whose well-being intrinsically includes relationships with others and membership in communities (beginning with the family) in which he or she has, as a matter of justice, both rights and responsibilities.[168]

Any moral theory that acknowledges the human capacities for reason and freedom has good grounds for affirming human dignity and basic human rights. Unfortunately for transhumanists, their materialism reduces rationality and free will to illusions. Further, if the nature of a human being is the unity of body and soul, the transhumanist who ultimately seeks to rid himself of his body and does not recognize the existence of an immaterial soul sets himself against this basic standard of human flourishing.

Conclusion

Roughly three hundred years ago modern scientists and philosophers rejected Aristotelian metaphysics to adopt a mechanistic view of the world. The dehumanizing effects of choosing this philosophical path have transpired gradually, largely because many philosophers have attempted to avoid or soften the implications of materialism as it relates to the human person. As shown in this chapter, transhumanists are fully committed to the materialist philosophy of human persons and aim to carry those ideals to their radical conclusions. Their idea to transform human beings into non-biological posthumans by using science and technology is fueled by

---

166 Feser, *Neo-Scholastic Essays*, 380.
167 Genesis 1:26-7.
168 Robert George, "Natural Law, God, and Human Dignity," *The Chautauqua Journal*, Volume 1 (2016), 1-2, https://encompass.eku.edu/cgi/viewcontent.cgi?article=1004&context=tcj (accessed July 19, 2020).

this materialistic, mechanistic view. My critique exposes the failures of materialism and the need for an alternative metaphysics. I recommend returning to the core ideas of Aristotelian metaphysics as a remedy for the inadequacies of materialism.

In the next two chapters I will turn to literature to extend my critique of transhumanism. In chapters two through four, I offered philosophical arguments against the materialist foundations of transhumanism. For chapters five and six, I will adopt the method of C. S. Lewis. He wrote, "For me, reason is the natural organ of truth, but imagination is the organ of meaning."[169] He argued that grasping the meaning of something is the preliminary condition of judging its truth or falsehood. He was convinced that when abstract arguments are "dipped in story," they come back to us powerfully and more clearly.[170] He demonstrated this method very effectively in his own works—*The Abolition of Man* is an extended philosophical argument, whereas *That Hideous Strength* represents those arguments in narrative form. In fact, Lewis writes in the preface to *That Hideous Strength*, "This is a "tall story" about devilry, though it has behind it a serious "point" which I have tried to make in my *Abolition of Man*."[171] Taking Lewis's approach, my next chapter will provide a Tolkienian perspective on transhumanism's project of cybernetic immortality and chapter six critiques transhumanism's project of superhappiness through the lens of selected dystopian works of literature.

---

169   C. S. Lewis, "Bluspels and Flalansferes," in C. S. Lewis, *Selected Literary Essays* (Cambridge, U.K.: Cambridge University Press, 1969), 265.

170   Walter Hooper, editor, *C. S. Lewis on Stories and Other Literature* (New York: First Harvest/HBJ edition, 1982), 90.

171   C. S. Lewis, *That Hideous Strength: A Modern Fairy-Tale for Grown-Ups* (New York: Scribner, 1945), Preface.

Chapter Five

Transhumanism's Superlongevity: A Tolkienian Critique

"To attempt by device or 'magic' to recover longevity is thus a supreme folly and wickedness of 'mortals.' Longevity or counterfeit 'immortality' (true immortality is beyond Eä) is the chief bait of Sauron—it leads the small to a Gollum, and the great to a Ringwraith."[1]

J. R. R. Tolkien

Introduction

TRANSHUMANISTS, BY THEIR very nature, share a basic conviction that distinguishes them from humanism and other ideologies: that is, a belief that it is possible and desirable to overcome biological aging and death by means of science and technology.[2] Transhumanists envision a triple 'S' techno-utopian civilization, where the second 'S' is superlongevity.[3] In the near future, their aim is life extension; their ultimate goal is cybernetic immortality.[4] The transhumanist ambition

---

[1] Humphrey Carpenter, ed., *The Letters of J. R. R. Tolkien* (New York: Houghton Mifflin Harcourt, 1995), 286.

[2] Max More and Natasha Vita-More, "Engines of Life: Identity and Beyond Death," in *The Transhumanist Reader*, 213.

[3] Transhumanism's triple 'S' civilization is a techno-utopia of superintelligence, superlongevity, and superhappiness.

[4] Ted Peters, "Progress and Provolution: Will Transhumanism Leave Sin Behind?," in Ronald Cole-Turner, editor, *Transhumanism and Transcendence: Christian Hope in an Age of Technological Enhancement* (Washington D.C.: Georgetown University Press, 2011), 64.

to extend life and preserve the self is at the heart of *The Transhumanist Declaration*:

> We favor morphological freedom—the right to modify and enhance one's body, cognition, and emotions. This freedom includes the right to use or not to use techniques and technologies to extend life, preserve the self through cryonics, uploading, and other means, and to choose further modifications and enhancements.[5]

Transhumanists use the following comparable terms to describe the aim of their project to overcome aging and death: biological immortality, radical life extension, indefinite lifespan, cybernetic immortality, and superlongevity.[6] In a broad sense, these terms describe the possibility of extending the human life span for as long as the universe endures.

Transhumanists expect to first achieve radical life extension through a combination of advances in biotechnology, regenerative medicine, genetic engineering, nanotechnology, and bionics. They see embodiment as the principal problem of the human condition, so death will ultimately be conquered through cybernetic immortality, or uploading a person's brain capacity and consciousness onto a computer. It should be noted that this scenario assumes the achievement of artificial general intelligence followed by a Singularity event.[7]

The transhumanist quest for superlongevity in this world is grounded in their materialist philosophy of mind and human persons. Whether this sort of immortality is beneficial or harmful for humanity is perhaps the

---

5 Max More and Natasha Vita-More, "The Transhumanist Declaration (2012)," in *The Transhumanist Reader*, 54-55. The original Transhumanist Declaration was crafted in 1998 by: Alexander Sasha Chislenko, Anders Sandberg, Arjen Kamphuiss, Bernie Staring, Bill Fantegrossi, Darren Reynolds, David Pearce, Den Otter, Doug Bailey, Eugene Leitl, Gustavo Alves, Holger Wagner, Kathryn Aegis, Keith Elis, Lee Daniel Crocker, Max More, Mikhail Sverdlov, Natasha Vita-More, Nick Bostrom, Ralf Fletcher, Shane Spaulding, T. Ol Morrow, Thom Quinn.

6 These terms are used interchangeably in the literature to describe the transhumanist project of superlongevity.

7 Previously, in chapters two and three, I argued that AGI, including the Singularity, is metaphysically impossible because the materialist philosophy of mind on which it is based is false. In chapter four, I argued that transhumanism's metaphysics of human persons cannot account for the existence of persons, enduring personal identity through technological enhancements or uploading, ethics, values, and duties, or individual autonomy, liberty, and rights.

most important and controversial question to answer when critiquing transhumanism. Responses vary widely from extreme optimism[8] to measured skepticism[9] to extreme fear.[10] I previously argued in chapters two through four that transhumanism's triple "S" techno-utopia will not be achieved because their materialist philosophy of mind and human persons is flawed and inadequate. In this chapter, I will take a different approach by critiquing transhumanism's quest for superlongevity from a Tolkienian perspective by using the mythology of Middle-earth.[11]

I will argue that transhumanism's solution to defeat death is harmful to humanity and this is the focus of my critique. I will proceed as follows: First, I will clarify transhumanism's views about death and immortality. Second, I will relate the powers of emerging technologies with the Rings of Power. Third, I will employ Tolkien's mythology of Middle-earth to argue that transhumanism's project of superlongevity is a counterfeit of true immortality and harmful to humanity. Finally, I will suggest a way forward to recover a proper perspective of human death and immortality.

---

8 Max Tegmark, *Life 3.0: Being Human in the Age of Artificial Intelligence* (New York: Alfred A. Knopf, 2017).

9 Jay Richards, ed., *Are We Spiritual Machines? Ray Kurzweil vs. the Critics of Strong A.I.* (Seattle, WA: Discovery Institute, 2002).

10 Bill Joy, "Why the Future Doesn't Need Us," *Wired*, Issue 8.04 (April 2000), https://www.wired.com/2000/04/joy-2/ (accessed July 25, 2020).

11 There is scholarship related to Tolkien's view of death and immortality, but few have related the mythology to transhumanism's unique version of immortality. Sources on Tolkien's view of death and immortality include: Daniel Helen, ed., *Death and Immortality in Middle-earth: Proceedings of The Tolkien Society Seminar 2016* (Edinburgh: Luna Press Publishing, 2017); Roberto Arduini and Claudio A. Testi, eds., *The Broken Scythe: Death and Immortality in the Works of J. R. R. Tolkien* (Zurich: Walking Tree Publishers, 2012); Gregory Bassham and Eric Bronson, eds., *The Lord of the Rings and Philosophy: One Book to Rule Them All* (Chicago: Open Court Publishing Company, 2003). Theodore Schick broaches transhumanism in his essay in the following book: Theodore Schick, "The Cracks of Doom: The Threat of Emerging Technologies and Tolkien's Rings of Power," in *The Lord of the Rings and Philosophy*, Gregory Bassham and Eric Bronson, eds. (Chicago: Open Court Publishing Company, 2003).

Transhumanism's View of Death and Immortality

The Desire to Overcome Death

The transhumanist campaign for superlongevity aims to rouse people out of their passive acceptance of aging and death to join the fight to overcome death with new technological solutions. In Max More's 1994 essay "On Becoming Posthuman," he maintains that "the technological conquest of aging and death stands out as the most urgent, vital, worthy quest of our time."[12] In Simon Young's "Transhumanist Manifesto," he writes "Death is an obscenity. The goal of life is survival—death is not part of the plan, so why take it lying down? Better to rage, rage, rage against the dying of the light!"[13] Yuval Noah Harari claims the Universal Declaration of Human Rights is the closest thing to a global constitution and it categorically states that 'the right to life' is humanity's most fundamental value. He then argues, "Since death clearly violates this right, death is a crime against humanity, and we ought to wage total war against it."[14]

Nick Bostrom's philosophical parable "The Fable of the Dragon-Tyrant" is a call to action in the fight against aging and death.[15] Bostrom's fable is the tale of a country's struggle against a vicious dragon that eats ten thousand people every day for centuries. The people come to accept that one day they will be food for the dragon. The oldest citizens are sacrificed to the dragon first, so the lives of the younger people are protected a little longer. The citizens to be sacrificed are herded every night onto a train leading to the dragon's abode. Very late in the story, the king commissions scientists to develop anti-dragon technologies. Using these technologies, the people finally slay the dragon. The moral of the story, says Bostrom, is that "de-

---

12   Max More, "On Becoming Posthuman," (1994), Scribd, https://www.scribd.com/document/354404944/On-Becoming-Posthuman (accessed August 8, 2020).

13   Simon Young, *Designer Evolution: A Transhumanist Manifesto* (New York: Prometheus Books, 2006), 42.

14   Yuval Noah Harari, *Homo Deus: A Brief History of Tomorrow* (New York: Harper Perennial, 2017), 21.

15   Nick Bostrom, "The Fable of the Dragon-Tyrant," *Journal of Medical Ethics*, 2005, Vol. 31, No. 5, pp 273-277, https://www.nickbostrom.com/fable/dragon.html (accessed August 13, 2020).

feating death is an urgent, screaming, moral imperative. The sooner we start a focused research program, the sooner we will get results."[16]

Bostrom sketches a two-tiered path to the future in his "Letter from Utopia." To reach Utopia, Bostrom instructs, you must realize your body is a deathtrap. First, by controlling your biochemical processes, you will vanquish illness and senescence. Second, you will move your mind to a more durable media and continue to improve the system, so death and disease keep receding. Finally, he promises, "Any death prior to the heat death of the universe is premature if your life is good."[17]

Ray Kurzweil emphasizes the transhumanist desire to conquer death in his 2005 book *The Singularity is Near: When Humans Transcend Biology*. He promises, "The Singularity will allow us to transcend the limitations of our biological bodies and brains. We will gain power over our fates. Our mortality will be in our own hands."[18]

Transhumanists often contrast their desire to overcome death with religious attitudes, especially Christianity, which they claim promote an attitude of acceptance and tolerance of death.[19] This is a mistaken caricature because Christians recognize death as a real tragedy, yet not to be feared, tolerated, or loved. Rather, God conquered death through the bodily resurrection of Christ from the dead and therefore, the Christian hope for eternity is also a bodily redemption and resurrection.[20] Christians understand that physical life without eternal spiritual life is the same as being dead in your sins.[21]

It is important to clarify that transhumanism's abhorrence of death and the desire to overcome it is not new, nor is it unfamiliar to Judeo-Christian

---

16   Nick Bostrom, "The Fable of the Dragon-Tyrant," *Journal of Medical Ethics*, 2005, Vol. 31, No. 5, pp 273-277, https://www.nickbostrom.com/fable/dragon.html (accessed August 13, 2020).

17   Nick Bostrom, "Letter from Utopia," *Studies in Ethics, Law, and Technology* (2008): Vol. 2, No. 1: pp. 1-7, https://www.nickbostrom.com/utopia.html (accessed August 9, 2020).

18   Ray Kurzweil, *The Singularity is Near: When Humans Transcend Biology* (New York: Penguin Books, 2005), 9.

19   Heidi Campbell and Mark Walker, "Religion and Transhumanism: Introducing a Conversation," *Journal of Evolution and Technology*, Vol. 14, Issue 2 (April 2005), https://www.jetpress.org/volume14/specialissueintro.html (accessed August 15, 2020). Although this volume was intended to explore the relations between religion and transhumanism, the reader will find that Christianity is discussed almost exclusively.

20   I Corinthians 15:42-57 (ESV).

21   Ephesians 2:1 (ESV).

thought. For example, King Solomon (c.990-931 B.C.) laments death saying, "All are from the dust, and to dust all return."[22] He writes that "[God] has put eternity into man's heart," which I take to mean our understanding of the concept of eternity, and our longing for it, is part of human nature.[23] In the rest of Ecclesiastes, Solomon explores alternative ways to satisfy this longing. Paul, in a letter to the Corinthians in c.55 A.D., writes, "The last enemy to be destroyed is death."[24] Saint Augustine (354-430 A.D.) observes it is natural to want to delay death and accept an offer of immortality. In *The City of God*, he notes that the very fact of existing is preferred to perishing:

> And, accordingly, when they know that they must die, they seek, as a great boon, that this mercy be shown them, that they may a little longer live in the same misery, and delay to end it by death. And so they indubitably prove with what glad alacrity they would accept immortality, even though it secured to them endless destruction.[25]

J. R. R. Tolkien (1892-1973), a professing Christian, reveals in a 1968 BBC documentary that the very keyspring of *The Lord of the Rings* is the concept that death is a violation. To make his point, he quotes a passage from Simone de Beauvoir's *A Very Easy Death*: "There is no such thing as a natural death: nothing that happens to a man is ever natural, since his presence calls the world into question. All men must die: but for every man his death is an accident, and even if he knows it and consents to it, an unjustifiable violation."[26] Tolkien affirms that human nature has both a natural and supernatural element and acknowledges that the separation of body and soul at death is a violation.

---

22   Ecclesiastes 3:20 (ESV).
23   Ecclesiastes 3:11 (ESV).
24   I Corinthians 15:26 (ESV).
25   Saint Augustine, *The City of God*, Book XI.27, in Mortimer Adler, editor, *The Great Books of the Western World*, Volume 16 (Chicago: Encyclopedia Britannica, Inc., 1990), 390.
26   Simone de Beauvoir, *A Very Easy Death*, translated by Patrick O'Brian (New York: Pantheon Books, 1965), 106, quoted in BBC "In Their Own Words" documentary via *Simone de Beauvoir and the Keyspring of Lord of the Rings*, https://apilgriminnarnia.com/2016/05/17/simone-de-beauvoirlotr/ (accessed August 12, 2020).

To underscore again, transhumanism's hatred of death and their desire to overcome it is not new, nor is it objectionable. However, their solution to defeat death is harmful to humanity and thus is the focus of my critique.

Death is a Technical Problem with a Technical Solution

It is important to clarify how transhumanists answer the question of *why* there is aging and death. In the "Transhumanist FAQ," Nick Bostrom explains that the origin of aging and death is simply a consequence of the evolutionary process:

> Average human lifespan hovered between 20 and 30 years for most of our species' history. Most people today are thus living highly unnaturally long lives. Because of the high incidence of infectious disease, accidents, starvation, and violent death among our ancestors, very few of them lived much beyond 60 or 70. There was therefore little selection pressure to evolve the cellular repair mechanisms (and pay their metabolic costs) that would be required to keep us going beyond our meager three scores and ten. As a result of these circumstances in the distant past, we now suffer the inevitable decline of old age: damage accumulates at a faster pace than it can be repaired; tissues and organs begin to malfunction; and then we keel over and die. Before transhumanism, the only hope of evading death was through reincarnation or otherworldly resurrection. Those who viewed such religious doctrines as figments of our own imagination had no alternative but to accept death as an inevitable fact of our existence.[27]

From a naturalistic evolutionary perspective, the problem of aging and death is the result of a technical glitch in the evolutionary process. Our ancestors died prematurely from diseases and accidents, which means the beneficial biological mechanisms needed for long life did not fully evolve. Transhumanists see faulty human biology as a technical problem with a technical solution. Therefore, transhumanists promote advances in bio-

---

[27] Nick Bostrom, "The Transhumanist FAQ," 36, https://www.nickbostrom.com/views/Transhumanist.pdf (accessed August 17, 2020).

technology, nanotechnology, cybernetics, and mind uploading as the solution to death.

This idea is promoted in the film *Transcendent Man*, a documentary about the life and work of Ray Kurzweil, who insists that death will be conquered by technology. In fact, he argues that the technology of the Singularity will create a new paradigm in which death will be treated merely as a disease to be cured.[28] The title of the documentary, *Transcendent Man*, reflects transhumanism's aim of immortality, which is to offer technologies that will help human beings rise above the limitations of their biology and become posthuman.

Transhumanist leaders Max More, Nick Bostrom, and James Hughes describe the transhumanist movement as a product of the Enlightenment humanist tradition; it is a secular philosophy of life that rejects blind faith, the supernatural, dogmas, and the afterlife.[29] Despite these claims, it is important to recognize that transhumanists hold many beliefs that seem to be quasi-religious: their focus on human improvement, their preoccupation with transcendence, their doctrinal statements in the *Transhumanist Declaration*, their vision of a posthuman immortality, their goal to eliminate suffering, their belief in the godlike power of technology to structure matter and recreate nature,[30] their belief that cryopreservation will ensure a resurrection of the dead,[31] and their transhumanist churches.[32]

---

28   *Transcendent Man*, directed by Barry Ptolemy, (Ptolemaic Productions, 2009 - US), YouTube Movies, (published on August 18, 2015), 1:23:48, https://www.youtube.com/watch?v=UCov79Blk9Q (accessed July 25, 2020). In chapter two, I argued that AGI is metaphysically impossible and therefore, the Singularity event will not happen.

29   More, *The Transhumanist Reader*, 4; Nick Bostrom, "The History of Transhumanist Thought," *Journal of Evolution and Technology*, Volume 14, Issue 1 (2005), https://jetpress.org/volume14/bostrom.html (accessed August 17, 2020); James J. Hughes, "The Politics of Transhumanism and the Techno-Millennial Imagination, 1626-2030," *Zygon*, Vol. 47, no. 4 (December 2012), https://www.trincoll.edu/Academics/centers/TIIS/Documents/Hughes--April%203.pdf (accessed August 17, 2020).

30   Tirosh-Samuelson, "Engaging Transhumanism," in Gregory R. Hansell and William Grassie, editors, *H+/- Transhumanism and its Critics* (Philadelphia, PA: Metanexus Institute, 2011), 25.

31   Max More and Natasha Vita-More, *The Transhumanist Reader* (West Sussex, UK: John Wiley & Sons, 2013), 214.

32   The Church of Perpetual Life website https://www.churchofperpetuallife.org/, (accessed August 15, 2020).

It is significant that Julian Huxley, who coined the term "transhumanism," considered himself a midwife delivering to the world a new ideology.[33] He clearly rejected Christianity and instead promoted science to address the human condition in his book, appropriately titled, *Religion Without Revelation*.[34] Russell Kirk, in *Enemies of the Permanent Things*, explores the nature of "Ideology." Kirk defines ideology as the belief that "human nature and society may be perfected by mundane, secular means . . . the ideologue immanentizes religious symbols and inverts religious doctrines."[35] Science and technology supplant God; the scientific manager of the new society replaces the religious teacher.[36] Applying Kirk's understanding, transhumanism represents an ideology that seeks to take the place of religion. Philosopher and transhumanist Patrick Hopkins acknowledges that transhumanism and traditional religions possess similar ideas, especially the desire for transcendence. The primary difference is that transhumanists believe that transcendence can be achieved through technology.[37] The notable obstacle to transcendence is that technology cannot solve the heat death of the universe.

To summarize, transhumanists believe technology will save us from death and our destiny is superlongevity in this world. In sharp contrast, Tolkien declares that the pursuit of superlongevity in this world is the ultimate enemy. What follows is a critique of the transhumanist view of superlongevity based on the themes and characters in Tolkien's mythology.

---

33   Julian Huxley, *New Bottles for New Wine* (London: Chatto & Windus, 1957), 13-17.

34   Julian Huxley, *Religion Without Revelation* (New York: Mentor Books, 1957).

35   Russell Kirk, *Enemies of the Permanent Things: Observations of Abnormity in Literature and Politics* (Illinois: Sherwood Sugden & Company, 1984), 154.

36   Ibid., 160-1.

37   Patrick D. Hopkins, "Transcending the Animal: How Transhumanism and Religion Are and Are Not Alike," *Journal of Evolution and Technology*, Volume 14, Issue 2 (August 2005), https://jetpress.org/volume14/hopkins.pdf (accessed August 17, 2020).

Tolkien's Rings of Power and the Powers of Emerging Technologies

The Theme of Tolkien's Mythology

In Tolkien's published letters, he addresses the overall message of his mythology. He emphasizes that the real theme is not mainly about Power and Dominion, but something much more permanent and difficult: "Death and Immortality: the mystery of the love of the world in the hearts of a race 'doomed' to leave and seemingly lose it; the anguish in the hearts of a race 'doomed' not to leave it, until its whole evil-aroused story is complete."[38] In another letter, he acknowledges this theme is not original because "most human art and thought is preoccupied with the theme of Death."[39] For example, in his famous essay "On Fairy-stories," Tolkien explains that one characteristic of Fantasy literature is that it functions as a medium of escape, and the oldest and deepest desire is "the Great Escape: the Escape from Death."[40] More specifically, Tolkien says he wrote a story that revealed that "Death is not the Enemy;" instead, the enemy is "the hideous peril of confusing true 'immortality' with limitless serial longevity."[41] As already noted, Tolkien acknowledged that Death was a hideous violation, but here he argues that the greater enemy is the danger of confusing superlongevity in this world with true immortality beyond this world.

One way Tolkien presents this theme about death and immortality is through the tale of the Rings of Power, which represent the advanced "technologies" of Middle-earth. Tolkien explains that "the chief power (of all the rings alike) was the prevention or slowing of decay..."[42] The preservative properties of the Elvish Rings were not meant for mortal Men; in fact, the final results were disastrous to them. The reader does not know exactly how Sauron deceived the men who later became the Nazgûl because there is no textual evidence, but we learn in Tolkien's long letter to Milton Waldman that the power of preservation made the Rings a tremen-

---

38   Carpenter, *Letters*, 246. Tolkien refers to the theme of Death and Immortality in the following letters: #186 (246-7), #203 (262), #208 (267), and #211 (277-84).

39   Ibid., 267.

40   J. R. R. Tolkien, "On Fairy-stories," in *The Tolkien Reader* (New York: Ballantine Books, 1966), 85.

41   Carpenter, *Letters*, 267.

42   Ibid., 152.

dous temptation to mortal Men who desired longevity within Arda like the Elves.[43] Given that the emerging technologies of biotechnology, nanotechnology, artificial general intelligence, and superintelligence are currently being lauded with the same unprecedented powers of superlongevity, a comparative analysis of the powers of the Rings and the powers of the emerging technologies will serve to frame the ultimate question of whether superlongevity in this world is beneficial or harmful to human beings.

The Powers of the Rings

The Rings of Power were forged in the Second Age of Middle-earth by elven Jewel-smiths, led by Celebrimbor (grandson of Fëanor) and guided by the knowledge and power of Sauron the Maia, the greatest of the servants of evil Melkor.[44] After Melkor was overthrown by the Valar, Sauron "determined to make himself master of all things in Middle-earth . . . and named himself Lord of the earth."[45] He deceived most of the peoples of Middle-earth by appearing fair and wise and offering his knowledge and help. Sauron suggested to the elves of Eregion that they could help heal Middle-earth and make it as beautiful as Valinor.[46] But secretly,

> Sauron made One Ring to rule all the others, and their power was bound up with it, to be subject wholly to it and to last only so long as it too should last. And much of the strength and will of Sauron passed into that One Ring . . . And while he wore the One Ring he could perceive all things that were done by means of the lesser rings, and he could see and govern the very thoughts of those that wore them.[47]

Sauron found that men were the easiest to ensnare of all the peoples of Middle-earth because "they desired secret power beyond the measure of their kind" and to them he gave the nine Rings of Power.[48]

---

43 Carpenter, *Letters*, 152-3.
44 J. R. R. Tolkien, *The Silmarillion*, second ed. (New York: Ballantine Books, 1977), 341-343.
45 Ibid., 346.
46 Carpenter, *Letters*, 152.
47 Ibid., 344.
48 Ibid., 345-6.

According to Tolkien, the chief power of all the Rings is the slowing of decay; that is, the preservation of what is desired or loved.[49] Gandalf warns Frodo that any mortal "who keeps one of the Great Rings does not die, but he does not grow or obtain more life, he merely continues until at last every minute is a weariness."[50] Gandalf further explains that anyone who often uses one of the Great Rings will "make himself invisible, he *fades*: he becomes in the end invisible permanently, and walks in the twilight under the eye of the Dark Power that rules the Rings."[51]

The Rings of Power enhance the natural power of the possessors; the nine Men with Rings became mighty, obtained glory and great wealth, and became kings, sorcerers, and warriors.[52] Eventually, all who wore the Rings were corrupted by evil and became the slaves of Sauron because he created the One Ring to control and dominate them all.[53] Sauron's lust for domination and control was so great that he did not tolerate any freedom or rivalry.[54] When Sauron wore the One Ring, he controlled and ruled Middle-earth, governing the very thoughts of those that wore the lesser rings. Further, the One Ring was unbreakable by any smithcraft and "anyone who used it became mastered by it; it was beyond the strength of any will to cast it away."[55]

To summarize, the powers of the Rings are as follows: immortality (as long as the One Ring endured), invisibility (fading), enhanced natural powers, corruption of the soul, and the One Ring rules them all.

The Powers of Emerging Technologies

The proposed benefits of emerging technologies are eerily similar to the powers of the Rings. In 2008, Peter Diamandis co-founded the Singularity University with Ray Kurzweil after being inspired by Kurzweil's book

---

[49] J. R. R. Tolkien, *The Silmarillion*, second ed. (New York: Ballantine Books, 1977), 152.

[50] Tolkien, *Silmarillion*, 346; Carpenter, *Letters*, 152. Despite the power of longevity provided by the Rings of Power, they were directly bound and controlled by the One Ruling Ring of Sauron. If the One Ring was unmade, Sauron and the nine mortal Men he enslaved would be annihilated.

[51] J. R. R. Tolkien, *The Lord of the Rings* (New York: Houghton Mifflin Harcourt, 2004), 47.

[52] Tolkien, *Silmarillion*, 346.

[53] Ibid.

[54] Ibid.

[55] Carpenter, *Letters*, 153-4.

The Singularity is Near.⁵⁶ The mission of Singularity University is to educate, inspire, and empower leaders in overlapping fields of technology to build breakthrough solutions to humanity's grand challenges.⁵⁷ Instead of experts in elven Jewel-crafting, the experts at Singularity University are entrepreneurs, corporations, development organizations, governments, investors, and academic institutions. Kurzweil and Diamandis attract experts in these fields to forge new powerful technologies no different from Sauron who attracted the elven Jewel-smiths to forge the Rings of Power. That is to say, Kurzweil and Diamandis draw many with their utopian vision of the future that does little to address the dangers that will surely accompany the new technologies.

Through the advanced research of Singularity University, Kurzweil and Diamandis seek to provide an interdisciplinary learning atmosphere that connects AGI, genetic engineering, nanotechnology, and robotics in order to develop technologies that will radically upgrade all of our physical and mental systems to a non-biological existence.⁵⁸ In other words, one of their goals is to merge human beings with powerful technology.⁵⁹ Kurzweil predicts simultaneous revolutions in three areas—biotechnology, nanotechnology, and AGI—that will usher in the Singularity by the year 2045 and change every aspect of our world forever.⁶⁰ According to Kurzweil, the

---

56 "Commonly Asked Questions," Singularity University website, https://su.org/about/faq/ (accessed August 17, 2020). Peter H. Diamandis is an international pioneer in the fields of innovation, incentive prize competitions, longevity, and commercial space. In 2014, he was named one of "The World's 50 Greatest Leaders" by Fortune Magazine. He serves as Founder and Executive Chairman of the XPRIZE Foundation, Co-Founder and Vice-Chairman of Human Longevity Inc. (HLI), Co-Founder/Co-Chairman of Planetary Resources and the Co-Founder of Space Adventures and Zero-Gravity Corporation. Peter is the New York Times Bestselling author of *Abundance – The Future Is Better Than You Think* and *BOLD – How to go Big, Create Wealth & Impact the World*.

57 James Barrat, *Our Final Invention: Artificial Intelligence and the End of the Human Era* (New York: Dunne Books, 2013), 59-60. Other organizations pursuing AGI projects are: Kernal company (Bryan Johnson), Neuralink (Elon Musk), National Nanotechnology Initiative (NNI), IBM, Numenta company, Artificial General Intelligence Research Institute (AGIRI), Carnegie Mellon's NELL and ACT-R, Cycorp's CYC project, Google, University of Michigan's SOAR project, Machine Intelligence Research Institute (MIRI).

58 Kurzweil, *Singularity*, 303.

59 Ray Kurzweil, "The Evolution of Mind in the Twenty-First Century" in *Are We Spiritual Machines?*, Jay Richards, ed. (Seattle: Discovery Institute, 2002), 55.

60 Kurzweil, *Singularity*, 136.

first two revolutions of biotechnology and nanotechnology will provide radical life extension to human beings by gradually merging humans with technology. The third revolution will achieve AGI, when computers will match and then supersede human intelligence; this will mark the Singularity.[61] I suggest that the powerful emerging technologies are comparable to the powers of the nine lesser rings and that the power of the Singularity is analogous to the power of the One Ring of Sauron.

According to transhumanists, the diverse field of biotechnology, which now includes genetic engineering, will provide the means to stop and also reverse disease and the aging process. Current research includes methods such as "RNA interference for turning off destructive genes, gene therapy for changing your genetic code, therapeutic cloning for regenerating your cells and tissues, smart drugs to reprogram your metabolic pathways, and somatic gene therapy, which replaces human DNA with synthesized genes."[62] These advances could continuously repair and replace the defective parts of our physical bodies in order to prolong life indefinitely. Like Sauron, transhumanists believe that people will be easily persuaded to merge with technology to radically prolong their lives just as the Men of Middle-earth accepted the nine Rings of Power to prolong their lives beyond their mortal nature.

For Kurzweil, this is only the beginning because nanotechnology will solve any remaining health problems by introducing nanobots and intelligence into our bodies and brains.[63] Nanobots injected into the bloodstream will "destroy pathogens such as bacteria, viruses, and cancer cells, and will be controlled via computer software and the internet."[64] For Kurzweil, the more important implication of nanotechnology is that we will "augment our thinking processes with nanobots that communicate with one another and with our biological neurons."[65] This technology will expand human potential because humans will think billions of times faster and be able to interface with all the information in the cloud. In addition, it will allow

---

61   Kurzweil, *Singularity*, 267.
62   Ibid., 256-7.
63   Kurzweil, *The Singularity is Near*, 206 and 506. Nanotechnology is based on the concept of tiny, self-replicating robots. "It will enable us to redesign and rebuild—molecule by molecule—our bodies and brains and the world with which we interact, going far beyond the limitations of biology."
64   Ibid., 255.
65   Ibid., 257.

wireless communication from one brain to another.[66] This technology that connects our thoughts to the cloud is not unlike the One Ring's ability to "see the thoughts of all those that used the lesser rings."[67]

Even though Kurzweil is leading the way in developing these technologies, there are many others right behind him. For example, in 2004, co-founder of Google, Larry Page, spoke about his vision for the future of the search engine: "Eventually you'll have the implant where if you think about a fact, it will just tell you the answer."[68] The research group at Facebook has a similar goal, to remove "the gap between your brain and the keyboard."[69] They call it the Brain Machine Interface (BMI) project.[70] The proponents of BMI gloss over one of the obvious dangers of merging our bodies and brains with technology—"neurocrime." BMI will make humans vulnerable to neural computer crimes, meaning crimes of illicit access to neural nanobots in our bodies and brains. If we find it difficult now to protect our computers from malicious malware and hackers, how much more should we be concerned about protecting our bodies and brains that are filled with nanotechnology?[71] Just as the Nazgul's choice to accept the Rings led to their corruption and destruction by Sauron, human beings who choose to submit to BMI will likely risk corruption and destruction through neurocrime.

Another important aspect that is de-emphasized by those who promote these emerging technologies to the mainstream public is the potential military application. The new development worth noting for our comparison to the Rings of Power is the use of nanomaterials to create cloaking technology for soldiers and vehicles that provide the power of invisibility.[72] In addition, engineered nanomaterials provide stronger, lightweight uniforms with en-

---

66   Kurzweil, *The Singularity is Near*, 309 and 316.
67   Carpenter, *Letters*, 152.
68   Steven Levy, 'We Are Entering the Era of the Brain Machine Interface," *Wired*, (April 17, 2017), https://www.wired.com/2017/04/we-are-entering-the-era-of-the-brain-machine-interface/ (accessed August 1, 2020).
69   Ibid., 2.
70   Ibid., 2.
71   Marcello Ienca & Pim Haselager, "Hacking the brain: brain–computer interfacing technology and the ethics of neurosecurity," *Ethics and Information Technology*, (April 2016), ResearchGate.com, https://www.researchgate.net/publication/301335762_Hacking_the_brain_brain-computer_interfacing_technology_and_the_ethics_of_neurosecurity (accessed August 17, 2020).
72   Steve Young, "Military Uses of Nanotechnology," *The Nanoage*, (December 2009), 2, http://thenanoage.com/military.htm (accessed August 17, 2020).

hanced properties that give soldiers almost superhuman properties, which compares to the power of the Rings to enhance the natural powers of the possessor. The world's major military strategists and scientists expect nanotechnology to change the future of warfare.[73] It is significant that Ray Kurzweil is one of five members on the Army Science Advisory Group (ASAG), which advises the U. S. Army on prioritizing their science research.[74]

Notwithstanding his enthusiasm over the three technological revolutions, Kurzweil's main focus remains on the Singularity event, the time when computers achieve human-level intelligence. At this time, he predicts an intelligence explosion because this self-aware AGI system will seek to self-improve again and again. This intelligence explosion will lead to artificial superintelligence, or ASI, which would mean there could be a thousand or ten thousand computers smarter than humans, hard at work 24/7, at a blinding rate, with total focus, swarming problems to solve.[75]

Kurzweil anticipates that ASI technology will enable him to transition to a completely non-biological existence by brain-porting himself to a hardware medium. This would mean "scanning his brain, capturing all of the salient details, and reinstantiating the brain's state in a different—most likely much more powerful—computational substrate."[76] This techno-utopia seems like it could quickly turn into a dystopian future when one realizes that whoever controls ASI controls the world, or worse, when one realizes that perhaps ASI cannot be controlled. Said differently, ASI has the power to rule us all, much like the One Ring rules them all.

To summarize, the powers of the emerging technologies are as follows: superlongevity in this world, enhanced natural powers, invisibility, corruption of software, and Artificial Superintelligence (ASI) that rules us all. Tolkien's Rings and transhumanism's emerging technologies offer similar powers, especially the power of radical longevity in this world. Specifically, the powers of transhumanism (the merging of technology and human beings) are comparable to the nine Rings of Power. The Superintelligence and the One Ring of Power are both capable of dominating human beings. One important dissimilarity between the One Ring and the Superintelligence is that AGI technology is still being developed, whereas the tale of the Rings has carried these issues to their logical conclusions. Tolkien's

---

73   Steve Young, "Military Uses of Nanotechnology," *The Nanoage*, (December 2009), 2, http://thenanoage.com/military.htm (accessed August 17, 2020)., 2-4.
74   Kurzweil, *Singularity*, 331.
75   Barrat, *Our Final Invention*, 195.
76   Kurzweil, *Singularity*, 324.

mythology demonstrates what this level of domination actually looks like when it is achieved and is therefore helpful in answering the question that transhumanism's Superintelligence is likely to be harmful to humanity.

A Tolkienian Critique of Transhumanism's Superlongevity

Why the Method of Literature is Needed

There is an increasing amount of scholarship devoted to critiquing the claims of transhumanism. Philosophical arguments and technical assessments abound that conclude their claims are not plausible.[77] I agree that philosophical arguments are successful in exposing the impossibility of transhumanism's techno-utopia because it is based on the flawed materialist philosophy of mind and human persons. However, these arguments have not curtailed researchers from pursuing transhumanist projects or from making outrageous claims about immortality. A similar situation occurred with the advent of logical positivism, which was soundly refuted by philosophers in the mid-twentieth century,[78] yet has survived and re-packaged as modern scientism. That is to say, a philosophically unsound ideology may persist when its assertions appeal to a culture that trusts science as its primary authority.[79] Hence, it is not surprising that philosophical arguments, though necessary, have not been enough to persuade transhumanists to abandon their dream of achieving immortality in this world.

---

77 Jay Richards, ed., *Are We Spiritual Machines: Ray Kurzweil vs. the Critics of Strong A.I.* (Seattle: Discovery Institute, 2002); Robert C. Koons and George Bealer, eds., *The Waning of Materialism* (Oxford: Oxford University Press, 2010).

78 Critiques can be found in essays and books: Willard V. O. Quine, "Two Dogmas of Empiricism," Philosophical Review 60 (1):20–43 (1951); Norwood Russell Hanson, *Patterns of Discovery* (New York: Cambridge University Press, 1958); Karl Popper, *The Logic of Scientific Discovery* (New York: Routledge, 2002); Thomas S. Kuhn, *The Structure of Scientific Discovery* (Chicago: The University of Chicago Press, 2012).

79 Richard N. Williams and Daniel N. Robinson, eds., *Scientism: The New Orthodoxy* (New York: Bloomsbury Academic, 2016), 6. Scientism and logical positivism both assert that only scientific knowledge counts as real knowledge; all else is mere opinion or nonsense.

Unlike discursive or scientific reasoning, the method of literature is able to awaken us to the truth of the matter through our imagination. Russell Kirk discusses the value of imagination in his famous 1977 essay "Teaching Humane Literature in High Schools."[80] He writes, "The purpose of literature is to develop the moral imagination. If human beings do not feel the touch of the moral imagination, they are as the beasts that perish."[81] The term moral imagination originated with Edmund Burke, but was popularized by Irving Babbitt and Russell Kirk.[82] I take moral imagination to mean that innate capacity to perceive ethical truths and permanent laws in the midst of confusing and chaotic times. Or put another way, being able to order your soul toward moral truths despite facing never-before-seen circumstances. For Kirk, literature develops the moral imagination by "teach[ing] human beings their true nature, their dignity, and their rightful place in the scheme of things. Such has been the end of poetry—in the larger sense of that word—ever since Job and Homer."[83]

Tolkien understood the value of the moral imagination and how literature could awaken and develop it in the reader. He briefly presents how the moral imagination works in *The Lord of the Rings* through Aragorn's dialogue with Eomer about their strange and unfamiliar circumstances. Eomer says, "It is hard to be sure of anything among so many marvels. The world is all grown strange . . . How shall a man judge what to do in such times?" Aragorn replies, "As he ever has judged. Good and ill have not changed since yesteryear; nor are they one thing among Elves and Dwarves and another among Men. It is man's part to discern them, as much in the gold wood as in his own house."[84] Tolkien demonstrates through Aragorn that permanent principles do not change even though our circumstances do. Tolkien's aim was "the elucidation of truth, and the encouragement of good morals in this real world, by the ancient device of exemplifying them in unfamiliar embodiments, that may tend to bring them home."[85]

For Tolkien, a temporary 'escape' to a fantasy secondary world is able to bring 'recovery,' that is, a renewed, clearer perspective to see things in the

---

80   Russell Kirk, "Teaching Humane Literature in High Schools" in *The Essential Russell Kirk: Selected Essays* (Delaware: ISI Books, 2007), 434-445.

81   Ibid., 436.

82   Kirk, "The Moral Imagination" in *The Essential Russell Kirk*, 205--218.

83   Kirk, "Teaching Human Literature in High Schools" in *The Essential Russell Kirk*, 436.

84   Tolkien, *The Lord of the Rings*, 438.

85   Carpenter, *Letters*, 194.

real world as we ought to see them.[86] Today we are faced with the question of whether superlongevity in this world is beneficial to us and we must answer using our moral imagination amidst rapidly changing technology and persuasive rhetoric from proponents. Tolkien sheds light on this question, not by philosophical argument, but by cultivating the reader's moral imagination through the thoughts and actions and consequences of the characters in Middle-earth.

Since many characters in Tolkien's mythology face the problem of death and immortality in some way, it is necessary to narrow my investigation to the given natures of the Elves and Men, the Númenóreans' pursuit of immortality, and the Nazgûls' escape from death. Each of these characters will develop the reader's moral imagination in response to our modern circumstances, namely engaging transhumanism's claim of superlongevity.

Death and Immortality for Elves

To better understand why Men lusted for immortality within the world, we start with investigating the Elves, the First-born incarnate beings of Arda, who were given immortal natures. It is through contact with Elves that Men became enamoured with limitless longevity within the world, which for Men is a false immortality and against their mortal nature. This was the beginning of what Tolkien calls their "hideous peril of confusing true 'immortality' with limitless serial longevity."[87] Or put another way, confusing the ultimate blessing of eternal life that transcends the world with endless existence within the world. This is the very same confusion that plagues transhumanists.

Ilúvatar, the Creator, gave the Elves an immortal nature, which consisted of longevity co-extensive with the life of Arda. Beyond the end of Arda, nothing was revealed to them.[88] Elves possess a dual nature of spirit (fëa) and body (hröa) that exists in unity. In the Creation myth, evil is built into the world from the beginning rather than emerging after the creative decree. Tolkien explains, "In this Myth the rebellion of created free-will precedes the creation of the World (Eä); and Eä has in it, sub-creatively

---

86 Tolkien, "On Fairy-stories," in *The Tolkien Reader*, 77.
87 Carpenter, *Letters*, 267.
88 Ibid., 285. Arda represents the world and consists of Middle-earth, and Aman, which consists of Valinor, the home of the Valar and some elves, and Eressea, an island inhabited by elves.

introduced, evil, rebellions, discordant elements of its own nature already when the Let it Be was spoken."[89]

Because Melkor's corruption and marring of Middle-earth was focused on matter, the Elves' bodies in Middle-earth were consequently affected, but not their spirits.[90] Even though they were not subject to deadly disease, their bodies could be destroyed by physical wounds or by grief. The violent severing of body and soul is a kind of death, but not an end for the Elves because their spirits are destined to dwell in Arda for the life of Arda.[91] These 'houseless' Elves received identical bodies to those lost and normally remained in Aman until the end of Arda.[92] They have the certain knowledge that if they experience the first kind of death, they will return to an incarnate life in Arda. Because their body and spirit are finite, they cannot experience the second kind of death, which would allow them to depart from Arda.

At first glance, one might envy the immortal nature of Elves, yet Tolkien allows the reader to experience this kind of endless serial living through the Elvish perspective. Transhumanists hold the simplistic view that this kind of longevity within the world should be preferred. Tolkien turns this view on its head because in Middle-earth the Elves envy the gift of death to Men, which is the ability to escape from the endless circles of the world. No one knows the future of Arda or how long it is ordained to endure, but the end will surely come and Elves must perish with it. No one speaks to the Elves of any hope beyond Arda.[93] There is the dread of ultimate loss, though it may be in the remote future; it is not necessarily easier to bear because a burden is heavier the longer it is borne.[94] Elves cannot escape Time, which is a great burden as the ages lengthen in a corrupt and marred world.[95] The progressive decline of the world away from the glowing past makes Elves dwell more in their memories and as Arda is marred they have great sorrow and resist change.[96] Finally, Elves must trust in Eru (Ilúvatar),

---

[89] Carpenter, *Letters*, 286; Tolkien, *Silmarillion*, 9. Eä represents the Universe.

[90] J. R. R. Tolkien, *Morgoth's Ring* (London: HarperCollins, 2015), 344-5.

[91] Ibid., 218.

[92] Ibid., 362-4. The Elvish spirit retains a memory, an imprint of its body. Eru gave Manwe authority to reconstruct an identical body so the Elves could return to incarnate life.

[93] Ibid., 311-12.

[94] Carpenter, *Letters*, 325; Tolkien, *Morgoth's Ring*, 312.

[95] Carpenter, *Letters*, 236.

[96] Ibid.

that whatever He has designed beyond the End will be wholly satisfying. Legolas explains the burden of being tied to Time and History this way:

> Nay, time does not tarry ever, but change and growth is not in all things and places alike. For the Elves the world moves, and it moves both very swift and very slow. Swift, because they themselves change little, and all else fleets by: it is a grief to them. Slow, because they need not count the running years, not for themselves. The passing seasons are but ripples ever repeated in the long stream. Yet beneath the Sun all things must wear to an end at last.[97]

A more thoughtful look at the Elves reveals that they found their immortal lives in the broken world of Arda increasingly burdensome and undesirable. Every negative aspect of the Elves' endless serial living also applies to transhumanism's superlongevity because, like the Elves, there would be no escape from Time, or from the burden of a corrupt world. Endless serial living in a broken world is not the same as eternal life in heaven. Grasping this difference is crucial to avoid the confusion between false and true immortality. However, it is equally important to understand that Elves are immortal in this world by nature while Men are not. Transhumanists put themselves in the place of the Creator by attempting to change humanity's mortal nature. It is also worth noting that Elves and Men in Middle-earth possess a body and soul, whereas transhumanists hold a materialist view of human nature in which there is no immaterial soul or mind.[98] Recognizing this helps make sense of transhumanism's singular focus on superlongevity in this world and the failure to consider true immortality, which transcends this world.

---

97   Tolkien, *The Lord of the Rings*, 388.
98   Robert C. Koons and George Bealer, eds., *The Waning of Materialism* (Oxford, UK: Oxford University Press, 2010), 5-8. Functionalism is the dominant theory in the philosophy of mind today and serves as the foundation and conceptual framework for AGI. Simply stated, functionalism is a materialistic understanding of the human mind that treats mental states akin to a computer program. A typical analogy of this view is: the mind is to brain as the program is to hardware. On this view, anything that has physical effects – for example mental events – must supervene on, or reduce to, or be identical with something physical.

Death and Immortality for Men

The Elves envy the Men of Middle-earth because Ilúvatar has given them the special gift of death, which is freedom beyond Arda and freedom to join in the Second Music of the Ainur.[99] Ilúvatar "willed that the hearts of Men should seek beyond the world and should find no rest therein; but they should have a virtue to shape their life, amid the powers and chances of the world, beyond the Music of Ainur, which is as fate to all things else."[100] Ilúvatar knew this gift of freedom would mean that Men "would stray often and would not use their gifts in harmony," so he gave them "a short life span in the world."[101] Through the Elves' envy of Men, Tolkien suggests that we should see death as a gift, which is central to developing our moral imagination about death and immortality.

Tolkien's refined thinking concerning the death and immortality for Men is reflected in the *Athrabeth Finrod Ah Andreth* (1959-60).[102] Through this philosophical debate between Andreth and Finrod in the First Age of Middle-earth, Tolkien affirms that Man's nature is a unity of body (hröa) and spirit (fëa). He makes a clear distinction between two kinds of deaths: the first death is the unnatural separation of body and spirit and the second death is a departure from Arda. The second death is Man's natural gift from Ilúvatar, which is to escape from the circles of the world. Transhumanists only focus on escaping the death of the physical body without recognizing the spirit of Man survives to escape the world.

Andreth shares with Finrod the wisdom and lore passed down to Man, which explains how the Fall of Men resulted in a change in their mortal nature. From the beginning Man was designed for the second type of death, which was akin to the Assumption of body and spirit together.[103] From The Tale of Adanel, Andreth tells how Melkor seduced Men, early in their ex-

---

99   Tolkien, *Morgoth's Ring*, 43; Tolkien, *The Silmarillion*, 36. The Second Music of the Ainur represents life beyond Arda, of which Iluvatar has not revealed any details.

100   Tolkien, *The Silmarillion*, 35-6.

101   Ibid.

102   Carpenter, *Letters*, 147-8. In his earlier writings, Tolkien does not give the details of the Fall of Men. In 1951, he wrote to Milton Waldman, "The first fall of Man ... nowhere appears—Men do not come on the stage until all that is long past, and there is only a rumour that for a while they fell under the domination of the Enemy and that some repented." The *Athrabeth* is Tolkien's way of addressing this 'rumour.'

103   Tolkien, *Morgoth's Ring*, 304-336.

istence, to turn away from the Voice (Ilúvatar) and worship Melkor as the Dark Lord. The consequence of this Fall was a change in their nature; Ilúvatar imposed the first kind of death on Men. Through Melkor's continuing corruptive influence, a two-fold fear developed in Men, which they refer to as the Shadow of Death: a fear of the unnatural separation of the body from the spirit and a fear of the unknown life beyond Arda.[104] This fear of the Shadow of Death drove Men to envy the Elves and pursue immortality in the world. I suggest that these same fears drive transhumanists to pursue superlongevity through technology.

The Downfall of Númenór: Men in Pursuit of Immortality

Tolkien's tale of the Númenóreans gives the reader the opportunity to experience how the Men of Middle-earth came to rebel against their mortal nature, the Valar, and their Creator by attempting to obtain immortality by force. These same developments can be found in transhumanism's abhorrence of death and pursuit of immortality by technological force. Near the end of the Second Age, the Men, who fought valiantly alongside the Elves and the Valar in the War of Wrath against Morgoth, were rewarded by the Valar with a land near the Undying Lands, known as the island of Númenor.[105] On a clear day, the Men could see the easternmost part of the Undying Lands, which was the shining city of Avalon in Eressëa, the haven of the Eldar.[106] The Valar and Elves enriched the Númenóreans with knowledge and instructed them in creative arts. The Men grew in wisdom, in creativity, and enjoyed a longer lifespan than Men had known, yet they still remained mortal.[107] They became mighty in crafts, above all ship-building and the art of sailing, voyaging across the surrounding seas.[108] The skills developed within the emerging technologies are comparable to the Numenorean creative arts.

As a condition of their close proximity to the Undying Lands, the Valar forbade men from sailing to the Blessed Realm. This Ban of the Valar was to ensure that the Númenóreans would not become "enamoured with the immortality of the Valar and the Eldar and the lands where all things endure."[109] Nevertheless, the Númenóreans developed an attitude of posses-

---

104 Tolkien, *Morgoth's Ring*, 310, 345-49.
105 Tolkien, *Silmarillion*, 310-11.
106 Ibid., 313-14.
107 Ibid., 311.
108 Ibid., 313.
109 Ibid.

siveness toward their artistic creations and skills, not wanting to leave all they had made and wishing for more time to enjoy them. The more joyful their life, the more they longed for immortality.[110] They murmured against the Valar because of the Ban, at first in their hearts, but then openly. "Why should we not envy the Valar, or even the least of the Deathless?" they asked. "For of us is required a blind trust, and a hope without assurance, knowing not what lies before us in a little while."[111] They wished to escape death in their own day, rather than trust in Ilúvatar for the hope that was beyond Arda. Similarly, transhumanists possess the same Númenórean will to take matters into their own hands and conquer death through technology.

At the height of his power, the Númenórean King Ar-Pharazôn challenged Sauron to a battle at Umbar in Middle-earth. So great was the might and splendor of Ar-Pharazôn's army that Sauron surrendered and begged for a pardon. Ar-Pharazôn brought Sauron back to Númenor as a prisoner, but after three years Sauron managed to beguile the King with his fair and wise counsel. Sauron lied to the King, first saying that Melkor, not Eru, is the Lord of All.[112] Then he declared "that everlasting life would be his who possessed the undying lands, and that the Ban was imposed only to prevent the Kings of Men from surpassing the Valar. But great Kings take what is their right."[113] The King was getting old and feared his own death, so he listened to Sauron's lies. He armed his ships for battle and set sail to break the Ban and "wrest everlasting life from the Lords of the West."[114] When the Númenóreans set foot on the shores of Aman in the Blessed Realm, the Valar called upon the One for help. Ilúvatar intervened in power and He changed the world forever, "a great chasm opened in the sea between Númenor and the Deathless Lands, and the water flowed down into it . . . and the world was shaken."[115] All the ships and men were drawn into the Abyss and utterly destroyed.

The ultimate Downfall of Númenor illuminates transhumanism's quest for superlongevity. The Númenóreans' pursuit of immortality was connected to their possessiveness of their long life span, achievements, and creations. Likewise, today our life expectancy has increased in the West, approaching eighty years and we enjoy greater achievements due to lon-

---

110 Tolkien, *Silmarillion*, 315; Tolkien, *The Lord of the Rings*, 1036.
111 Tolkien, *The Silmarillion*, 317.
112 Ibid., 325.
113 Tolkien, *The Lord of the Rings*, 1036-7.
114 Ibid., 1037.
115 Tolkien, *Silmarillion*, 334.

ger productivity. Consequently, transhumanists promote a Númenórean attitude by promising superlongevity as the way to preserve our skills, our lives, our history, and our intellectual property.[116]

The Númenóreans did not understand that death was a gift from Ilúvatar, bestowed on them because Arda was not their home. They did not have faith in Ilúvatar, a faith necessary to accept that death is the beginning of a blessed eternity beyond Arda. Similarly, transhumanists only view death as a tragedy and see the "primary role of religion as deathist rationalization—that is, rationalizing the tragedy of death as a good thing."[117] At the climax of technology, transhumanists believe the Singularity event will usher in victory over death, which means we will "no longer need to rationalize death as a primary means of giving meaning to life."[118]

King Ar-Pharazôn believed it was his right to obtain immortality by force. In like manner, it is interesting that transhumanists view enhancements as their right and refer to each major advance of technology as a *revolution*. Kurzweil writes, "The first half of the twenty-first century will be characterized by three overlapping revolutions—in Genetics, Nanotechnology, and Robotics."[119]

The Ban of the Valar fueled the desires of the Numenoreans to pursue immortality to an even greater degree. In similar fashion, some critics of transhumanism suggest there should be a ban on all research of emerging technologies.[120] Theodore Schick, a Tolkien scholar who writes about the relationship between the Rings and emerging technologies, discusses the inherent dangers we face today and how we should respond. In his essay "The Cracks of Doom: The Threat of Emerging Technologies and Tolkien's Rings of Power," he notes that one solution is to "throw them back into the fire, or at least not forge them in the first place, for they have the potential to destroy the human race."[121] This solution would likely drive researchers underground into the shadows, which would make the technology even more vulnerable to a criminal element. In response to this, the required enforcement of a ban on research would approach tyrannical control, restricting human

---

116   Tolkien, *Silmarillion*, 326-30.
117   Kurzweil, *Singularity*, 372.
118   Ibid., 326.
119   Kurzweil, *Singularity*, 205.
120   Bill Joy, "Why the Future Doesn't Need Us," *Wired*, Issue 8.04, April 2000, https://www.wired.com/2000/04/joy-2/ (accessed August 17, 2020).
121   Theodore Schick, "The Cracks of Doom: The Threat of Emerging Technologies and Tolkien's Rings of Power," in *The Lord of the Rings and Philosophy: One Book to Rule Them All*, Greg Bassham and Eric Bronson, eds. (Chicago: Open Court Publishing, 2003), 22.

freedom. Schick agrees the sacrifice of privacy and freedom is too high, but some critics like Bill Joy, co-founder of Sun Microsystems, are "willing to make the sacrifice for the sake of preventing greater harm."[122]

The Nazgûl: Men Escaping Death

Tolkien's story of the Nazgûl, also known as Ringwraiths or Black Riders, offers valuable insight about pursuing an unnatural existence. Bill Davis connects Tolkien's treatment of the Nazgûl to Aristotle's conclusion that every natural thing has a nature, a way they are supposed to be. Hence, Davis says "only *natural* existence is a good thing. Continuing to exist in any other way—any *unnatural way*—is worse than death."[123] Prior to the Downfall of Númenor, Sauron had distributed the Rings of Power to nine great men, among whom were three great lords of Númenor.[124] These Men accepted the Rings because they "desired secret power beyond the measure of their kind."[125] Their desires were initially fulfilled as they became mighty Men in their day, obtaining glory, great wealth, and unending life.[126] As time passed, their unending life became a prolonged death, as their physical bodies transformed into nothingness; they became invisible and entered the realm of shadows.[127] One by one, according to the natural strength and the good or evil of their wills, the nine great Men fell under the enslavement and domination of Sauron, who corrupted and controlled them by the power of the One Ring; they became his terrible servants.

By the time the reader encounters the Nazgûl in *The Lord of the Rings*, they have lost their humanity. Most of Tolkien's descriptions of the Nazgûl are explanations of *what* they are rather than *who* they are. For example, at the Siege of Gondor, when Gandalf faces the Lord of the Nazgûl, he shouts: "'Go back! Fall into the nothingness that awaits you and your Master. Go!' The Black rider flung back his hood, and behold he had a kingly crown;

---

122 Theodore Schick, "The Cracks of Doom: The Threat of Emerging Technologies and Tolkien's Rings of Power," in *The Lord of the Rings and Philosophy: One Book to Rule Them All*, Greg Bassham and Eric Bronson, eds. (Chicago: Open Court Publishing, 2003), 31.

123 Bill Davis, "Choosing to Die," in *The Lord of the Rings and Philosophy: One Book to Rule Them All*, eds., Gregory Bassham and Eric Bronson, eds. (Chicago: Open Court Publishing, 2003), 126.

124 Tolkien, *Silmarillion*, 320.
125 Ibid., 345.
126 Ibid., 346.
127 Ibid., 346.

and yet upon no head visible was it set. The red fires shone between it and the mantled shoulders vast and dark. From a mouth unseen there came a deadly laughter."[128] The description is more about what is absent rather than his presence. The Nazgûl no longer had the will to think or act on their own, but "uttered only [Sauron's] will and his malice."[129]

Not only have the Nazgûl lost their physical form and freedom, but their names and personal identities are gone. On this point, Tolkien scholar Amy Amendt-Raduege notes, "In an epic work where hundreds of characters are named, where complex genealogies provide the names of individuals not otherwise mentioned, and where several characters carry multiple names in multiple countries, the *absence* of any name at all is surely significant."[130] Amendt-Raduege observes that "the lack of name signals the lack of individuality, of uniqueness, and personhood."[131] When the One Ring is finally destroyed, the Nazgûl perish also: "And into the heart of the storm, with a cry that pierced all other sounds, tearing the clouds asunder, the Nazgûl came, shooting like flaming bolts, as caught in the fiery ruin of the hill and sky they crackled, withered, and went out."[132] Their final end seems more a relief than a tragedy and no one mourns their passing. The most crucial lesson from the Ringwraiths is the realization that their fate could have been avoided. Each chose to accept the Ring that promised immortality, but instead they endured a fate more terrible than death.

The tale of the Nazgûl has much to teach us about the consequences of desiring and submitting to artificial longevity against one's mortal human nature. The following description of transhumanism closely resembles what could be called unnatural existence:

> Artificial materials will be integrated into the body more and more... Organs could be replaced by super-advanced machine versions that would run forever and never fail. Red blood cells could be perfected by red blood cell nanobots, who could power their own movement, eliminating

---

128   Tolkien, *The Lord of the Rings*, 829.
129   Ibid., 823.
130   Amy Amendt-Raduege, "Better Off Dead," *Fastitocalon: Studies in Fantasticism Ancient to Modern*, Volume 1.1 (Bergstrabe: WVT Wissenschaftlicher Verlag Trier, 2010), 75. Even the Chief of the Ringwraiths is identified as a title, the King of Angmar. Only one is given a hint of a name and it serves as his title--Khamul, the Black Easterling.
131   Ibid., 76.
132   Tolkien, *The Lord of the Rings*, 947.

the need for a heart at all ... Eventually, Kurzweil believes humans will reach a point when they're entirely artificial, a time when we'll look back at biological material and think how unbelievably primitive it was that humans were ever made of that and that humans aged, suffered from cancer, allowed random factors like microbes, diseases, accidents to harm us or make us disappear.[133]

If we grant that the powers of the emerging technologies are comparable to the powers of the nine lesser rings and that the power of the Singularity is similar to the power of the One Ring of Sauron, then the consequences of transhumanism's superlongevity is akin to trading your personhood, individuality, freedom, and ultimately your body to achieve an unnatural, unbearable existence. As I have demonstrated previously in chapter four, the concept of personhood becomes problematic when humans submit to merging themselves with technology. There would be a loss of individuality if our brains were augmented by nanobots to enhance natural abilities and then merged with the Internet. Considering the inherent dangers of an Artificial Superintelligence controlling our bodies and brains, we would inevitably lose our freedom to think and act on our own. Thankfully, the fate just described can be prevented. Just as the Nazgûl had a choice to accept or reject the technology of the Ring, we also have a choice today regarding our acceptance of applying the emerging technologies to ourselves.

A Way Forward: Sam and Aragorn as Exemplars

Our critique so far has focused on comparing transhumanism's emerging technologies to the Rings of Power, the differing natures of Elves and Men, and the negative examples of how the Númenóreans and the Nazgûl suffered horrific consequences in their pursuit of immortality. Tolkien also offers positive role models of characters who respond to the problem of death and immortality as they ought, namely Samwise Gamgee and Aragorn.

Tolkien considered Sam "the jewel among the hobbits"[134] and "a more representative hobbit than any others."[135] Through Sam, Tolkien reveals

---

133 Tim Urban, "The AI Revolution: Our Immortality or Extinction," *Wait But Why*, January 27, 2015, The Artificial Intelligence Revolution: Part 2, (accessed August 1, 2020).

134 Carpenter, *Letters*, 88.

135 Ibid., 329.

how people should respond to their longing for immortality in this world. Tolkien scholar Gaelle Abalea argues that Tolkien shows how to obtain immortality in this world through memory and transmission.[136] By *memory* he means remembering people by the telling of tales. By *transmission*, Abalea means that artistic creation can be a means of transmitting part of ourselves as a legacy.[137] Tolkien referred to this activity as sub-creation, which he considered "a human right: we make in our measure and in our derivative mode, because we are made: and not only made, but made in the image and likeness of a Maker."[138]

An illustration of how memory satisfies the impulse for immortality is when Sam reminds Frodo of the value of telling tales as they make their way to Mordor. Sam says the tales that really matter are the ones where "folk seem to have been just landed in them, usually—their paths were laid that way, as you put it."[139] They both come to realize they have landed in a great tale that never ends. Frodo wisely adds, "But the people in [the tale] come and go when their part's ended. Our part will end later—or sooner."[140] They both acknowledge their finite lives will be remembered as part of a much bigger story that will continue.

Another example of memory is the Red Book, which is the written record of their adventures. Before Frodo leaves for the Grey Havens, he tells Sam, "[Y]ou will read things out of the Red Book, and keep alive the memory of the age that is gone, so that people will remember the Great danger and so love their beloved land all the more."[141] Cultivating memory of this sort has a greater purpose than personal glorification and is more like passing one's wisdom and knowledge to the next generation.

Sam obtains immortality through transmission in two ways: artistic sub-creation and parenting. After the battle for the Shire was won, Sam began his forestry work, re-making the Shire as it ought to be. Using the gift from Galadriel, Sam "planted saplings in all the places where specially beautiful or beloved trees had been destroyed, and he put a grain of the

---

136   Gaelle Abalea, "Transmission: an escape from death in Tolkien's work?" in *Death and Immortality in Middle-earth: Proceedings of The Tolkien Society Seminar 2016*, Daniel Helen, ed. (Edinburgh: Luna Press Publishing, 2017), 135.
137   Ibid., 135-6, 141.
138   Tolkien, "On Fairy-stories," in *The Tolkien Reader*, 74-5.
139   Tolkien, *The Lord of the Rings*, 711.
140   Ibid., 712.
141   Ibid., 1029.

precious dust in the soil at the root of each."¹⁴² Sam knew it would take time for the trees to grow, but was satisfied that "his great-grandchildren, he thought, would see the Shire as it ought to be." I take Sam's gardening skill as his means of artistic sub-creation and through it he transmitted a part of himself to his progeny.

Parenting children is also a form of transmission for Sam; he and Rosie welcome their first child, Elanor, to their family and look forward to many more children.¹⁴³ Anna Mathie contends that this is the Hobbit's great strength: "This fertility, this willingness to pass life on to a new generation rather than grasping for "endless life unchanging," should likewise be mankind's proper strength."¹⁴⁴ Sam was more hopeful about transmitting his wisdom to his offspring than he was about endlessly perfecting and preserving himself.

Sam's proper fulfillment of obtaining immortality in this world through memory and transmission is in sharp contrast to transhumanist ideals. Through whole brain emulation, transhumanists hope to upload their minds to a computer and eventually transition to a completely non-biological existence.¹⁴⁵ Their hope for cybernetic immortality in this world is actually no hope at all, but rather a dead end; that is, a path that turns in on itself.

Aragorn, the heir of Isildur and a Númenórean, accepts death as a gift from Ilúvatar, something his ancestors could not accept. He believed death was the path to true immortality beyond Arda. Aragorn is called Estel, which means hope.¹⁴⁶ This hope that Aragorn personifies is not an expectation of good based on experience of what is known in the world. Rather, Estel means trust and comes from one's nature as a Child of the One.¹⁴⁷ Aragorn saw death as a gift because he trusted that his Creator had a good purpose and plan, a higher hope for Men beyond Arda.

Nevertheless, for Tolkien, death is still a cruel and tragic loss and he portrays it as such.¹⁴⁸ In fact, on Aragorn's deathbed, he says to Arwen, "I

---

142   Tolkien, *The Lord of the Rings*, 1023.
143   Tolkien, *The Lord of the Rings*, 1029.
144   Anna Mathie, "Tolkien and the Gift of Mortality," *First Things*, November 2003, https://www.firstthings.com/article/2003/11/tolkien-and-the-gift-of-mortality (accessed August 15, 2020).
145   Kurzweil, *Singularity*, 324.
146   Tolkien, *The Lord of the Rings*, 1057.
147   Tolkien, *Morgoth's Ring*, 320.
148   Ibid., 324.

speak no comfort to you, for there is no comfort for such pain within the circles of the world."[149] Arwen expresses the loss and separation caused by death when she says, "[T]he gift of the One to Men, it is bitter to receive."[150] Yet at the end, Aragorn expresses hope in the midst of sadness, "In sorrow we must go, but not in despair. Behold! We are not bound for ever to the circles of the world, and beyond them is more than memory. Farewell!"[151] Through Aragorn's death, Tolkien achieves what he calls eucatastrophe, the sudden joyous turn and deliverance from sorrow.[152] Aragorn accepted death as a gift because he believed his mortal nature was from his Creator and he believed his destiny beyond Arda was part of the blessed plan of Ilúvatar. In contrast to Aragorn, transhumanists deny their mortal nature and reject any hope of an afterlife. These beliefs drive them to grasp for cybernetic superlongevity in this world.

Conclusion

Time spent in Tolkien's world of Middle-earth helps us recover a clear view of how we ought to view death and immortality in the real world. My aim in investigating Tolkien's legendarium was to help shed light on the crucial question of whether transhumanism's pursuit of superlongevity in this world is beneficial or harmful for human beings. I conclude that the project to merge human beings with technology to achieve artificial superlongevity in this world is definitely harmful for several reasons. To accept transhumanism's superlongevity would be to mistake longevity in this world for true immortality that transcends this world. The supposed radical life extension through technological enhancements and mind-uploading would be unnatural and dehumanizing, resulting in the loss of personhood, identity, individuality, embodiment, and free will. Finally, the effect of a Superintelligence on humans would likely mean their complete domination and servitude, not unlike that demanded by Sauron. The unnatural existence that transhumanism promotes is actually a fate worse than death. For these reasons, the pursuit of immortality in this world is, as Tolkien says, "a supreme folly and wickedness."[153] The proper satisfac-

---

149 Tolkien, *The Lord of the Rings*, 1062.
150 Ibid., 1063.
151 Ibid.
152 Tolkien, "On Fairy-stories," in *The Tolkien Reader*, 86.
153 Carpenter, *Letters*, 286.

tion of the longing for immortality in this world should be fulfilled through telling of tales, artistic sub-creation, and parenthood.

Throughout his legendarium, Tolkien urges the reader to consider death as a gift. The Men of Middle-earth struggled to accept death as the path to eternal life beyond Arda because their knowledge was limited to a vague notion of the afterlife and the Second Music of the Ainur. However, people today have something they did not have, religion with revelation—that is, special revelation in the Bible, which contains God's offer of eternal life. "This is eternal life, that they know the only true God, and Jesus Christ whom you have sent."[154] We live in a world where Jesus Christ, God incarnate, rose from the dead and made this promise, "I am the resurrection and the life. Whoever believes in me, though he die, yet shall he live, and everyone who lives and believes in me shall never die."[155] This is true immortality that transcends death and this world. For the followers of Christ, physical death is the path to true immortality. For anyone who does not have hope for eternity beyond this world, Tolkien's epic stirs up a longing to find out the truth of the matter. Thankfully, since Jesus entered time and history, His evidential claims can be investigated.[156]

---

[154] John 17:4, ESV.
[155] John 11:25-26, ESV.
[156] N. T. Wright, *The Resurrection of the Son of God: Christian Origins and the Question of God* (Minneapolis: Fortress Press, 2003); Michael R. Licona, *The Resurrection of Jesus: A New Historiographical Approach* (Downers Grove, IL: InterVarsity Press, 2010); Gary R. Habermas and Michael R. Licona, *The Case for the Resurrection of Jesus* (Grand Rapids, MI: Kregel Publications, 2004).

Chapter Six

Transhumanism's Superhappiness: Making Dystopian Fiction A Reality

"It's beautiful because it's so simple. All scientific breakthroughs are simple."[1]
Scientist Bob Comeaux

Introduction

TRANSHUMANISTS SEEK TO TRANSFORM human persons through the use of science and technology. They hope to radically improve health and lifespans, enhance our intellectual and physical capacities, and increase our control over mental states and moods.[2]

Simply put, they hope to engineer happiness. As materialists, transhumanists hold that mental and emotional states, like happiness, are strictly determined by neurochemical functions of the brain. In his book *The Hedonistic Imperative*, philosopher David Pearce, who is the co-founder of Humanity+, presents the transhumanist project to abolish human suffering and secure happiness.[3] According to Pearce, through genetic engineering

---

1   Walker Percy, *The Thanatos Syndrome* (New York: Picador USA, 1987), 196.
2   Nick Bostrom, "In Defense of Posthuman Dignity," in *H+/- Transhumanism and Its Critics*, edited by Gregory R. Hansell and William Grassie (Philadelphia: Metanexus Institute, 2011), 55.
3   Science, Technology, and the Future, The Hedonistic Imperative -

and neuropharmacology, future "paradise engineering specialists" will eliminate aversive experience from the living world.[4]

Transhumanists have an evolutionary explanation for the origin of humanity's aversive mental and emotional states. According to Pearce, humans have a relatively stable level of happiness around which they fluctuate throughout their lives, despite their experiences of positive or negative events.[5] This means that even though events can affect happiness in the short term, people return to their stable level of happiness, also called their hedonic set-point. This general baseline of happiness is lower than it could be because our neural metabolic pathways evolved with pain and unhappiness. These were selected for survival and reproduction, not for happiness.[6] Given this understanding of the hedonic set-point, Pearce emphasizes that no amount of human enhancement related to superintelligence and superlongevity will guarantee a greater degree of happiness. If the triple 'S' civilization is going to succeed as a techno-utopia, a direct biological solution is necessary to raise the hedonic set-point and achieve global superhappiness.

Transhumanists characterize this project as a "naturalisation of heaven," an alternative to the afterlife promised in certain traditional religions.[7] They perceive the project to abolish human suffering as a moral imperative because "human beings are entitled to lifelong well-being in this world, rather than the next."[8] Pearce writes, "If we get things right, the future of

---

Youtube Mini Documentary, https://www.youtube.com/watch?v=dLtC-5olrK4 (accessed August 22, 2020).

4   David Pearce, *The Hedonistic Imperative*, HedWeb.com, Introduction, https://www.hedweb.com/hedethic/hedonist.htm (accessed August 1, 2020). David Pearce's overall strategy encompasses the entire sentient world, which includes abolishing non-human animal suffering. This project proposes redesigning traditional eco-systems and genetically engineering animals. This paper's focus is limited to an evaluation of transhumanism's project related to human beings.

5   Ibid.
6   Ibid.
7   Ibid.
8   Pearce, *The Hedonistic Imperative*, Chapter 3, "Our Emotional Future," Hedweb.com, https://www.hedweb.com/hedethic/hedon3.htm#emotional (accessed August 1, 2020). As I argued in chapter four, transhumanists have no philosophical grounds for their appeal to individual autonomy, free will, or individual rights. The inadequacy of their materialist philosophy to account for individual autonomy and liberty is one of the reasons why there is a blatant inconsistency between defending individual autonomy and upholding their utilitarian ethic.

life in the universe can be wonderful beyond the bounds of human imagination: a triple 'S' civilisation of superlongevity, superintelligence, and superhappiness."⁹

In this chapter, I will evaluate this project of superhappiness through the lens of the following dystopian works of literature: Jonathan Swift's *Gulliver's Travels* (1726), Aldous Huxley's *Brave New World* (1932), and Walker Percy's *The Thanatos Syndrome* (1987). I begin by explaining the reasons for selecting these three literary works for my critique of transhumanism. Next, I will critique transhumanism's superhappiness project by posing three core questions to the dystopian texts and to transhumanism. The answers to these questions will shed light on the motivation, methods, and the human cost of implementing the project of superhappiness. Just as evil can be understood as a privation of good, I will argue that the human goods deprived by transhumanism's pursuit of superhappiness would likely result in a dystopian future.¹⁰ Finally, I will offer a virtue-based approach to human flourishing as an alternative to transhumanism's superhappiness.

The Rationale for Selecting the Dystopian Literature

This chapter draws on resources from dystopian literature to illustrate the truth and consequences of the superhappiness project. My goal is to inspire the reader's moral imagination by exploring the motives, actions, and consequences of the selected literary characters. Literature is often used as an intellectual tool to critique utopian ideas because fiction writers who explore utopian themes stir the reader's imagination. In Marcus Rockoff's essay "Literature," he examines the role of literature in critiquing transhumanism and identifies three classes.¹¹ Literary works in the first class have central ideas, messages, or themes analogous to transhumanism. This class may include literary works from time periods before modern technology was available. The second class of literature includes novels with specific technologies and methods comparable to transhumanism, or extrapolations of technologies that will develop in the future. The third class, which

---

9   David Pearce, "What is Transhumanism? The 3 Supers," *Institute for Ethics and Emerging Technologies*, September 16, 2014, https://ieet.org/index.php/IEET2/print/9543 (accessed August 21, 2020).
10 Augustine, *The City of God*, in Mortimer Adler, editor, *Great Books of the Western World, Volume 16* (Chicago: Encyclopedia Britannica, Inc., 1990), 380.
11 Marcus Rockoff, "Literature," in Robert Ranissch and Stefan Lorenz Sorgner, editors, *Post- and Transhumanism: An Introduction* (New York: Peter Lang Edition, 2014), 254.

is rare, refers to literature that explicitly portrays transhumanism as a movement or has a transhumanist character in the plot.[12] This class of novels make direct references and correlations to transhumanism and require less moral imagination from the reader.[13]

For this critique, I selected works from the first two classes of transhumanist literature: *Gulliver's Travels*, which represents Rockoff's first class, and *Brave New World* and *The Thanatos Syndrome*, which fall into the second class. What follows is a brief overview of each work and my reasons for selecting it to critique transhumanism's superhappiness.

Jonathan Swift's Gulliver's Travels

In Jonathan Swift's 1726 classic *Gulliver's Travels* (Part III), he depicts the unhindered progress of science and technology and its effects on human beings and society. The book represents the fictional travel record of Gulliver's voyages to four established societies that were previously unknown to his home country. Within this context, Swift satirizes human nature, politics, religion, as well as the ill effects of science and technology.[14] Gulliver's third voyage takes him to the country of Laputa, where he documents the

---

12   Marcus Rockoff, "Literature," in Robert Ranissch and Stefan Lorenz Sorgner, editors, *Post- and Transhumanism: An Introduction* (New York: Peter Lang Edition, 2014), 254.

13   An example of the third class of literature is Zoltan Istvan, *The Transhumanist Wager* (Futurity Imagine Media L.L.C., 2013). The novel tells the story of transhumanist Jethro Knights and his unwavering quest for immortality via science and technology. Fighting against him are fanatical religious groups, economically depressed governments, and mystic Zoe Bach: a dazzling trauma surgeon and the love of his life, whose belief in spirituality and the afterlife is absolute. Exiled from America and reeling from personal tragedy, Knights forges a new nation of willing scientists on the world's largest seasteading project, Transhumania. When the world declares war against the floating city, demanding an end to its renegade and godless transhuman experiments and ambitions, Knights strikes back, leaving the planet forever changed.

14   Franssen, Maarten, Lokhorst, Gert-Jan and van de Poel, Ibo, "Philosophy of Technology," *The Stanford Encyclopedia of Philosophy* (Fall 2018 Edition), Edward N. Zalta (ed.), Section 2.3, https://plato.stanford.edu/archives/fall2018/entries/technology/ (accessed August 25, 2020). The distinction between science and technology: science aims to understand the world as it is and technology aims to change the world. Laputa represents the development of science and Lagado represents the development of technology. This chapter will focus on Laputa.

Laputans' obsession with the scientific conception of the world and the resulting consequences to their people and society.

In his book *Irrational Man*, William Barrett claims that the whole movement of Romanticism was at bottom an attempt to escape from Laputa.[15] The science-minded Laputans were so devoted to abstract mathematics and astronomy they became detached from ordinary common sense activities. For example, Barrett notes that a Laputan tailor fitted Gulliver with a suit of clothes by means of a sextant, quadrant, and other scientific gadgets. The result was a very ill-fitting garment. Geometry does not provide an accurate means of measuring the organic human form. The implication is that human persons cannot be fully accounted for using scientific reason.

Swift's early literary work falls into Rockoff's first class of transhumanist literature because it conveys the general message that implementing a scientific utopia can have disastrous human consequences. In 1726, modern physical science was just emerging and machine-powered technology was yet to develop in the second half of the eighteenth century.[16] The Laputans' scientific mindset corresponds to the current-day transhumanist technological worldview in the following ways: their mechanical world picture, their view that man can master nature, their aim to unitize, mathematize, and technologize everything, and their tendency to objectify the world and one another.[17] Gulliver's assessment of the consequences of science and technology in Laputa can be a model for us to proactively evaluate the philosophy that undergirds transhumanism and envision its consequences.

Aldous Huxley's Brave New World

Aldous Huxley's *Brave New World* falls into Rockoff's second class of transhumanist literature because it portrays specific technological methods and procedures that correspond to the transhumanist project of superhappiness. The Controllers in *Brave New World* share the transhumanist pursuit of global happiness, including using genetic engineering and neuropharmacology as scientific solutions.

---

15   William Barrett, *Irrational Man: A Study in Existential Philosophy* (New York: Anchor Books, 1958), 123.

16   Craig M. Gay, *Modern Technology and the Human Future* (Downers Grove, Illinois: IVP Academic, 2018), 121.

17   Gay, *Modern Technology and the Human Future*, 99, 105, 102, 121, 122, 129; Jonathan Swift, *Gulliver's Travels*, Book III, in Mortimer Adler, editor, *The Great Books of the Western World, Volume 34*, (Chicago: Encyclopedia Britannica, Inc., 1990), 93-8, 102-3.

The Controllers in *Brave New World* are the ruling elite who have eliminated suffering and perfected the goal of universal human happiness by taking control of the entire population, not by violent force but by means of science and technology. Like transhumanists, the Controllers are materialists who reduce the human mind and emotions to neurochemical functions of the brain. They understand happiness and well-being strictly in terms of attaining pleasure and avoiding pain. The technologies employed are similar to the emerging technologies of transhumanism: artificial reproduction, genetic engineering, and mood altering drugs. In *Brave New World*, a person's life is predetermined by genetic engineering and he is conditioned to enjoy it; if this fails, there is always the drug soma. Huxley illustrates that a techno-utopia of superhappiness achieves only the shallow illusion of happiness because it is based on a flawed materialist view of human persons.

David Pearce acknowledges that several critiques comparing transhumanism's project of superhappiness to *Brave New World* have been so effective that they had to "delay research into paradise engineering."[18] This admission confirms that analogizing the transhumanist agenda to dystopian literature is fruitful in frustrating transhumanism's progress.

Walker Percy's The Thanatos Syndrome

The Thanatos Syndrome belongs in Rockoff's second class of transhumanist literature because it addresses a specific scientific method. Unlike *Brave New World*, which is set in the distant future, this story is set, like the television series *Max Headroom*, twenty minutes into the future.[19] A group of scientists devise a program to alter human behavior by changing brain chemistry, much like David Pearce's solution. Walker Percy draws attention to the scientists' reductionist view of human persons—they believe that changing human brain chemistry will magically solve society's complex social and moral problems, such as crime, child abuse, teenage suicide, and teenage

---

18   David Pearce, "Brave New World? A Defense of Paradise-Engineering," *LIfeboat Foundation* website, https://lifeboat.com/ex/brave.new.world (accessed September 2, 2020).

19   *Max Headroom* TV Series, Each episode begins with a curious reminder that what viewers were about to witness was just "20 minutes into the future." That is to say, much closer than you might imagine. https://www.wnycstudios.org/podcasts/otm/articles/212461-max-headroom (accessed September 4, 2020).

pregnancies. Similarly, transhumanists see human suffering, both physical and mental, as a "technical problem with a technical solution."[20]

Transhumanists, like the scientists in *The Thanatos Syndrome*, attempt to build an ideal society, but they reject traditional methods to eliminate suffering and achieve happiness. They dismiss virtue-based ethics and socio-economic reforms that improve the external environment. Transhumanists argue that traditional methods fail because they do not solve humanity's main problem, which is that we are all genetically constrained by our hedonic set-point.[21] Accordingly, a direct biological solution to abolish suffering using fine-tuned pharmacology, genetic engineering, and germline gene editing, is most reasonable and feasible.[22]

In Percy's essay "Notes for a Novel About the End of the World," he describes the novelist as a prophet, "writing about the coming end in order to warn about present ills and so avert the end."[23] The novelist, says Percy, is the canary in a coal mine. When a canary detects harmful conditions and cries out and then collapses, it may be time for the miners to surface and think things over.[24] Percy identifies the present ill of society as "the absorption by the layman not of the scientific method but rather of the magical aura of science, whose credentials he accepts for all sectors of reality."[25] Percy's "scientists" are akin to Swift's "projectors" on the island of Laputa and Huxley's "Controllers" in *Brave New World*, all of whom misuse science and technology in an attempt to solve humanity's problems with little regard for the human cost.

Summary

Transhumanism's never-before-seen techno-utopian engineered superhappiness calls for a critical evaluation using dystopian literature, in particular the above mentioned choices that deal with similar themes, ideas, and methods. Imagining dystopias that misuse science and technology

---

20   David Pearce, "Brave New World? A Defense of Paradise-Engineering," *Lifeboat Foundation* website, https://lifeboat.com/ex/brave.new.world (accessed September 2, 2020).

21   David Pearce, "The Abolitionist Project," *Abolitionist* website, 2007, 1-2. https://www.abolitionist.com/ (accessed September 8, 2020).

22   Ibid.

23   Walker Percy, *The Message in the Bottle* (Open Road Media, Kindle Edition), 101.

24   Ibid., 101-2.

25   Percy, *The Message in a Bottle*, 113.

force us to rethink our current assumptions and expectations about science, technology, and progress and their effects on human nature and society.

Critiquing Transhumanism's Project of Superhappiness

Transhumanism forces us to assess the consequences of applying science and technology to the human person. This critique of transhumanism's superhappiness project seeks to answer three core questions: Why undertake a global utopian project? How is this utopia to be achieved? What is the cost to humanity if the proposed technologies are implemented? Examining transhumanism through the lens of each selected text will shed light on whether the human cost of superhappiness will likely lead to a future dystopian reality.

Jonathan Swift's Gulliver's Travels

Question #1: Why undertake a utopian project?

In the country of Laputa, people are obsessed with all kinds of scientific speculations, which fuel their desire for power and control. The Laputan scientists had mastered the technology of magnetic levitation, making it possible for the king to rule from a floating island two miles above the realm of Balnibarbi. The king used this levitation technology to control the people below by blocking sunlight and rain as punishment for insurrections.[26]

Additionally, the scientific elite controlled Balnibarbi by establishing scientific academies in every city,[27] the purpose being to abolish traditional methods of agriculture, building, and learning and enact new rules and methods based on speculative experimental science and technology. None of these projects succeeded, and as a result, the whole country lay in a miserable waste.[28] It is significant that in 1726, three centuries before transhumanism's speculative idea of using genetic engineering to secure human happiness, Jonathan Swift imagined a ruling elite, motivated by a desire for

---

26   Swift, *Gulliver's Travels*, Book III, 102-3.
27   Jonathan Swift's portrayal of the Academies in *Gulliver's Travels* is similar to Francis Bacon's description of Salomon's House in his 1627 book *A New Atlantis*. See Sir Francis Bacon, *A New Atlantis* (Minervapublishing.net, 2018), 33-45. Both the projectors of the Academies and the scientists of Salomon's House are charged with increasing scientific knowledge in order to solve the problems of society.
28   Swift, *Gulliver's Travels*, 105-6.

power and control, that misused science and technology with disastrous consequences to the people and their society.

Question 2: How is this utopia to be achieved?

On Gulliver's visit to the floating island of Laputa, he observed the people were enamored and focused only on scientific speculations, such as mathematics, geometry, astrology, and astronomy, at the expense of all other forms of knowledge.[29] With their materialistic view of the world, they sought scientific solutions to all their problems.

In the land of Balnibarbi, which was ruled from above, Gulliver found that scientific speculations were put into practice at the grand academy of the city Lagado. Traditional methods were rejected in favor of new scientific rules and methods for everything from agriculture to building, manufacturing, and learning.[30] A broad range of absurd, speculative techniques were attempted with the ambition of improving society, such as extracting sunbeams out of cucumbers, reducing human excrement to its original food, building houses from the roof down to the foundation, and abolishing all spoken words to save breath, purportedly as a health advantage.[31] One can only imagine that David Pearce and his speculative project of superhappiness would be welcomed with open arms at the grand academy of Lagado.

Question #3: What is the human cost of this Utopia?

The devastating aftermath of the failures at the grand academy in Lagado affected the people, the land, and the society. The fertile land did not produce food, despite much labor, because the new speculative methods and tools were absurd and inadequate for farming.[32] The people were unhappy, without food, wore rags for clothes, and their strangely built houses lay in ruins.[33] Even after many years of repeated failures, the academy's projectors did not consider returning to the traditional rules and methods, but were driven all the more to make their speculative schemes work.[34] There is nothing progressive about these scientists refusing to admit their mistakes. Recalling the wisdom of C.S. Lewis, "If you are on the wrong road, progress

---

29 Swift, *Gulliver's Travels*, 97.
30 Ibid., 106.
31 Ibid., 107-111.
32 Swift, *Gulliver's Travels*, 104.; 112.
33 Ibid., 104.-5.
34 Ibid., 106.

means doing an about-turn and walking back to the right road; and in that case the man who turns back soonest is the most progressive man."[35]

The scientists of the academies of Laputa suffered from their singular focus. They were so distracted with speculative thought that they lost their communication skills and normal public discourse deteriorated; servants were hired to rouse their attention during conversations by flapping their mouths or ears.[36] Husbands were so wrapped up in scientific speculations that they ignored their wives, who then resorted to pursuing repeated adulterous affairs for attention.[37] Gulliver observed that the people experienced much dread and anxiety over their calculations of the earth approaching the sun and comets approaching the earth. They became perpetually alarmed and unhappy, unable to sleep or enjoy the common pleasures of life.[38]

All of their scientific speculation failed to make them happy. Their singular scientific focus led them to a form of egoism that retarded their communication skills, destroyed their marriages, crippled their community, and caused widespread anxiety and depression.

Aldous Huxley's Brave New World

Question #1: Why did the Controllers undertake a utopian project?

In Aldous Huxley's *Brave New World*, the Controllers are the ruling elite who have eliminated suffering and perfected universal human happiness by taking control of the entire population by means of science and technology. The Controllers employ artificial reproduction technology, genetic engineering, behavioral conditioning, propaganda through hypnopaedia, and the mood altering drug soma to achieve a five-caste stable society of uniform, happy, complacent, and enslaved workers.[39]

The Controller Mustapha Mond exclaims, "People are happy; they get what they want, and they never want what they can't get . . . And if anything should go wrong, there's soma."[40] In other words, a person's life is predetermined by genetic engineering and he is behaviorally conditioned to enjoy his lot in life. Providing people with the illusion of happiness is critical in *Brave New World* for the stability of the State.

---

35   C. S. Lewis, *Mere Christianity* (New York: HarperCollins, 1980), 28.
36   Swift, *Gulliver's Travels*, 94-5.
37   Ibid., 98.
38   Ibid.
39   Huxley, *Brave New World*, 3-63.
40   Ibid., 220.

The Controllers justified pursuing their utopian project because the people had voluntarily chosen to submit to the Controllers after The Nine Years War and the Economic Collapse. "There was a choice between World Control and destruction."[41] When political and economic solutions failed, the people submitted to the Controllers' program to use direct biological solutions.

Controller Mustafa Mond's real motivation is revealed when he confesses he had a chance to be sent to an island, where some freedom and individuality were allowed, but he chose instead the Controllership, preferring his power to control people to be artificially happy in a determined society.[42]

Question #2: How is this Brave New World to be achieved?

The Controllers engineer a stable society of happy citizens by harnessing the technologies of artificial reproduction, artificial wombs, genetic engineering, behavioral conditioning, and the euphoriant drug soma.[43] By controlling each person's biology, his life is predetermined to enjoy his work and social class and happiness is always available through consuming goods, playing sports, engaging in unlimited promiscuous sex, and submitting to the perfect pleasure-drug soma.

Soma offers artificial happiness via a mindless escape that dulls a person's sense of reality and makes him content with his lack of freedom. Controller Mustapha Mond promotes the beauty of soma saying, "Take a holiday from reality whenever you like, and come back without so much as a headache or a mythology."[44] He says with soma, "stability was practically assured," implying that the illusion of happiness was essential for the success of their stable society.[45] In *Brave New World*, gene editing technology was not yet advanced to genetically engineer the brain for happiness, but soma kept people from suffering by providing the illusion of happiness.

Question #3: What is the human cost of the Brave New World?

The Controllers were benevolent dictators who boasted of achieving an efficient, stable welfare state, consisting of five castes, no poverty, no crime, no war, a consumer economy, and most of all, a happy citizenry. However,

---

41 Huxley, *Brave New World*, 48.
42 Ibid., 226-228.
43 Ibid., 3-63.
44 Ibid., 54.
45 Ibid.

as Controller Mustapha Mond says, "One can't have something for nothing. Happiness has got to be paid for."[46]

In *Brave New World*, the currency of payment is the loss of human goods starting before birth. Embryos are genetically engineered and controlled from fertilization until birth and afterward undergo behavioral conditioning. All aspects of a person's life are predetermined, all for the good of society: intellect, personality, skills, and physical traits are assigned in accordance with his assigned caste.[47] People are deprived of their individuality, personal freedom, self-determination, and autonomy. They are conditioned to be loyal to the State, which takes precedence over the individual and any other relationship. Hence, babies are made, not born so there is no motherhood, no marriage, no home or child-rearing or family, and no love of God or others. Instant gratification through promiscuous sex is the substitute for love.[48] In *Brave New World* "every one belongs to every one else."[49]

The drug soma is the opiate of the people, keeping the citizenry content with their lack of freedom and providing an escape from their meaningless lives. Soma is dehumanizing because it dulls the intellect, sedates a person into contentment, flattens the emotions, and distracts a person from thinking. People are conditioned to hate solitude, which deprives them of reading, deep thought, and reflection. The Controllers knew that contemplation often leads a person to discover truth, goodness, and beauty in the world and ultimately to know God, all of which were forbidden.[50]

The Controllers conditioned the people to equate happiness with pleasurable feelings, so no one developed moral or intellectual virtues; for example, there was no need for courage, nobility, or heroism.[51] Finally, the cost of stability meant the banning of knowledge—of science, art, literature, and religion—because this kind of knowledge is incompatible with emotional ease and artificial happiness.[52]

---

46   Huxley, *Brave New World*, 228.
47   Ibid., 3-63.
48   Ibid.
49   Ibid., 45.
50   Ibid., 234-5.
51   Ibid., 220-1; 236-7.
52   Ibid., 225-240.

Walker Percy's The Thanatos Syndrome

Question #1: Why did the scientists undertake a utopian project?

In *The Thanatos Syndrome*, two scientists conspire to execute a social experiment to improve society by secretly adding heavy sodium to the water supply of the town of Feliciana. Their goal was to modify human brain chemistry by suppressing the prefrontal cortical neuron function of the townspeople. The scientists reasoned, much like the transhumanists, that "a segment of the human neocortex and of consciousness itself is not only an aberration of evolution but is also the scourge and curse of life on this earth, the source of wars, insanities, perversions— in short, those very pathologies which are peculiar to *Homo sapiens*."[53]

The scientists claim to be motivated by humanitarian goals, such as suppressing anti-social behavior, reducing violent crime, and curing pathologies that thwart human happiness, but nonetheless they were blind to the dehumanizing effects on their victims.[54] In reality, their real motivation was fame; they believed that their experiment was a scientific breakthrough, the beginning of a scientific revolution to end all revolutions.[55] The two scientists suffered from hubris and a false optimism about their power and ability to improve society.

Question 2: How is this utopia achieved?

The two scientists who collaborated to drug the town's drinking water based their project on new research that revealed a connection between heavy sodium and cortical neurons in the brain that suppress anti-social behavior. Their ambitious goal was to instantly improve the behavior of citizens in a community that was riddled with high crime, drug addiction, teenage pregnancies, and mental health problems by changing the townspeople's brain chemistry—without their consent.[56]

The scientists boast, "It's beautiful because it's so simple. All scientific breakthroughs are simple."[57] Scientist Bob Comeaux lamented that traditional methods of reforming society had failed, but their neurochemical solution had spectacular results, "such as reducing the suffering in the

---

53 Walker Percy, *The Thanatos Syndrome* (New York: Picador USA, 1987), 195.
54 Ibid., 21-2, 68-9.
55 Ibid., 60, 194-6.
56 Percy, *The Thanatos Syndrome*, 191-193.
57 Ibid., 196.

community and making criminals behave themselves."[58] David Pearce would undoubtedly agree about the beautiful simplicity of improving human behavior via scientific solutions.

Question #3: What is the human cost of this utopia?

By secretly introducing heavy sodium into the water supply of Feliciana, the two scientists not only violated the human rights of the townspeople, but the side effects of the chemical were horrific and dehumanizing.[59] The observable side effects were: animal-like unfocused vacancy, shedding of guilt, childlike speech and thinking, change in personality, bland flat tone, promiscuous animal sexuality, loss of context, and immediate computer-like recall of factual information. The scientists reasoned, from their utilitarian ethic, that the greater good of suppressing criminal and antisocial behavior in society as a whole outweighed the harm done to individuals.[60]

Transhumanism's Superhappiness Project

Question #1: Why do transhumanists undertake a utopian project?

Transhumanists argue that humanity has failed to achieve happiness. They assume that psychological hedonism is substantially true, meaning humans are psychologically constructed to desire and pursue pleasure.[61] "At present, [human beings] pursue the many faces of happiness avidly but with frighteningly irrational, and not infrequently murderous, levels of ineptitude."[62] The reason human beings cannot attain lasting happiness is the fault of Darwinian evolution. Our biochemical systems evolved to increase our chances of survival and reproduction, not to give us lasting happiness.[63] Therefore, manipulation of the external environment alone cannot achieve happiness.[64]

---

58   Percy, *The Thanatos Syndrome*, 347.
59   Ibid., 191-3, 21-2, 68-9.
60   Ibid., 346-7.
61   Stanford Encyclopedia of Philosophy, "Psychological Hedonism," https://plato.stanford.edu/entries/hedonism/#PsycHed (accessed August 22, 2020).
62   Pearce, *The Hedonistic Imperative*, Chapter 2, "The Psychology of Armchair Hedonism," HedWeb.com, https://www.hedweb.com/hedethic/hedon2.htm (accessed August 29, 2020).
63   Pearce, *The Abolitionist Project*, 1-2.
64   Pearce, *The Hedonistic Imperative*, Chapter 2, "Let's Get Rational," HedWeb.com, https://www.hedweb.com/hedethic/hedon2.htm (accessed August 30, 2020).

Armed with these assumptions, transhumanists conclude that the only reasonable solution to attain happiness is the direct biological route wherein the brain's hedonic set-point is reset by genetic engineering and neuropharmacology.[65] Pearce claims that the vision of paradise engineering "stems from a deep sense of compassion at the unimaginable scale and dreadful intensity of suffering in the world."[66] When asked in an interview if the transhumanist is motivated by religion, David Pearce responded, "I think it's hard to reconcile transhumanism and revealed religion. If we want to live in paradise, we will have to engineer it ourselves. If we want eternal life, then we'll need to rewrite our bug-ridden genetic code and become god-like . . . Sadly, only hi-tech solutions can ever eradicate suffering from the living world. Compassion alone is not enough."[67] Thus, underneath the deep sense of compassion belies their desire to have god-like control to re-create humanity in order to create god-like posthumans.

By exploring the fictional dystopias alongside transhumanism's vision of paradise, it is evident that the underlying motive for pursuing such a society is power. The speculative scientists of Laputa, the Controllers of *Brave New World*, the two scientists of Feliciana, and transhumanists like David Pearce, are all motivated by the power to control others using science and technology.

Question #2: How is this superhappiness utopia achieved?

Transhumanists claim their biological program for superhappiness is technically feasible, in principle, based on two assumptions. First, there is a neurobiological foundation to all emotional life and second, the continued trajectory of current developments in neuro-chemical drugs and gene therapies.[68] After all, Pearce writes, "An earthly paradise can be achieved only by the profane application of science."[69]

---

65   Pearce, *The Hedonistic Imperative*, Chapter 2, Section 2.7 "Why Be Negative," https://www.hedweb.com/hedethic/hedon2.htm (accessed August 31, 2020).

66   Ibid.

67   David Pearce, "Interview with Nick Bostrom and David Pearce," *Cronopis*, December 2007, https://www.hedweb.com/transhumanism/ (accessed September 1, 2020).

68   Pearce, *The Hedonistic Imperative*, Chapter 1, Section 1.0 "Sabotage at the Mill," Section 1.1 "The Biological Program," HedWeb.com, https://www.hedweb.com/hedethic/hedon1.htm (accessed September 15, 2020).

69   Ibid., Chapter 1, Section 1.1 "The Biological Program."

Transhumanism's plan to engineer happiness will progress in three stages, ranked in order of difficulty. The first stage begins with utopian designer drugs, which Pearce describes as long-acting, delayed action, non-neurotoxic mood-brighteners.[70] The strategy is to modify the meso (cortico-) limbic dopamine system, which means multiplying the number of mesolimbic dopamine and serotonin cells because they are the cells that call the shots.[71] Modifying this biochemical system is key, says Pearce, "If the [dopamine and serotonin cells] are not happy, the whole organism will be miserable as well until they've got their psychochemical fix."[72]

The second stage of the program is somatic gene therapy aimed at permanently restructuring the brain's reward pathways by disabling the countervailing inhibitory feedback processes.[73] Somatic gene therapy treats non-reproductive cells and therefore affects only the individual patient, not the patient's descendants. Therefore, in order to achieve the ambitious goal of abolishing suffering, transhumanists depend on the development of germline gene therapy, which is the next stage of their program.

In this third stage, germline gene editing will focus on early-stage embryonic cells, which ensures that genes are permanently corrected in all cells of the patient's body, making happiness a heritable trait. The mapping of the entire genome will presumably reveal which combinations of genes code for structures and proteins that depress mood; these will need to be taken out or repressed. The genes associated with hyperthymia, a mental state of feeling consistently happy, will be introduced, reduplicated, and expressed in progressively larger numbers of the population and their germlines.[74] Re-engineering the brain requires introducing more nerve cells, which enlarges the prefrontal cortex beyond the size of the birth canal. With the advent of artificial womb technology, there will be no constraints on brain size and it will then be feasible to control all the processes of fetal growth and enhancement from conception to birth.

Today, gene editing and artificial womb technologies for therapeutic uses are advancing rapidly and transhumanists are poised to use these same

---

70   Pearce, *The Hedonistic Imperative*, Chapter 1, Section 1.3 "The Civilising Neurotransmitter." HedWeb.com, https://www.hedweb.com/hedethic/hedon1.htm (accessed September 15, 2020).

71   Ibid., Chapter 1, Section 1.2 "Pumping Up The Volume."

72   Ibid., Chapter 2, Section 2.3 "Vacuous Desires?"

73   Ibid., Chapter 1, Section 1.5 "The Molecular Genetics Of Paradise."

74   Ibid., Chapter 3, Section 3.3 "Good Code Gets Better," HedWeb.com, https://www.hedweb.com/hedethic/hedon3.htm (accessed September 3, 2020).

technologies as stepping stones for their project of human enhancement.[75] When it comes to the ethics of superhappiness, David Pearce responds rhetorically, "If it's technically feasible, what's wrong with using biotechnology to get rid of mental pain altogether?"[76]

David Pearce's explanation of the superhappinesss project is reminiscent of Gulliver's account of the research projects at the grand academy of Lagado. Both David Pearce and the projectors at the academy are driven by their scientific materialism to pursue scientific solutions to all problems, forsaking all other traditional forms of wisdom and knowledge on the matter. It is interesting that a mistaken assumption of materialism leads both to such absurd pursuits, like genetically engineering superhappiness and extracting sunbeams out of cucumbers.

Even though transhumanists rarely compare paradise engineering to *Brave New World*, David Pearce does not object, in principle, to Huxley's idea of achieving utopia through neuropharmacology, gene editing, cloning, artificial wombs, and germline genetic engineering. Much like Controller Mustapha Mond, Pearce agrees that people are motivated by psychological hedonism and will overwhelmingly choose technologically engineered happiness over suffering. Pearce admits that Huxley's vision of technology is inadequate. For example, he says the pleasure drug soma is underwhelming and one-dimensional as a utopian euphoriant.[77] Pearce goes on to say that "Huxley does an effective hatchet-job on the very sort of "unnatural" hedonic engineering that most of us so urgently need."[78] Assuming that most people are alarmed by the dystopia in *Brave New World*, it is shocking that Pearce approves of Huxley's scientific utopia, in principle. Specifically, he agrees that technology should be used to secure happiness and get rid of mental pain, but thinks Huxley's envisioned technologies are woefully inadequate and primitive for achieving utopia.

David Pearce also shares common ground with the two scientists in *The Thanatos Syndrome* in three important respects. First, both promote pro-

---

75 Rana and Samples, *Humans 2.0:Scientific, Philosophical, and Theological Perspectives on Transhumanism* (Covina, CA: Reasons to Believe Press, 2019), 31-65; 239-56. For example, a therapeutic use of gene editing would be curing monogenetic disorders like Leber's congenital amaurosis. A therapeutic use of artificial womb technology would be to improve the outcome of premature births, extending the survival of infants born prior to 22 weeks.

76 Pearce, "Brave New World? A Defense of Paradise-Engineering," 1.

77 Ibid., 2.

78 Pearce, "Brave New World? A Defense of Paradise-Engineering," 2.

grams built on new high-risk research technology.[79] Second, the method of covertly adding heavy sodium to the water supply and the method of germline gene editing both violate the human rights and free will of their victims. Even more so for germline gene editing because it violates the rights of the patient's descendents. Any mistakes or unintended consequences will be generationally permanent. Lastly, all hold a utilitarian ethic, which means the end goal of abolishing suffering and securing global happiness justifies any disadvantage or harm done to individuals.

Question #3: What human goods are deprived in this utopia of superhappiness?

According to transhumanism's materialist philosophy, the human person is strictly physical and is defined by biology and genetics. Persons are not inherently valuable as rational, moral, free creatures made in the image of their Creator. I argue that the human cost of transhumanism's superhappiness utopia will degenerate into a dystopia. First of all, their philosophy of materialism, in principle, exacts a high human cost. That is to say, a strict materialist is deprived of an adequate account of the self-evident features of human persons, such as the enduring self, consciousness, free will, mind/soul, moral knowledge, rationality, inherent value, human dignity, equal rights, meaning, and purpose.[80]

Transhumanism's superhappiness project assumes this inadequate materialist view of the mind and human persons and carries it to extreme conclusions, specifically that suffering will be abolished and global happiness achieved by using biochemical and genetic engineering. If this superhappiness utopia is implemented, human well-being and flourishing will be diminished. In what follows, I explain seven human goods that will likely be deprived, resulting in a dystopian future comparable to the fictional dystopias examined.

1. Parental reproductive rights will be denied; reproduction will be state-controlled.

---

79   Fazale R.Rana and Kenneth R. Samples, *Humans 2.0*, 52-65. Gene editing using CRISPR-Cas9 faces many challenges: cutting and splicing genomes may introduce new cell mutations by mistake, hundreds of off-target sites with similar DNA sequences may be altered during the process, the Cas9 enzyme sometimes attacks the target site over and over until it is damaged, there is a lack of understanding about the relationships between information housed in the genome and biological traits and behaviors, and gene editing technology is now available to amateur biologists and biohackers, thanks to the DIY biological movement.

80   In chapters two through four, I argued that the philosophy of materialism is inadequate to account for the human mind and person.

Germline gene editing is the most radical feature of the transhumanist project. Transhumanists expect a reproductive revolution of "designer babies" where preimplantation genetic screening will be standard practice and artificial wombs will be available and recommended.[81] Pearce writes, "Future parents who decide, whether in deference to God or Nature, to decline gene-therapy for a child they know will likely grow up depressive, for example, may be open to accusations of child-abuse. Responsible parents, on the other hand, will want to get their kids the best happiness money can buy."[82]

Further, since Pearce believes transhumanists will succeed in conquering death with their superlongevity project, population control will become a necessity. He assumes the state will take control over reproduction because "decisions about reproduction cannot be left to the discretion of individual couples alone."[83] At this stage of the transhumanist project, the freedom *not* to enhance will be challenged and the state will be in charge of reproduction. Therefore, a human cost of superhappiness will be the decline of parental reproductive rights.

Pearce's eagerness to rely on state-controlled reproduction evokes C. S. Lewis's man-moulders of the new age who use prenatal conditioning to control human nature. "[They] will be armed with the powers of an omnicompetent state and an irresistible scientific technique: we shall get at last a race of conditioners who really can cut out all posterity in what shape they please."[84]

2. Enhanced children will have diminished agency, autonomy, and moral responsibility.

The enhanced children "made" as the result of the reproductive revolution will be objects of their parent's design, products of their parent's will, and later the products of the will of the state. These children will have a genetically enhanced hedonic set-point, which means they are engineered with an optimal temperament of patience, empathy, sense of humor, and optimism. Parents will be masters over their children's genome, usurping their children's right to autonomy. The enhanced children will presumably have the genetic basis for the "best life," but will have lost the proper stance

---

81   Pearce, *Hedonistic Imperative*, Chapter 1, Section 1.0 "Sabotage At The Mill"; Section 1.13 "The Growing Pleasures of Homunculi."
82   Ibid., Chapter 3, Section 3.3 "Good Code Gets Better."
83   Pearce, "Brave New World? A Defense of Paradise-Engineering," 14.
84   Lewis, *The Abolition of Man*, 60.

of the natural giftedness of life and the right to an open future.[85] As a result, they will experience diminished human agency, autonomy, and moral responsibility.

    3. The parent-child relationship will become disfigured.

Michael J. Sandel, in his book *The Case Against Perfection*, explores how reproductive genetic engineering threatens our human flourishing. Although Sandel agrees there will be an erosion of human freedom and moral responsibility for enhanced children, he argues these are lesser problems compared to the main problem—that is, reproductive engineering promotes in parents a desire for mastery and control over their children instead of accepting children as gifts.[86] The giftedness of life is threatened when children become objects of our design, products of our will, and instruments of our ambition. Parenthood is meant to teach us to be open to the unbidden and to restrain our impulse to control.[87] Reproductive engineering disfigures the relationship between the parent and child; most notably, according to Sandel, it deprives the parent of learning humility that "openness to the unbidden can cultivate."[88] Enhanced children will be deprived of the sense of parental unconditional love.[89] The children will likely not view their character and talents as gifts from God or nature, but feel overly responsible and indebted to their parents. Hence, Sandel argues that one of the main human costs will be the disfigurement of the parent-child relationship.

    4. Gene-editing is high-risk and mistakes will be irreversible and generational.

The project of targeted germline gene-editing is a high-risk technology, requiring a high degree of specificity and precision to identify, cut, splice, delete, and insert genes. This technology is prone to error and these mistakes are irreversible, wide-ranging, and generational.[90] Understanding this gives new meaning to the word if in Pearce's proviso "if we get things right . . . "[91] The Controllers in *Brave New World* resolved genetic mistakes by

---

85   Michael J. Sandel, *The Case Against Perfection: Ethics in the Age of Genetic Engineering* (Cambridge, Massachusetts: The Belknap Press of Harvard University Press, 2007), 8-9.

86   Sandel, *The Case Against Perfection*, 45-6.

87   Ibid., 45.

88   Ibid., 46.

89   Ibid., 49.

90   Rana and Samples, *Humans 2.0*, 52-65.

91   Pearce, "What is Transhumanism? The 3 Supers,"

sending unorthodox individuals to remote islands.⁹² It is unclear whether the transhumanist superhappiness engineers will be as benevolent in resolving genetic mistakes.

There are also risks from criminal bio-hackers and novice biologists who are not motivated to act justly. They will likely gain access to gene-editing technology and engineer dangerous super-viruses to warp and harm the human genome.⁹³ These criminal biohackers would seek to destroy the project of superhappiness. Transhumanists rarely mention the threat of evil-doers in any of their projects, largely because they have no solution to the depravity of the human condition.

5. Negative emotions valuable for human flourishing and well-being will be abolished.

Transhumanists promise to achieve long-term global happiness with future designer drugs and genetic engineering. Negative emotions, like anger, anxiety, sadness, depression, jealousy, guilt, shame, and fear will be abolished and positive emotions will be secured, like kindness, empathy, patience, and pleasure. According to Pearce's hedonistic view of happiness, only positive feelings are good and negative feelings are bad for a person's well-being. This view of happiness is shallow and fails to account for the complexity and depth of well-being, namely that negative emotions are valuable for true happiness.

Philosophers Julien Deonna and Fabrice Teroni argue in their essay "Feel Bad, Live Well! The Value of Negative Emotions for Well-being" that negative emotions, like anger, guilt, shame, and embarrassment, are fundamentally valuable for well-being.⁹⁴ Recent research on the role that emotions play in well-being has demonstrated that negative emotions, even emotions like contempt, anxiety, and disgust are intentional states that provide information to us about the world and ourselves and are critical in leading a good life.⁹⁵

---

92   Huxley, *Brave New World*, 226-7-9.

93   Alexandra Ossola, "You Could Soon Use CRISPR to Biohack in Your Own Home," *Popular Science*, November 9, 2015, https://www.popsci.com/you-could-soon-become-biohacker-at-home-using-crispr/ (accessed September 1, 2020).

94   Julien Deonna and Fabrice Teroni, "Feel Bad, Live Well! The Value of Negative Emotions for Well-being," University of Geneva Philosophy Department, 2020, https://www.unige.ch/lettres/philo/recherche/research-groups/thumos/projects/feel-bad-live-well-value-negative-emotions-well-being/ (accessed September 13, 2020).

95   Ibid., 2.

Deonna and Teroni investigate how negative emotions can provide evaluative knowledge and understanding about the world. For example, our moral anger can draw our attention to genuine injustices and how we should respond.[96] They also illustrate how negative emotions can provide self-knowledge and self-understanding. For example, by experiencing guilt I am provided with a signal that I have done something wrong. This can initiate self-reflection about my integrity and possibly self-reform.[97]

It is reasonable to expect that, if the transhumanists succeed in abolishing negative emotions, people will be deprived of valuable evaluative knowledge and understanding about the world and themselves that is necessary for happiness and well-being.

Robert Nozick makes a similar point in *Anarchy, State, and Utopia* with his thought experiment called the Experience Machine.[98] He argues that there is more that matters to us than our feelings. Even if we had the option to plug into an Experience Machine that would give us any experience we desired, we would likely realize that what matters more is that we want to do certain things, not just have an experience of doing them. We want to be a certain sort of person, not just have an experience of being that person.[99] What we are is important to us. Nozick concludes by saying, "Perhaps what we desire is to live (an active verb) ourselves, in contact with reality. (And this, machines cannot do for us.)"[100] If what we are is important, then transhumanism's paradise engineers cannot genetically engineer happiness for us. By imagining the kind of artificial happiness offered to us by David Pearce, we realize, like Nozick, that living our lives in contact with reality matters more.

6. Art and literary culture will become obsolete.

After our human brains are enriched with happiness, Pearce expects that the art and literature we once enjoyed in our unenhanced state will seem perverted. Much like Mustapha Mond's assessment of the cost of happiness, Pearce expects "the classical literary canon may fall into obscurity."[101] He as-

---

96 Julien Deonna and Fabrice Teroni, "Feel Bad, Live Well! The Value of Negative Emotions for Well-being," University of Geneva Philosophy Department, 2020, 14-15, https://www.unige.ch/lettres/philo/recherche/research-groups/thumos/projects/feel-bad-live-well-value-negative-emotions-well-being/ (accessed September 13, 2020)

97 Ibid., 16-18.

98 Robert Nozick, *Anarchy, State, and Utopia* (New York: Basic Books, 1974), 42-45.

99 Ibid., 43.

100 Ibid., 45.

101 Pearce, "Brave New World? A Defense of Paradise-Engineering," 21-22.

sumes we will not "be edified by the cultural artifacts of a bygone era."[102] Anticipating that our moral sense will change if suffering is abolished, Pearce argues that "morality in the contemporary sense may no longer be needed."[103]

If philosophers Deonna and Teroni are right about the human cost of abolishing negative emotions, Pearce's expectation that art and literature will become obsolete seems plausible. Consider these excerpts from Naomi Nye's poem "Kindness,"

>Before you know kindness as the deepest thing inside,
>You must know sorrow as the other deepest thing.
>You must wake up with sorrow.
>You must speak to it till your voice
>Catches the thread of all sorrows
>And you see the size of the cloth.
>
>Then it is only kindness that makes sense anymore,
>Only kindness that ties your shoes
>And sends you out into the day to mail letters and purchase bread,
>Only kindness that raises its head
>From the crowd of the world to say
>It is I you have been looking for,
>And then goes with you everywhere
>Like a shadow or a friend.[104]

Imagine that you are an enhanced "superhappy" person, having never felt great sorrow or loss. Read the lines of the poem again. It is easy now to see how the meaning of kindness is lost as reflected in this poem, along with the meaning of much of the literary canon.

7. The superhappiness project will ultimately become obsolete.

We cannot forget that the ultimate goal of transhumanism is to get rid of human biology altogether by uploading our minds to computers. If, on materialism, our emotional and mental states are determined solely by our neurobiology, then the superhappiness project will become obsolete in the last phase of transhumanism. This exposes the superhappiness project for what it is, a flimsy bridge until the last phase of mind-uploading can be de-

---

102 Pearce, "Brave New World? A Defense of Paradise-Engineering," 21-22.
103 Pearce, "A Brave New World? A Defense of Paradise-Engineering," 9.
104 Naomi Nye, "Kindness," Poets.org, https://poets.org/poem/kindness (accessed September 13, 2020).

veloped and perfected.[105] Transhumanists realize that the project of super-longevity will never succeed unless an artificial happiness is engineered to pacify those who are ensnared in the triple 'S' dystopian civilization.

Imagining the human cost of transhumanism's superhappiness project is sobering because it reveals how their promised utopia could easily become a dystopian reality. If human persons are more than physics and chemistry, and if happiness is more than genetically-controlled biochemistry and neurons firing in the brain, then transhumanism's solution for securing superhappiness with genetic engineering and neuropharmacology is inadequate and dehumanizing. Moreover, the human goods deprived as a result of superhappiness engineering are essential to human flourishing.

Based on my comparative critique using dystopian literature, it is reasonable to oppose transhumanism's superhappinesss project because of the foreseeable human cost. But more importantly, by recognizing that transhumanism is based on a materialist philosophy of human persons, the transhumanist is disqualified from claiming a complete understanding of human nature and therefore, is precluded from claiming their project will achieve superhappiness. Transhumanism's project of superhappiness serves as a *reductio ad absurdum* argument against the materialist view of human persons by demonstrating how reductive methods of genetic engineering to achieve superhappiness lead to dangerous and extreme absurdities when carried to their logical conclusions.

Human Happiness: An Alternative Theory

A Brief History of a Philosophical Mistake

Mortimer Adler argues that modern thinkers made a serious philosophical mistake when they began conceiving of human happiness as a subjective psychological state of *feeling good* instead of an objective ethical state of *being good*.[106] Adler traces this major shift in the understanding of happiness back to the eighteenth century Enlightenment utilitarians.[107] Jeremy Bentham (1748-1832) was one of the first to propose the principle of utility, "the greatest happiness for the greatest number," as a powerful tool to judge the

---

105 I argued in chapters 2, 3, and 4, that mind-uploading is metaphysically impossible.

106 Mortimer Adler, *Ten Philosophical Mistakes* (New York: Simon & Schuster Inc., Touchstone Edition, 1985), 131-2.

107 Ibid., 140-44.

usefulness of every action.[108] He argued that sensations of pleasure and pain determine how we act in the world and represent the standards of right and wrong. Therefore, happiness became simply the balance of pleasure over pain.[109] Many Enlightenment thinkers, such as Claude-Adrien Helvetius, declared the eighteenth century the "century of happiness," largely because they thought that the key obstacles to happiness were declining, namely religious superstition, classical beliefs, and the struggle for existence.[110]

Historian Darrin McMahon, in his book *Happiness: A History*, also traces the history of this shift, like Adler, to the eighteenth century, when philosophers separated happiness from the virtuous life. Instead of a reward for living well, happiness was seen as a natural human endowment, a self-evident truth, which all human beings could attain in this life.[111] More and more, happiness was seen as a natural right. McMahon characterizes the progression in human expectations this way: "We can be happy, we will be happy, we should be happy. We have a right to happiness."[112]

On the other hand, the classical and Judeo-Christian view of happiness was linked to virtue, right action, and goodness. The flourishing life requires self-control, commitment, reason, judgment, and is often painful.[113] Feeling good is not the standard measure of being good. McMahon follows the development of the Enlightenment view of happiness, defined as *feeling* good, forward to the present age of neuroscience, genetics, and biotechnology.[114] He cites a number of happiness studies that conclude that moods and feelings of well-being are primarily a function of the evolutionary development of human genetics and brain chemistry.[115] The focus on good feelings coupled with the idea that it might be possible to manipulate our genes and biochemistry to enhance happiness seems to be propelling us toward the

---

108 Darrin M. McMahon, *Happiness: A History* (New York: Grove Press, 2006), 212-3

109 Ibid., 212-3, 222, 345-53 Other philosophers and scientists of the Enlightenment used this phrase in various forms: Frances Hutcheson, Gottfried Wilhelm von Leibniz, Claude-Adrien Helvetius, Julien Offray de la Mettrie, and John Stuart Mill.

110 Ibid., 205, 216-7.

111 Ibid., 13, 247.

112 Ibid., xii.

113 Ibid., 233.

114 Ibid., 253-480.

115 Ibid., 472-4. Like transhumanist David Pearce, psychologists propose that happiness is less dependent on circumstances and more dependent on what psychologists call the hedonic setpoint.

transhumanist project of superhappiness, the very world that Aldous Huxley once feared.[116]

My critique of the transhumanist project of superhappiness illustrates the value of imagining Huxley's dystopia. A common reaction to transhumanism's superhappiness resembles the response of John the Savage in *Brave New World*, who witnesses the dehumanizing effects of engineered "happiness" and defiantly claims his "right to be unhappy."[117] He knows there is more to life than good feelings: "I don't want comfort. I want God, I want poetry, I want real danger, I want freedom, I want goodness. I want sin."[118] The price is too high for a shallow happiness based only on feeling good. I suggest turning away from transhumanism's road to shallow happiness and returning to the ancient road that leads to the life of virtue and human flourishing.

A Virtue-Based Theory of Happiness

In ancient Athens, Socrates (c.470-399 BC) and Plato (c.428 -348 BC) began to rationally inquire about the definition, pursuit, and attainment of human happiness, or in Greek, *eudaimonia*, which means complete well-being or human flourishing.[119] Socrates believed that "the unexamined life is not worth living" and he spent his life questioning his own conventional beliefs and those of his fellow citizens, including their beliefs about happiness.[120] Socrates and Plato rejected the previous conceptions of happiness that were linked to hedonism, pleasure, power, riches, fame, health, and familial love.[121] They concluded that human happiness is chiefly a function of virtue, where virtues are understood as human excellences

---

116   Darrin M. McMahon, *Happiness: A History* (New York: Grove Press, 2006), 475.
117   Huxley, *Brave New World*, 240.
118   Ibid.
119   Plato, *Phaedrus, Symposium, The Republic Book 10*, in Mortimer Adler, editor, *Great Books of the Western World*, Volume 6 (Chicago: Encyclopedia Britannica, 1990), 124-129, 164-165, 437-441.
120   Plato, *Apology*, in Mortimer Adler, editor, *Great Books of the Western World*, Volume 6, 210, 38a.
121   Plato, *Philebus*, in Mortimer Adler, editor, *The Great Books of the Western World, Volume 6* Chicago: Encyclopedia Britannica, 1990), 609-639.

that define the good man and the good life.¹²² The virtues serve as the means to the ultimate end—happiness.¹²³

Aristotle (385-325 BC) formulated a theory of happiness grounded in the central elements found in Socrates and Plato. First, he agreed that happiness is the ultimate human good, "It is that for the sake of which everything else is done."¹²⁴ Second, he affirmed that human happiness is primarily a function of virtue; it is the moral excellence of a whole life well lived.¹²⁵ "Happiness is the activity of the soul in accordance with the best virtue in a complete life."¹²⁶ Aristotle saw virtue, not merely as a passive state or possession, but rather as an activity practiced throughout a lifetime.¹²⁷ Aristotle's point of departure from Socrates and Plato is his placement of happiness within his overall teleological metaphysics.

Aristotle asserts that everything in nature has an internal principle of change and a telos, and those ends benefit the natural thing itself.¹²⁸ Thus, human beings have a telos, a purpose to fulfill. The general principle is that different kinds of things, whether vegetative, animal, or human, are perfected by different things and thus, each kind of thing has individual virtues.¹²⁹

Aristotle identified rationality as the distinguishing feature of human beings.¹³⁰ The exercise of reason is essential for happiness because by it we know and choose how we ought to live; specifically, reason gives us the capacity to judge between needs and wants and between real and apparent goods. Therefore, knowledge and virtue are connected in this way: a virtuous person combines theoretical knowledge and practical knowledge to particular situations. The result is an action done with the right motive, at the right time, and in the right way. Humans use their rational faculty to modify their desires and deliberate about the best means to achieve their ends.

---

122   Plato, *Apology*, 206, 30a.
123   Mortimer Adler, "Virtue and Vice: Introduction," *The Great Books of the Western World,* The Syntopicon II (Chicago: Encyclopedia Britannica, 1990), 776.
124   Aristotle, *Nicomachean Ethics*, in Mortimer Adler, editor, *Great Books of the Western World, Volume 8* (Chicago: Encyclopedia Britannica, 1990), 1097a, 1097b.
125   Ibid., 1098a.
126   Ibid., 343, 1098a,15-20.
127   Ibid., 1099a.
128   Monte Ransome Johnson, *Aristotle on Teleology* (Oxford: Oxford University Press, 2005), 6.
129   Ibid., 222.
130   Aristotle, *Nicomachean Ethics*, 343, 1098a.

Theoretical and practical knowledge correspond to the two parts of the rational soul: the contemplative (theoretical) intellect aims at truth and the practical intellect aims at right action. These, in turn, relate to the two types of virtues, intellectual (e.g., wisdom and understanding) and moral (e.g., courage, temperance, justice, and liberality).[131] Aristotle ranked the activity of the intellect in contemplation as the most excellent virtue contributing to happiness because it is the most continuous, divine-like, and self-sufficient.[132] He maintained that moral virtues, ranking second, are acquired by habituation. We do not possess them by nature, yet every person has the capacity for moral virtue.[133] Aristotle believed education and training are central to the virtuous life, which is necessary for happiness. However, he acknowledged that some possess a natural giftedness toward happiness, but still need education and training to develop their capacities.[134]

In Aristotle's rational account of happiness, the virtues are necessary, but not sufficient. Other goods are required for complete happiness: friends, moderate wealth, good birth, and other external blessings of good fortune.[135] Complete happiness, for Aristotle, is the philosopher's intellectual activity of god-like contemplation of truth and the Divine.[136] This contemplative mode of life is sustained and made possible by the stable character of the morally virtuous life.[137]

Saint Thomas Aquinas (1225-1274) refined Aristotle's theory of happiness in light of Christian theology by adding the theological virtues of faith, hope, and charity.[138] These virtues transcend man's natural capacities and therefore, are gifts of God's grace to direct man to Himself.[139] Aquinas reasoned that earthly happiness is imperfect and falls short of true happiness.

> For this present life is subject to many unavoidable evils: to ignorance on the part of the intellect, to disordered af-

---

131   Aristotle, *Nicomachean Ethics*, 1103a.
132   Ibid., 1177a,b.
133   Ibid., 1103a,b.
134   Ibid., 345, 1099b10-15.
135   Ibid., 344-345, 1099b5. For example, women cannot be happy to the same degree as men and natural slaves have no capacity for happiness at all.
136   Ibid., 432-433, 1177b15-30, 1178a1-5.
137   Ibid., 432, 1177b26-1178a22.
138   Thomas Aquinas, *Summa Theologica*, Mortimer Adler, editor, *Great Books of the Western World*, Volume 18 (Chicago: Encyclopedia Britannica, 1990), 44, 60-64.
139   Ibid., 60.

fection on the part of the appetite, and to many penalties on the part of the body... Likewise neither can the desire for good be satiated in this life. For man naturally desires the good which he has to be abiding. Now the goods of the present life pass away, since life itself passes away, which we naturally desire to have, and would wish to hold abidingly, for man naturally shrinks from death.[140]

Aquinas argues that true happiness is ultimately found in knowing God and in beholding the vision of God's essence in the afterlife.[141] Aquinas explains that the telos of human nature toward virtue is diminished by the effects of the fall. We need divine grace to heal our corrupted human nature.[142] Therefore, for Aquinas, we require God's grace to lead a good life on earth and to experience a life of eternal blessedness.

Conclusion: A Virtue-based Theory of Happiness

Transhumanism's hedonistic project of superhappiness is the logical progression and outcome of the Enlightenment utilitarian philosophical mistake. Transhumanists make *feeling* good the central focus of achieving superhappiness. Both Aristotle and Aquinas understood that pleasure is not the supreme good because it is the result of a supreme good, the virtuous life.[143] C. S. Lewis wrote, "Every preference of a small good to a great, or a partial good to a total good, involves the loss of the small or partial good for which the sacrifice was made... You can't get second things by putting them first; you can get second things only by putting first things first."[144] Lewis calls this a universal law. Aristotle and Aquinas understand this law as pointing to the telos of human nature. *Feeling* good is a second thing that can only be realized by putting first things first, which is *being good*. The happy life is the virtuous life.

---

140   Thomas Aquinas, *Summa Theologica*, Mortimer Adler, editor, *Great Books of the Western World*, Volume 17 (Chicago: Encyclopedia Britannica, 1990), 638.

141   Ibid., 629.

142   Thomas Aquinas, *Summa Theologica*, Mortimer Adler, editor, *Great Books of the Western World, Volume 18* (Chicago: Encyclopedia Britannica, 1990), 179-180.

143   Thomas Aquinas, *Summa Theologica*, Mortimer Adler, editor, *Great Books of the Western World, Volume 17*, 620; Aristotle, *Nicomachean Ethics*, Book 10, 430-431.

144   C. S. Lewis, "First and Second Things," in Walter Hooper, editor, *God in the Dock: Essays on Theology and Ethics* (Grand Rapids, Michigan: William B. Eerdmans Publishing Company, 1970), 280.

Chapter Seven

Conclusion

"The question of what humanity is to be is going to be decided in the next sixty years."[1]

Lord Feverstone

Summary of Thesis

THE PHILOSOPHICAL FOUNDATION of transhumanism is materialism, which means transhumanists are committed to a strictly physical story about reality and how things came to be. It is from this mistaken philosophy that transhumanists boldly pursue their projects of superintelligence, superlongevity, and superhappiness. The ultimate aim of the transhumanist is to become posthuman by ridding himself of his biology in order to attain cybernetic immortality through uploading his mind to a computer.

Transhumanism's techno-utopian project reminds me of the meme that highlights the difference between science and the humanities: "SCIENCE can tell you how to clone a Tyrannosaurus Rex; HUMANITIES can tell you why this might be a bad idea."[2] If I presented this book as a meme, it would say: "Transhumanists want to tell you how to become a posthuman; I want

---

1   C. S. Lewis, *That Hideous Strength: A Modern Fairy-Tale for Grown-ups* (New York: Scribner, 1945), 39.
2   Illuminating Your World website, https://www.google.com/search?rlz=1C5CHFA_enUS833US834&sxsrf=ALeKk0ozZ0yh7EUcuRv-JmoTHj-uAwAqmBw:1602619607995&source=univ&tbm=isch&q=illuminating+your+world+memes&sa=X&ved=2ahUKEwis48ajr7LsAhUEPqoKHa1x-AIwQjJkEegQIChAB&biw=1431&bih=742#imgrc=PEK9900rNIU-GM&imgdii=E3fbdHSEAiy_qM (accessed October 12, 2020).

to tell you why this is not only a bad idea, but metaphysically impossible." My thesis is that transhumanism's proposed triple 'S' techno-utopian projects are metaphysically impossible because they are founded on a flawed and inadequate materialist philosophy of mind and human persons and are undesirable because of the human goods lost if implemented.

Many modern thinkers for the last four hundred years have made a philosophical mistake by embracing ontological materialism. Transhumanism is the culmination of a commitment to carry to completion the application of the materialistic metaphysical picture of reality to humanity, specifically to remake humans into posthumans. The failure of the materialist philosophy of transhumanism should cause its proponents to reconsider the Aristotelian metaphysical picture of reality, which offers essentialism, teleology, and a virtue-based view of human flourishing.[3]

As C. S. Lewis said: "Progress means getting nearer to the place you want to be. And if you have taken a wrong turn, then to go forward does not get you any nearer. If you are on the wrong road, progress means doing an about-turn and walking back to the right road; and in that case the man who turns back soonest is the most progressive man."[4] I provide the reader with good reasons to turn back from transhumanism and return to the ancient road that leads to human flourishing. What follows is a summary of my arguments from each chapter that support my thesis.

Summary of Arguments

In chapter one, I investigate the key historical figures that influence transhumanism, showing how contemporary transhumanism has arrived in the present from its history. Transhumanism's history reveals that it is firmly rooted in ideas from ancient literature, the Renaissance, the Enlightenment, and the early twentieth century eugenics movement. Its core tenets amplify three historical ideas: a desire to control nature and the human condition, a mechanistic and materialist picture of the world, and a technological view of progress. The desire to control nature has the oldest pedigree; however, all three central tenets of transhumanism can be traced back to Francis Bacon in the early seventeenth century. Bacon is

---

3   Metaphysics is the science of the first principles of being, the fundamental issues in ontology, such as causation, substance, essence, modality, identity, persistence, and teleology.

4   C. S. Lewis, *Mere Christianity* (New York: HarperCollins Publishers, 1952), 28-29.

seen as a precursor to transhumanism and proponents see him as a pivotal figure in their ideological history.

Bacon and other early modern philosophers and scientists replaced classical Aristotelian metaphysics with what they called the mechanical philosophy. This is the condensed story, according to Ed Feser:

> After rejecting Aristotelian formal and final causes in the natural world, the early moderns recognized only material and efficient causes (not the Aristotelian kind). Matter, at bottom, was unobserved particles having mathematically quantifiable features. Cause and effect relations had nothing to do with teleology, but merely related to regularities depicted in the laws of nature. Therefore, material reality is simply physical particles interacting according to meaningless laws of nature. There is ultimately nothing over and above the particles of which they are made. The mechanical philosophy was aimed at increasing human utility and power through technology, whereas classical philosophy was aimed at wisdom and understanding.[5]

For the ensuing four hundred years, philosophers and scientists have continued down the mechanistic/materialist path, attempting to give everything a purely materialistic explanation in order to complete the scientific image of the world. From Descartes, Locke, Hume, and going forward, most anything that was not material was explained as a projection of the mind. As Ed Feser says, "Everything that doesn't fit the mechanistic model has been swept under the rug of the mind."[6]

Accordingly, contemporary philosophers and scientists have been left with a gigantic dirt pile under the rug (mind), so to speak. No materialist attempt to explain the human mind has been successful because mental states, such as consciousness, intentionality, rationality, and creativity, cannot be explained strictly in terms of physical processes, properties, and causes. This ideological history of transhumanism set the stage for my critique of its materialist philosophy, which undergirds the projects of superintelligence, superlongevity, and superhappiness.

---

5   Edward Feser, *The Last Superstition: A Refutation of the New Atheism* (South Bend, Indiana: St. Augustine's Press, 2008), 175- 179.
6   Ibid., 192-3.

In chapter two, I investigated the transhumanist goal of achieving AGI, meaning AI with human level intelligence, which is the crucial step in transhumanism's anticipation of a Superintelligence and after that, the Singularity event.[7] Transhumanists are wholly committed to attaining AGI, as evidenced by their numerous think tanks and research labs that are focused entirely on its realization.[8] Transhumanists predict the Singularity event is near because they believe the achievement of AGI is imminent. For this reason, I began my investigation of transhumanism by critiquing the philosophy of AGI. I argue that belief in the Singularity is not reasonable based on the metaphysical impossibility of AGI. I critique the philosophy of AGI in relation to its major theories: the principle of causal closure, functionalism, and computationalism. My argument is:

1. If AGI is metaphysically possible, then the materialist philosophy of mind is possible.
2. The materialist philosophy of mind is false and self-defeating.
3. Therefore, AGI is metaphysically impossible.[9]

The term 'materialism' has been used in diverse ways in philosophy; however, traditionally in philosophy of mind it represents a mechanistic view, meaning that mental states are either dependent on or reduced to physical states. In other words, materialism entails that there is no aspect

---

7   The Singularity event is generally defined as the future period during which the pace of technological change will be so rapid, its impact so deep, that human life will be irreversibly transformed.

8   "A Timeline of Transhumanism," *The Verge*, https://www.theverge.com/a/transhumanism-2015/history-of-transhumanism (accessed March 29, 2020). Transhumanist AGI research centers include: Singularity University, Machine Intelligence Research Institute, Novamente, Center for Applied Rationality, Thiel Fellowship, Global Brain Institute, OpenCogBot, and The Future of Life Institute.

9   J. P. Moreland & William Lane Craig, *Philosophical Foundations for a Christian Worldview*, (Downers Grove, Illinois: IVP Academic, 2003), 50, 257, 497, and 503. There are no clear criteria which can be applied mechanically to determine whether a proposition is metaphysically possible/impossible. I take metaphysical possibility to mean broad logical possibility in terms of actualizability. Metaphysical possibility is not the same as conceivability, which means you can imagine it can occur. Rather, for something to be a real possibility, there has to be an actual potential or ability for it to occur.

of the mind that cannot be ultimately explained by physical forces.[10] Philosopher Jerry Fodor (1935-2017) explains the materialist view succinctly: "Physics fixes all the facts in the world. Physics determines chemistry; chemistry determines biology; biology determines brain science; and brain science determines the mental life."[11]

The proponents of AGI hold that "the appropriately programmed computer really is a mind in the sense that computers, given the right programs, can literally be said to understand and have cognitive states."[12] I establish the first premise of my argument by explaining how AGI is predicated on three materialist philosophies: the causal closure principle, the functionalist philosophy of mind, and the computational theory of mind. If AGI is achieved, then materialist philosophy of mind is possible (since the actual proves the possible). What follows is a summary of my critique of the three philosophies, which establish the second premise of my argument, that the materialist philosophy of mind is false and self-defeating.

The principle of causal closure is the major premise in the argument for materialism. In fact, it is presented as a universal principle "fully established by empirical research," yet physics lacks the completeness that is needed for such a claim. The thesis assumes the existence of a successful, completed, general reductionist theory that fully accounts for our conscious mental states. To establish causal closure, "the physicalist would still have to demonstrate, step by step, that all causal roles which our explanations confer to our conscious states, do in fact belong to something physical (or do not exist)."[13] This work is yet to be done. My critiques demonstrate that the principle of causal closure should instead be consid-

---

10   Victor Reppert, "The Argument from Reason," in William Lane Craig and J. P. Moreland, editors, *The Blackwell Companion to Natural Theology*, (West Sussex, UK: John Wiley & Sons Ltd, 2009), 344-6.

11   Jerry Fodor, "Look!" *London Review of Books*, Vol. 20 No. 21 (October 29, 1998): 2. https://www.lrb.co.uk/v20/n21/jerry-fodor/look, (accessed Feb. 20, 2020).

12   Howard E. Gardner, *The Mind's New Science: A History of the Cognitive Revolution* (United States: Basic Books, 1985) 140. Weak AI holds that "the programmed computer simulates human intelligence in a specific domain with restricted applicability."

13   Carlo Gabbani, "The Causal Closure of What? An Epistemological Critique of the Principle of Causal Closure," (January 2013), 157, *ResearchGate*, https://www.researchgate.net/publication/280562788_The_Causal_Closure_of_What_An_Epistemological_Critique_of_the_Principle_of_Causal_Closure (accessed April 13, 2020).

ered a research hypothesis in the case for materialism and not a decisive universal principle and major premise of the argument.

Next, I argue that the functionalist philosophy of mind does not account for the fundamental and conspicuous feature of internal rational thought processes, namely consciousness. I incorporate the philosophical arguments of Thomas Nagel, David Chalmers, Saul Kripke, Immanuel Kant, and John Searle to demonstrate that functionalism is false and self-defeating. I conclude that transhumanism's predictions of conscious machines will never be realized because it is based on the functionalist philosophy of mind, which offers no account of the fundamental feature of internal thought processes, namely consciousness.

Lastly, I argue that the computational theory of mind is false. This theory is at the heart of AGI; it is referred to as the Basic Model and is the core doctrine of computer science. The general idea is that thinking and computing are the same thing. If the internal processes of a computer are equivalent to human mental processes, then the machine can be understood to have a mind.

My line of argument against the computational theory of mind is twofold. First, human thinking operates as a semiotic (sign-using) system. Second, computers function as physical symbol systems, not as semiotic (sign-using) systems. Therefore, thinking is not computing and computers are not thinking things. While computers function causally on the basis of symbols, even to the extent of simulating human behavior in their outputs, they do not qualify as semiotic, sign-using, systems. Therefore, machines do not possess minds and the Basic Model that equates thinking and computing is false.

For transhumanists whose goal is to build a machine to be a person, these three flawed materialistic philosophies of mind fuel a belief that cannot be actualized. I argue that machines will not become conscious beings with minds and therefore, AGI is metaphysically impossible.

In spite of the arguments posed against AGI, transhumanists still predict the overwhelming success of AGI, claiming that computers and robots will soon exceed human persons in virtually all domains, including creativity.[14] In chapter three, I argue that creativity is the unique human advantage, one

---

14   See the following books that promote AGI: Hans Moravec, *Robot: Mere Machine to Transcendent Mind* (New York: Oxford University Press, 1999); John Pollock, *How To Build a Person: A Prolegomenon* (Cambridge, Massachusetts: The MIT Press, 1989); Ray Kurzweil, *How to Create a Mind: The Secret Of Human Thought Revealed* (New York: Penguin Books, 2012).

that machines will never have. I provide evidence for this fact by demonstrating that literary creativity is the sole province of humans.

Selmer Bringsjord, director of the Rensselaer AI and Reasoning (RAIR) Laboratory at Rensselaer Polytechnic Institute in New York, set out with his team to answer the creativity question by designing a computer program that generates original short stories; they named their artificial literary agent BRUTUS1.[15] The RAIR team's attempt to build an artificial author exposed two conscious mental states that are required for literary creativity, but cannot be reduced to computation: the experience of TEMIs and imagining the points of view of literary characters. Both of these mental states require conscious introspection, meaning the author represents the experiences to himself, which BRUTUS1 cannot do. To explain and defend my conclusion, I turn to the work of philosophers Gottfried Leibniz, Frank Jackson, Thomas Nagel, and John Searle.

I argue that BRUTUS1 does not possess genuine literary creativity, which illustrates that human creativity is a recalcitrant obstacle for achieving AGI. But equally important, since BRUTUS1 and other machines will increasingly appear to be creative, I offer the Lovelace Test as the best way to judge machine creativity. In essence, to pass the Lovelace Test, AGI researchers must create a machine that "breaks the bounds of mindless symbol manipulation to think for itself."[16]

In chapter four, I critique three distinctive features of transhumanism's metaphysics of the human person: an evolving human nature, a patternist view of personal identity, and a techno-gnostic view of embodiment. I demonstrate that their materialist, mechanistic, reductionist metaphysics of the human person cannot adequately account for the existence of persons, enduring identity, ethics, values, duties, individual autonomy, liberty, or rights. Even if we grant their materialist view can somehow account for these things, none will survive the proposed trajectory of enhancements. Since their philosophy offers an inadequate understanding

---

15   Bringsjord and Ferricci, *What Robots Can and Can't Be*, preface. BRUTUS is a system architecture for story generation. BRUTUS1 is the initial implementation of this architecture, with future versions expected.

16   Bringsjord, Bello, and Ferrucci, "Creativity, the Turing Test, and the (Better) Lovelace Test," 10. The following are examples of AGI computers attempting to pass the Lovelace Test: a screenplay written using AGI methods https://www.youtube.com/watch?v=LY7x2Ihqjmc&t=194s and a song composed using AGI methods https://www.youtube.com/watch?v=lcGYEXJqun8 (accessed April 15, 2020).

of the human person, there is no justification that their proposed trajectory of enhancements to transform humans into posthumans will succeed. More importantly, if attempted, such a pursuit will not be good for human flourishing.

I turn to literature in chapters five and six to extend my critique of transhumanism. C. S. Lewis argues that when philosophical arguments are "dipped in story," they come back to us powerfully and more clearly.[17] Taking Lewis's approach, I provide a Tolkienian critique of transhumanism's project of superlongevity in chapter five. Superlongevity is the term transhumanists use to describe their aim to overcome aging and death through cybernetic immortality, or uploading a person's brain capacity and consciousness onto a computer.[18] I compare the powers of emerging technologies that enable superlongevity with the Rings of Power in Middle Earth, and then liken transhumanists to the Númenóreans and the Nazgûl.

I argue that the project to merge human beings with technology to achieve artificial superlongevity in this world is harmful for several reasons. To choose transhumanism's superlongevity would be to mistake longevity in this world for true immortality that transcends this world. Radical life extension through technological enhancements and mind-uploading would be unnatural and dehumanizing, resulting in the loss of personhood, identity, individuality, embodiment, and free will. Finally, the effect of a Superintelligence on humans would likely result in complete domination and servitude, not unlike that demanded by Sauron. The unnatural existence that transhumanism promotes is actually a fate worse than death. The pursuit of immortality in this world, as Tolkien says, is "a supreme folly and wickedness."[19]

In Chapter six, I critique the transhumanist project of superhappiness through the lens of the following dystopian works of literature: Jonathan Swift's *Gulliver's Travels*, Aldous Huxley's *Brave New World*, and Walker Percy's *The Thanatos Syndrome*. As materialists, transhumanists hold that

---

17   C. S. Lewis, edited by Walter Hooper, *C. S. Lewis on Stories and Other Literature* (New York: First Harvest/HBJ edition, 1982), 90.

18   Superlongevity assumes a materialist philosophy of mind and human persons. I presented philosophical arguments in chapters two through four against materialism, concluding that achieving AGI is metaphysically impossible and transhumanism's metaphysics of human persons cannot account for the existence of persons or enduring personal identity through technological enhancements and mind uploading.

19   Carpenter, *Letters*, 286.

mental and emotional states, like happiness, are strictly determined by neurochemical functions of the brain. The aim of the transhumanist project of superhappiness is to abolish human suffering and secure happiness through genetic engineering and neuropharmacology.[20]

Transhumanism assumes an inadequate materialist view of the mind and human person and carries it to extreme conclusions, specifically that suffering can be abolished and that global happiness can be achieved by using biochemical and genetic engineering. My critique reveals that in a superhappiness utopia, the following essential human goods will be diminished or lost: (1) Parental reproductive rights will be denied and controlled by the state; (2) Enhanced children will have diminished agency, autonomy, and moral responsibility; (3) The parent-child relationship will become disfigured; (4) High-risk gene-editing mistakes will be irreversible and generational; (5) Negative emotions that are essential for human flourishing and well-being will be abolished; (6) Art and literary culture will become obsolete.

In the end, the superhappiness project itself will become obsolete because the goal of transhumanism is to get rid of human biology altogether by uploading our minds to computers. If, on materialism, our emotional and mental states are determined solely by our neurobiology, then the superhappiness project will become obsolete in the last phase of transhumanism. This exposes the superhappiness project for what it is: a flimsy bridge until the last phase of mind-uploading can be developed and perfected.[21] I conclude that the human cost of transhumanism's superhappiness utopia will degenerate into a dystopia.

A Philosophical Alternative to Materialism: Aristotelian Metaphysics

In these six chapters, I show how transhumanists undertake to put the philosophy of materialism into practice in their projects of superintelli-

---

20   David Pearce, *The Hedonistic Imperative*, HedWeb.com, Introduction, https://www.hedweb.com/hedethic/hedonist.htm (accessed August 1, 2020). David Pearce's overall strategy encompasses the entire sentient world, which includes abolishing non-human animal suffering. This project proposes redesigning traditional eco-systems and genetically engineering animals. This paper's focus is limited to an evaluation of transhumanism's project related to human beings.

21   I argued in chapters 2, 3, and 4, that mind-uploading is metaphysically impossible.

gence, superlongevity, and superhappiness. Their philosophy fails to give an adequate account of the mind and human person and therefore, their projects are not only metaphysically impossible, but undesirable for human flourishing. For transhumanists, the material world is reduced to the blind laws of nature governing the behavior of inherently meaningless and purposeless physical particles. Hence, they conclude that a human person is a bundle of molecular and cellular complexes with no fixed nature, essence, or teleology. The things materialism leaves out—the conscious substantial self, enduring identity, rationality, free will, morality—are the things that Aristolelian metaphysics of the human person seeks to explain.

Aristotelian metaphysics maintains that a human being is a single substance that is a composite of body (matter) and soul (form), with a rational nature as its substantial form. The rationality of human beings calls for a special classification distinct from animals, plants, and inorganic substances.[22] On Aristotle's view, the powers of the intellect are immaterial and do not directly depend on bodily organs for their operation. That is, the intellect grasps forms, essences, universals, and other abstract concepts like propositions. Therefore, a purely naturalistic evolutionary origin of the human essence is ruled out. The soul (form) is the bearer of identity, but I am not strictly identical with my soul. I am not reducible to my soul because my body is essential. Because of this, the transhumanist ambition to rid himself of his body is incompatible with Aristotle's view of the embodied human person.

A key concept in Aristotelian metaphysics is that teleology is inherent in the natural order.[23] That is, the telos or purpose of a material substance in nature exists inherently because of the kind of thing it is. Thomas Aquinas carried Aristotle's fundamental concept of inherent natural teleology to the theological conclusion that a divine intelligence (God) is necessary to impart intrinsic natural teleology and to order things to their ends.[24] A man-made artifact (e.g., a computer), on the other hand, is made of parts

---

22   The power, or potential, of rational thought should not be confused with the exercise of rational thought. The capacity for rationality is built into the human embryo from the moment it comes into existence. A human being can have the power of rationality without having the use or exercise of that power.

23   Edward Feser, *Neo-Scholastic Essays* (South Bend, Indiana: St. Augustine's Press, 2015), 147.

24   While Aristotle did argue that the motion we observe in the world must be sustained by an Unmoved Mover, he did not assume a divine intelligence was necessary to impart intrinsic natural teleology to things. Aquinas and the Scholastics carried Aristotle's philosophy further.

and has no inherent tendency to perform its function. Transhumanists view the body as a material collection of parts, devoid of inherent teleology. Instead, they impose their will and purpose on the body externally.

Contrary to transhumanism's view that human happiness is a subjective psychological state of *feeling* good, Aristotle views human happiness as an objective ethical state of *being good*.[25] For Aristotle, happiness is primarily a function of virtue, the moral excellence of a whole life well lived.[26] The exercise of reason is essential for happiness because by it we know and choose how we ought to live; specifically, reason gives us the capacity to judge between needs and wants and between real and apparent goods.

Complete happiness, for Aristotle, is the intellectual activity of god-like contemplation of truth and the Divine.[27] This contemplative mode of life is sustained and made possible by the stable character of the morally virtuous life.[28] Saint Thomas Aquinas (1225-1274) refined Aristotle's theory of happiness in light of Christian theology by adding the theological virtues of faith, hope, and charity.[29] These virtues transcend man's natural capacities and therefore, are gifts of God's grace to direct man to Himself.[30] Aquinas reasoned that earthly happiness is imperfect and falls short of true happiness, which is ultimately found in knowing God and in beholding the vision of God's essence in the afterlife.[31] Divine grace is needed and available to heal our corrupted human nature.[32] For Aquinas, God's grace is needed to lead a good life on earth and to experience a life of eternal blessedness.

Transhumanists make *feeling* good the central focus of achieving superhappiness. Both Aristotle and Aquinas understood that pleasure is not the supreme good because it is the result of a supreme good, the virtuous life.[33]

---

25 Mortimer Adler, *Ten Philosophical Mistakes* (New York: Simon & Schuster Inc., Touchstone Edition, 1985), 131-2.
26 Aristotle, *Nicomachean Ethics*, in Mortimer Adler, editor, *Great Books of the Western World*, Volume (Chicago: Encyclopedia Britannica, 1990), 1098a.
27 Ibid., 432-433, 1177b15-30, 1178a1-5.
28 Ibid., 432, 1177b26-1178a22.
29 Thomas Aquinas, *Summa Theologica*, Mortimer Adler, editor, *Great Books of the Western World*, Volume 18 (Chicago: Encyclopedia Britannica, 1990), 44, 60-64.
30 Ibid., 60.
31 Ibid., 629.
32 Ibid., 179-180.
33 Thomas Aquinas, *Summa Theologica*, Mortimer Adler, editor, *Great Books of the Western World*, Volume 17, 620; Aristotle, *Nicomachean Ethics*, Book 10, 430-431.

C. S. Lewis wrote, "You can't get second things by putting them first; you can get second things only by putting first things first."[34] *Feeling* good is a second thing that can only be realized by putting first things first, which is *being* good. Therefore, the happy life is the virtuous life.

My explanation of Aristotle's key concepts of essentialism, teleology, and his virtue-based theory of human flourishing provides the reader with reasons to investigate Aristotelian metaphysics further as an alternative to the materialistic/mechanistic reductionist philosophy of materialism. The overall aim of my dissertation is to help the reader critique transhumanism's materialist philosophy and analyze the human cost of its projects in order to expose how, by design, they will alienate a person from his or her humanity. I have offered sufficient reasons to reject the materialist philosophy of transhumanism and reconsider Aristotle's metaphysics of the human person.

---

34   C. S. Lewis, "First and Second Things," in Walter Hooper, editor, *God in the Dock: Essays on Theology and Ethics* (Grand Rapids, Michigan: William B. Eerdmans Publishing Company, 1970), 280.

Bibliography

Abalea, Gaelle. "Transmission: an escape from death in Tolkien's work?" *Death and Immortality in Middle-earth: Proceedings of the Tolkien Society Seminar 2016*, edited by Daniel Helen. Edinburgh: Luna Press Publishing, 2017.

Adler, Mortimer J. *Ten Philosophical Mistakes*. New York: Simon & Schuster Inc., Touchstone Edition, 1985.

———. "Virtue and Vice: Introduction." Syntopicon II. *The Great Books of the Western World*, edited by Mortimer Adler. Chicago: Encyclopedia Britannica, 1990.

Aeschlman, Michael D. *The Restitution of Man: C. S. Lewis and the Case against Scientism*. Grand Rapids, Michigan: William B. Eerdmans Publishing Company, 1983.

Aeschylus, *"Prometheus Bound." The Great Books of the Western World*, edited by Mortimer Adler. Chicago: Encyclopedia Britannica, 1990.

Allison, Henry E. "Kant's Refutation of Materialism." The Monist, Vol. 72, Issue 2 (April 1, 1989).

———. "Kant's Theory of Freedom." Cambridge: Cambridge University Press, 1990.

Amendt-Raduege, Amy. "Better Off Dead." *Fastitocalon: Studies in Fantasticism Ancient to Modern*, Vol. 1.1. Bergstrabe: WVT Wissenschaftlicher Verlag Trier, 2010.

Ariely, Dan. *The (Honest) Truth About Dishonesty: How We Lie to Everyone—Especially Ourselves*. New York: Harper, 2013.

Arduini, Roberto and Claudio A. Testi. *The Broken Scythe: Death and Immortality in the Worlds of J. R. R. Tolkien.* Zurich: Walking Tree Publishers, 2012.

Aristotle. "Metaphysics." *The Great Books of the Western World, Volume 7,* edited by Mortimer Adler. Chicago: Encyclopedia Britannica, 1990.

———. "Nicomachean Ethics." *The Great Books of the Western World, Volume 8,* edited by Mortimer Adler. Chicago: Encyclopedia Britannica, Inc., 1990.

———. "On the Soul." *The Great Books of the Western World, Volume 7,* edited by Mortimer Adler. Chicago: Encyclopedia Britannica, Inc., 1990.

Aquinas, Thomas. *Summa Theologica. The Great Books of the Western World, Volume 17,* edited by Mortimer Adler. Chicago: Encyclopedia Britannica, 1990.

Augustine. "The City of God." *The Great Books of the Western World, Volume 16,* edited by Mortimer Adler. Chicago: Encyclopedia Britannica, Inc., 1990.

Babbitt, Irving. *Literature and the American College: Essays in Defense of the Humanities.* New York: Houghton, Mifflin, and Company, 1908.

Bacon, Francis. *Novum Organum.* In *Great Books of the Western World, Volume 28,* edited by Mortimer Adler. Chicago: Encyclopedia Britannica, Inc., 1990.

———. "The Advancement of Learning." *The Great Books of the Western World, Volume 28,* edited by Mortimer Adler. Chicago: Encyclopedia Britannica, Inc., 1990.

———. *The Great Instauration.* Constitution Society website https://www.constitution.org/bacon/instauration.htm (accessed March 5, 2020).

———. "New Atlantis." *The Great Books of the Western World, Volume 28,* edited by Mortimer Adler. Chicago: Encyclopedia Britannica, 1990.

Bamford, Sim. "A Framework for Approaches to Transfer of a Mind's Substrate." International Journal of Machine Consciousness, Vol. 4, No. 1 (2012), 23-34. https://pdfs.semanticscholar.org/36cd/238588dee2b-7fa36ef2c3a0a80447b30b96a.pdf (accessed June 18, 2020).

Bashford, Alison. "Julian Huxley's Transhumanism." *Crafting Humans: From Genesis to Eugenics and Beyond*, edited by Marius Turda. Goettingen: V&R Unipress, 2013.

———. "Where Did Eugenics Go?" *The Oxford Handbook of the History of Eugenics*, edited by Alison Bashford and Philippa Levine. New York: Oxford University Press, 2010.

Barrat, James. *Our Final Invention: Artificial Intelligence and the End of the Human Era*. New York: Thomas Dunne Books, 2013.

Barrett, William. *Irrational Man: A Study in Existential Philosophy*. New York: AnchorBooks, 1958.

Beauvoir, Simone de. *A Very Easy Death*, translated by Patrick O'Brian. New York: Pantheon Books, 1965.

Bernal, J. D. The World, the Flesh and the Devil. *Marxist.org*, https://www.marxists.org/archive/bernal/works/1920s/soul/ (accessed March 11, 2020)

Boden, Margaret A. "Could a Robot Be Creative— And Would We Know?" *Android Epistemology*, edited by Kenneth M. Ford, Clark Glymour, and Patrick J. Hayes. Menlo Park, CA: American Association for Artificial Intelligence, 1995.

Boden, Margaret A. "Creativity and Artificial Intelligence." *The Philosophy of Creativity: New Essays*, edited by Elliot Samuel Parul and Scott Barry Kaufman. New York: Oxford University Press, 2014.

Borchert, Donald M., and David Stewart, eds. *Being Human in a Technological Age*. Athens, Ohio: The Ohio University Press, 1979.

Bostrom, Nick. "A History of Transhumanist Thought." *Journal of Evolution and Technology*, Vol. 14, Issue 1, April 2005, https://www.nickbostrom.com/papers/history.pdf (accessed February 2, 2020.

———. "In Defense of Posthuman Dignity." *H+/- Transhumanism and Its Critics*, edited by Gregory R. Hansell and William Grassie. Philadelphia: Metanexus Institute, 2011.

———. "Letter from Utopia." *Studies in Ethics, Law, and Technology* (2008): Volume 2, No. 1. https://www.nickbostrom.com/utopia.html (accessed August 9, 2020).

———. *Superintelligence: Paths, Dangers, Strategies.* Oxford, UK: Oxford University Press, 2014.

———, "The Fable of the Dragon-Tyrant." *Journal of Medical Ethics* (2005) Volume 31, No. 5. https://www.nickbostrom.com/fable/dragon.html (accessed August 13, 2020).

———. "The Transhumanist FAQ: A General Introduction, Version 2.1." 2003, https://nickbostrom.com/views/transhumanist.pdf (accessed September 14, 2019).

———. "Transhumanist Values." *Ethical Issues for the 21st Century.* Reprinted in *Review of Contemporary Philosophy.* Volume 4, May 2005. https://nickbostrom.com/ethics/values.pdf (accessed November 12, 2019).

———. "What is a Singleton?" *Linguistic and Philosophical Investigations*, Vol. 5, No. 2 (2006). https://www.nickbostrom.com/fut/singleton.html (accessed June 25, 2020).

Bringsjord, Selmer. "Is the Connectionist-logicist Clash One of AI's Wonderful Red Herrings?" *Journal of Experimental & Theoretical AI*, 1 (1991).

Bringsjord, Selmer and David A Ferrucci. *Artificial Intelligence and Literary Creativity: Inside the Mind of BRUTUS, a Storytelling Machine.* Mahwah, NJ: Lawrence Erlbaum Associates, Inc. Publishers, 2000.

———. *What Robots Can and Can't Be.* Dordrecht, The Netherlands: Kluwer Academic Publishers, 1992.

Bringsjord, Selmer, Alexander Bringsjord, and Paul Bello. "Belief in The Singularity isFideistic." RPI.edu. (January 25, 2012). http://kryten.mm.rpi.edu/SB_AB_PB_sing_fideism_022412.pdf (accessed April 19, 2020).

Bringsjord, Selmer, Paul Bello, and David Ferrucci. "Creativity, the Turing Test, and the (Better) Lovelace Test." *Minds and Machines*, June 2008, https://www.researchgate.net/profile/Paul_Bello2/publication/2430434_Creativity_the_Turing_Test_and_the_Better_Lovelace_Test/links/00b7d534feb157a685000000/Creativity-the-Turing-Test-and-the-Better-Lovelace-Test.pdf (accessed March 10, 2020).

Bringsjord, Selmer and Naveen Sundar Govindarajulu, "Are Autonomous and Creative Machines Intrinsically Untrustworthy?" *Foundations of Trusted Autonomy*, edited by Hussein A. Abbass Jason Scholz Darryn J. Reid Editors. Cham, Switzerland: Springer International Publishing Company, 2017. http://kryten.mm.rpi.edu/SB_NSG_aut2dishon.pdf (accessed April 25, 2020).

Buckner, Cameron and James Garson. "Connectionism." *The Stanford Encyclopedia of Philosophy* (Fall 2019 Edition), Edward N. Zalta, editor. https://plato.stanford.edu/archives/fall2019/entries/connectionism/ (accessed April 16, 2020).

Burtt, E. A. *The Metaphysical Foundations of Modern Science*. New York: Dover Publications, Inc., 2003.

Campbell, Heidi and Mark Walker, "Religion and Transhumanism: Introducing aConversation." *Journal of Evolution and Technology*, Vol. 14, Issue 2 (April 2005). https://www.jetpress.org/volume14/specialissueintro.html (accessed August 15, 2020).

Carnap, Rudolf, "The Logical Foundations of the Unity of Science." Reprinted from *International Encyclopedia of Unified Science*: Vol. I. Edited by Otto Neurath, Rudolf Carnap, and Charles Morris. Chicago: University of Chicago Press, 1938-55.

Carr, Nicholas. "Is Google Making Us Stupid?" *TheAtlantic - Technology*, July/August 2008. https://www.theatlantic.com/magazine/archive/2008/07/is-google-making-us-stupid/306868/ (accessed May 28, 2020).

_____. *The Glass Cage: How Our Computers are Changing Us*. New York: W.W. Nortonand Co., Inc.: 2015.

Carpenter, Humphrey, ed. *The Letters of J. R. R. Tolkien*. New York: Houghton Mifflin Harcourt, 1995.

Chalmers, David J. "Consciousness and its Place in Nature." *Blackwell Guide to Philosophy of Mind*, edited by Steven Stich & Ted Warfield. Massachusetts: Blackwell Publishing, 2003. http://consc.net/papers/nature.pdf (accessed March 15, 2020).

Chesterton, Gilbert K. *Orthodoxy*. United States: Simon & Brown, 2010.

———. *The Everlasting Man*. New York: Dodd, Mead and Company, 1925.

Chisholm, Roderick. "Human Freedom and the Self." The Lindley Lecture, University of Kansas (April 23, 1964). *KUScholarWorks*. https://kuscholarworks.ku.edu/bitstream/handle/1808/12380/Human%20Freedom%20and%20the%20Self-1964.pdf?sequence=1 (accessed April 13, 2020).

Condorcet, Marquis de. *Sketch for a Historical Picture of the Progress of the Human Mind: Tenth Epoch*, translated by Keith Michael Baker. *Daedalus*, 133, no.3, 2004. http://www.jstor.org/stable/20027931 (accessed March 1, 2020).

Copan, Paul, Tremper Longman, Christopher Reese, and Michael Strauss, Editors. *Dictionary of Christianity and Science*. Michigan: Zondervan, 2017.

Copeland, Jack. "The Church-Turing Thesis." *AlanTuring.net: Reference Articles on Turing*. June 2000. http://www.alanturing.net/turing_archive/pages/reference%20articles/The%20Turing-Church%20Thesis.html (accessed April 15, 2020).

Copleston, Frederick. *A History of Philosophy: Volume III: Late Medieval and Renaissance Philosophy*. New York: Doubleday, 1993).

Council, Jared. "Can an AI System Be Given a Patent?" *The Wallstreet Journal* (October 11, 2019), https://www.wsj.com/articles/can-an-ai-system-be-given-a-patent-11570801500 (accessed October 15, 2019).

Csikszentmihalyi, Mihaly and Judith LeFevre."Optimal Experience at Work and Leisure," *Journal of Personality and Social Psychology* (1989), Vol. 56, No. 5, 815-822. https://pdfs.semanticscholar.org/2c19/82f8de71b-73771cb11ba192c10c30d92cd58.pdf (accessed July 7, 2020).

Danaylov, Nikola. "A Transhumanist Manifesto." *Singularity* blog, March 15, 2016. https://www.singularityweblog.com/a-transhumanist-manifesto/ (accessed June 10, 2018).

Darwin, Charles. *Descent or Origin of Man*. In *Great Books of the Western World, Volume 49*, edited by Mortimer Adler, 253-265. Chicago: Encyclopedia Britannica, Inc., 1990.

Davis, Bill. "Choosing to Die." In *The Lord of the Rings and Philosophy: One Book to Rule Them All*. Gregory Bassham and Eric Bronson, eds. Chicago: Open Court Publishing, 2003.

Dembski, William. "Converting Matter into Mind: Alchemy and the Philosopher's Stone in Cognitive Science." *Perspectives on Science and Christian Faith* Vol. 42, No. 4, (1990). http://www.arn.org/docs/dembski/wd_convmtr.htm (accessed March 30, 2020).

Dennett, Daniel. *Consciousness Explained*. New York: Back Bay Books, 1991.

____. *From Bacteria to Bach and Back Again: the Evolution of MInds*. New York: W.W. Norton & Company, Inc., 2017.

Dennett, Daniel C. and Alvin Plantinga. *Science and Religion: Are They Compatible?* Oxford: Oxford University Press, 2011.

Deonna, Julien and Fabrice Teroni. "Feel Bad, Live Well! The Value of NegativeEmotions for Well-being." University of Geneva Philosophy Department (2020) https://www.unige.ch/lettres/philo/recherche/research-groups/thumos/projects/feel-bad-live-well-value-negative-emotions-well-being/ (accessed September 13, 2020).

Descartes, Rene. "Discourse on the Method." *The Great Books Of the Western World, Volume 28*, edited by Mortimer Adler, 265-291. Chicago: Encyclopedia Britannica, Inc., 1990.

____. "Meditations VI." *The Great Books of the Western World, Volume 28*, edited by Mortimer Adler. Chicago: Encyclopedia Britannica, Inc., 1990.

____. *Treatise of Man*, translated by Thomas Steele Hall. New York: Prometheus Books, 2003.

Dewey, John. *Democracy and Education*. New York: The Free Press, 1916.

____. *The Influence of Darwin on Philosophy and Other Essays*. New York: Henry Holt and Co., 1910.

Diderot, Denis. *Rameau's Nephew/D'Alembert's Dream*, translated by Leonard Tancock. London: Penguin Books, 1966.

Diderot and D'Alembert. *Encyclopédie,* "Bulletin." *Classiques Garnier,* https://classiques-garnier.com/editions-bulletins/Encyclopedie_Diderot_D-Alembert_WEB.pdf, (accessed March 6, 2020).

Drexler, Eric K. *Engines of Creation.* Garden City, NY: Anchor Press/Doubleday, 1986.

_____. *Nanomedicine: Volume I Basic Capabilities.* Georgetown, TX: Landes-Bioscience, 1999. online book. http://www.nanomedicine.com/NMI/Foreword.htm (accessed June 15, 2020).

Ellul, Jacques. "On the Aims of a Philosophy of Technology." *Philosophy of Technology,* edited by Robert c. Scharff and Val Dusek. UK: John Wiley & Sons, 2014.

Esfandiary, F. M. *Up-Wingers: A Futurist Manifesto.* E-Reads, https://slowlorisblog.files.wordpress.com/2015/05/esfandiary-up-wingers-a-futurist-manifesto.pdf, (accessed on March 13, 2020).

Essinger, James. *Ada's Algorithm: How Lord Byron's Daughter Ada Lovelace Launched the Digital Age.* Brooklyn: Melville House, 2014.

Ettinger, Robert. "The Prospect of Immortality." cryonics.org, https://www.cryonics.org/images/uploads/misc/Prospect_Book.pdf (accessed March 14, 2020), 11.

Ettinger, Robert. *Man to Superman: The Startling Potential of Human Evolution—and How to Be Part of It.* New York: St. Martin's Press, 1972.

Ferkiss, Victor. *Nature, Technology, and Society: Cultural Roots of the Current Environmental Crisis.* New York: New York University Press, 1993.

Feser, Edward. "Aquinas on the Human Soul." *The Blackwell Companion to Substance Dualism,* edited by Jonathan J. Loose, Angus J. L. Menuge, and J. P. Moreland. Hoboken, NJ: John Wiley & Sons, Inc., 2018.

_____. *Aristotle's Revenge: the Metaphysical Foundations of Physical and Biological Science.* Germany: Editiones Scholasticae, 2019.

———, *Neo-Scholastic Essays*. South Bend, Indiana: St. Augustine's Press, 2015.

———. "One Long Circular Argument." *The Claremont Institute* Vol. XVII, No. 4 (Fall 2017). http://www.claremont.org/crb/article/one-long-circular-argument/ (accessed March 15, 2020).

———. *Philosophy of Mind: A Beginner's Guide*. Oxford: Oneworld Publications, 2006.

———. "Reading Rosenberg, Part II," *EdwardFeser.blogspot.com*, November 3, 2011. http://edwardfeser.blogspot.com/2011/11/reading-rosenberg-part-ii.html (accessed February 15, 2020).

———. *The Last Superstition: A Refutation of the New Atheism*. South Bend, Indiana: St. Augustine's Press, 2008.

Fetzer, James H. *Artificial Intelligence: Its Scope and Limits*. Boston: Kluwer Academic Publishers, 1990.

———. *Computers and Cognition: Why Minds Are Not Machines*. Boston: Kluwer Academic Publishers, 2001.

Feynman, Richard. "There's Plenty of Room at the Bottom." Transcript of his 1959 speech at Caltech. https://www.zyvex.com/nanotech/feynman.html (accessed June 15, 2020).

Firth, Joseph and John Torous, Brendon Stubbs, Josh A. Firth, Genevieve Z. Steiner, LeeSmith, Mario Alvarez Jimenez, John Gleeson, Davy Vancampfort, Christopher J. Armitage, Jerome Sarris. "The Online Brain: How the Internet May be Changing our Cognition." *World Psychiatry*, June 2019. Published online May 6, 2019. https://www.ncbi.nlm.nih.gov/pmc/articles/PMC6502424/ (accessed May 28, 2020).

Firth-Butterfield, Kay and Yoon Chae. "Artificial Intelligence Collides with Patent Law." World Economic Forum, White Paper (April 2018), http://www3.weforum.org/docs/WEF_48540_WP_End_of_Innovation_Protecting_Patent_Law.pdf (accessed April 20, 2020).

Flieger, Verlyn and Douglas A. Anderson, editors. *Tolkien On Fairy-stories*. London: HarperCollins Publishers, 2014.

Fodor, Jerry. "Look!" *London Review of Books* Vol. 20, No. 21 (October 29,1998). https://www.lrb.co.uk/v20/n21/jerry-fodor/look (accessed February 11, 2018).

Fukuyama, Frances. *Our Posthuman Future: Consequences of the Biotechnology Revolution.* New York: Farrar, Straus and Giroux, 2002.

———. "Transhumanism: The World's Most Dangerous Idea." *Foreign Policy* no.144 (2004). https://www.au.dk/fukuyama/boger/essay/ (accessed May 28, 2020).

Gabbani, Carl. "The Causal Closure of What? An Epistemological Critique of the Principle of Causal Closure." *ResearchGate* (January 2013). https://www.researchgate.net/publication/280562788_The_Causal_Closure_of_What_An_Epistemological_Critique_of_the_Principle_of_Causal_Closure (accessed April 13, 2020).

Gardner, Howard. *The Mind's New Science: A History of the Cognitive Revolution.* United States: Basic Books, 1985.

Garreau, Joel. *Radical Evolution: The Promise and Peril of Enhancing Our Minds, Our Bodies--and What It Means to be Human.* New York: Broadway Books, 2005.

Gay, Craig M. *Modern Technology and the Human Future: A Christian Appraisal.* Downers Grove: IVP Academic, 2018.

George, Robert. "Natural Law, God, and Human Dignity." *The Chautauqua Journal,* Volume 1 (2016). https://encompass.eku.edu/cgi/viewcontent.cgi?article=1004&context=tcj (accessed July 19, 2020).

Gilkey, Langdon. *Religion and the Scientific Future: Reflections on Myth, Science, and Theology.* New York: Harper & Row, 1970.

Goertzel, Ben. "Encouraging a Positive Transcension." *Singularity Stewardship and the Global Brain MIneplex* (2004). https://goertzel.org/dynapsyc/2004/PositiveTranscension.htm#_4._Singularity_Stewardship (accessed June 16, 2020).

———."Superintelligence: Fears, Promises and Potentials," *Journal of Evolution & Technology,* Vol. 24, Issue 2 (November 2015). https://jetpress.org/v25.2/goertzel.htm (accessed March 28, 2020).

Goetz, Stewart, and Charles Taliaferro. *Naturalism*. Grand Rapids: Wm. B. Eerdmans Publishing Co., 2008.

Good, Irving John. "Speculations Concerning the First Ultraintelligent Machine." Conference on the Conceptual Aspects of Biocommunications, October 1962, University of California, Los Angeles, Draft of this monograph, May 1964. http://acikistihbarat.com/dosyalar/artificial-intelligence-first-paper-on-intelligence-explosion-by-good-1964-acikistihbarat.pdf (accessed March 28, 2020).

Grant, George. *Technology and Empire: Perspective on North America*. Toronto: House of Anansi, 1969.

Habermas, Gary. "The Minimal Facts Approach to the Resurrection of Jesus." *Southeastern Theological Review*, Summer 2012. https://www.garyhabermas.com/articles/southeastern_theological_review/minimal-facts-methodology_08-02-2012.htm (accessed April 25, 2020).

Hahn, Hans, Otto Neurath, and Rudolf Carnap. "Wissenschaftliche Weltauffassung: Der Wiener Kreis," 1929. English translation: "The Scientific Conception of the World: The Vienna Circle," in Sahotra Sarkar, Editor, *Science and Philosophy in the Twentieth Century, Vol.I: The Emergence of Logical Empiricism: from 1900 to the Vienna Circle*. New York: Garland Publishing, 1996.

Haldane, J. B. S. "Daedalus: or Science and the Future." *Marxists.org*, https://www.marxists.org/archive/haldane/works/1920s/daedalus.htm (accessed March 11, 2020).

Hansell and William Grasssie, editors. *H+/-: Transshumanism & Its Critics*. Philadelphia: Metanexus Institute, 2011.

Harari, Yuval Noah. *Homo Deus: A Brief History of Tomorrow*. New York HarperCollins, 2017.

Harris, Michael. *The End of Absence: Reclaiming What We've Lost in a World of Constant Connection*. New York: Penguin, 2014.

Haugeland, John. *Artificial Intelligence: The Very Idea*. Cambridge, Massachusetts: The MIT Press, 1986.

———. "Semantic Engines: An Introduction to Mind Design," *Mind Design*. Cambridge, MA: MIT Press, 1981. https://cse.buffalo.edu/~rapaport/575/F01/haugeland.pdf (accessed April 15, 2020).

Hauskeller, Michael. "Prometheus Unbound: Transhumanist argument from (human) nature." *Ethical Perspectives* (March 2009), 11, *ResearchGate*. https://www.researchgate.net/publication/232770169_Prometheus_unbound_Transhumanist_arguments_from_human_nature (accessed March 2, 2020).

Hempel, Carl G. "Comments on Goodman's Ways of Worldmaking." *Synthese* (1980) 45: 193-199, quoted in Carlo Gabbani. "The Causal Closure of What? An Epistemological Critique of the Principle of Causal Closure." *ResearchGate*. https://www.researchgate.net/publication/280562788_The_Causal_Closure_of_What_An_Epistemological_Critique_of_the_Principle_of_Causal_Closure (accessed April 11, 2020).

Hesiod, *The Theogony*, translated by Hugh G. Evelyn-White. *Sacred Texts* website (1914). https://www.sacred-texts.com/cla/hesiod/theogony.htm (accessed November 20, 2020).

Hobbes, Thomas. "Leviathan: Of Man." *The Great Books of the Western World, Volume 21*, edited by Mortimer Adler. Chicago: Encyclopedia Britannica, Inc., 1990.

Hoffman, Steven A. "Transhumanist Materialism: A Critique from Immunoneuropsychology." *Building Better Humans? Refocusing the Debate on Transhumanism*, edited by Hava Tirosh-Samuelson and Kenneth L. Mossman. Frankfurt: Peter Lang, 2012.

Homer, "The Iliad." *The Great Books of the Western World Volume 3*, edited by Mortimer Adler. Chicago: Encyclopedia Britannica, Inc., 1990.

———, "The Odyssey." *The Great Books of the Western World Volume 3*, edited by Mortimer Adler. Chicago: Encyclopedia Britannica, Inc., 1990.

Hooper, Walter. *C. S. Lewis on Stories and Other Literature*. New York: First-Harvest/HBJ edition, 1982.

Hopkins, Patrick D. "Transcending the Animal: How Transhumanism and Religion Are and Are Not Alike." *Journal of Evolution and Technology*, Volume 14, Issue 2 (August 2005). https://jetpress.org/volume14/hopkins.pdf (accessed August 17, 2020).

Horgan, John. "David Chalmers Thinks the Hard Problem is Really Hard," *Scientific American*, April 10, 2017, https://blogs.scientificamerican.com/cross-check/david-chalmers-thinks-the-hard-problem-is-really-hard/, (accessed April 2, 2020).

Hughes, James. "Contradictions from the Enlightenment Roots of Transhumanism." *Journal of Medicine and Philosophy*, 0: 1-19, 2010. http://citeseerx.ist.psu.edu/viewdoc/download?doi=10.1.1.993.3636&rep=rep1&type=pdf (accessed June 28, 2020).

____."Embracing Change with All Four Arms: A Posthumanist Defense of Genetic Engineering." http://www.changesurfer.com/Hlth/Genetech.html (accessed June 14, 2020).

____."The Future of Death: Cryonics and the Telos of Liberal individualism." *Journal of Evolution and Technology*, Volume 6, July 2001. https://www.jetpress.org/volume6/Death.htm (accessed June 28, 2020).

____. "Transhumanism and Personal Identity." In *The Transhumanist Reader*, edited by Max More and Natasha Vita-More, 227-233. Philadelphia: Metanexus Institute, 2011.

____. "The Politics of Transhumanism and the Techno-Millennial Imagination,1626-2030." *Zygon Journal of Religion and Science*, Vol. 47, No-4December 2012, https://www.trincoll.edu/Academics/centers/TIIS/Documents/Hughes—April%203.pdf (accessed February 2, 2020).

Hume, David. "Essay Concerning Human Understanding." *The Great Books of the Western World, Volume 33*, Mortimer Adler, editor. Chicago: Encyclopedia Britannica, 1990.

Huxley, Aldous. *Brave New World*. New York: HarperCollins, 2017.

Huxley, Julian. *New Bottles for New Wine*. New York: Harper & Brothers Publishers, 1957.

____. *Evolutionary Humanism* (New York: Prometheus Books, 1992), 268.

———. "Race in Europe," (1936), Rare Books and Manuscripts, https://digital.kenyon.edu/rarebooks/16 (accessed March 13, 2020).

———. *Religion Without Revelation.* New York: Mentor Books, 1957.

Ibsen, Henrik. *Four Major Plays: Volume I.* New York: A Signet Classic, 1992.

Ienca, Marcello, and Pim Haselager. "Hacking the brain: brain-computer interfacing technology and the ethics of neruosecurity." *Ethics and Information Technology.* April 2016. https://www.researchgate.net/publication/301335762_Hacking_the_brain_brain-computer_interfacing_technology_and_the_ethics_of_neurosecurity (accessed June 15, 2020).

Jackson, Frank. "Looking Back on the Knowledge Argument." *There's Something About Mary*, edited by Peter Ludlow, Yujin Nagasawa, and Daniel Stoljar. Cambridge, Mass.: The MIT Press, 2004.

———. "Epiphenomenal Qualia." *There's Something About Mary*, edited by Peter Ludlow, Yujin Nagasawa, and Daniel Stoljar. Cambridge, Mass.: The MIT Press, 2004.

James, William. "The Will to Believe." *Gateway to the Great Books,* edited by Robert M. Hutchins and Mortimer J. Adler. Chicago: Encyclopedia Britannica, Inc., 1963.

Jefferson, Geoffry. "The Mind of Mechanical Man." *British Medical Journal,* June 25, 1949. https://www.ncbi.nlm.nih.gov/pmc/articles/PMC2050428/?page=6 (accessed April 26, 2020).

Johnson, Monte Ransome. *Aristotle on Teleology.* New York: Oxford University Press, 2005.

Jonas, Hans. *Philosophical Essays: From Ancient Creed to Technological Man.* Englewood Cliffs, NJ: Prentice-Hall, Inc., 1974.

Joy, Bill. "Why the Future Doesn't Need Us." *Wired,* Issue 8.04 (April 2000). 1-18.

Kant, Immanuel. "The Metaphysics of Morals." *The Great Books of the Western World, Volume 39,* edited by Mortimer J. Adler, editor. Chicago: Encyclopedia Britannica, Inc., 1990.

Kirk, Russell. *Enemies of the Permanent Things: Observations of Abnormity in Literature and Politics*. Illinois: Sherwood Sugden & Company, 1984.

———. "Teaching Humane Literature in High Schools." In *The Essential Russell Kirk: Selected Essays*. Delaware: ISI Books, 2007.

———. "The Moral Imagination." In *The Essential Russell Kirk: Selected Essays*. Delaware: ISI Books, 2007.

Kitcher, Philip. *Vaulting Ambition*. Cambridge, Massachusetts: The MIT Press, 1990,.

Koene, Randal A. "Uploading to Substrate-Independent Minds." In *The Transhumanist Reader*, edited by Max More and Natasha Vita-More, 146-156. Sussex, UK: John Wiley & Sons, 2013.

———."What Does it Mean For a Mind to be Substrate-Independent?" *Carboncopies,* FAQ, https://carboncopies.org/faq (accessed May 29, 2020).

Koons, Robert C. and George Bealer, editors. *The Waning of Materialism*. Oxford: Oxford University Press, 2010.

Kosslyn, Stephen M. *Image and Brain: The Resolution of the Imagery Debate*. Cambridge, Massachusetts: The MIT Press, 1994.

Kripke, Saul. *Naming and Necessity*. Oxford UK: Blackwell Publishing, 1972.

Kurzweil, Ray. "The Coming Merging of Mind and Machine." *Scientific American*, (March 23, 2009). https://www.scientificamerican.com/article/merging-of-mind-and-machine/ (accessed April 1, 2020).

———. *How to Create a Mind: The Secret of Human Thought Revealed*. NewYork:Penguin Books, 2013.

———. *The Singularity is Near: When Humans Transcend Biology*. New York: Penguin Books, 2005.

Langley, Pat and Randolph Jones. "A computational model of scientific insight." *The Nature of Creativity,* edited by Robert J. Sternberg. New York: Cambridge University Press, 1988.

———. "Retrieval and Learning in Analogical Problem Solving." *Researchgate*, May 1997. https://www.researchgate.net/publication/2663663_Retrieval_and_Learning_in_Analogical_Problem_Solving (accessed April 22, 2020).

Larson, Erik. "The Limits of Modern AI: A Story." *The Best Schools*, June 2016. https://thebestschools.org/magazine/limits-of-modern-ai/ (accessed February 18, 2020).

Le Rond d'Alembert, Jean-Baptiste. *Preliminary Discourse to the Encyclopedie*, translated by Richard N. Schwab and Walter E. Rex. Ann Arbor, Michigan: University of Michigan Library, 2009.

Leibniz, Godfried W. *The Principles of Philosophy known as Monadology. Early Modern Texts* website (2017). https://www.earlymoderntexts.com/assets/pdfs/leibniz1714b.pdf (accessed April 28, 2020).

Lemonick, Michael D. "J. Craig Venter: Gene Mapper." *Time Magazine*, December 25, 2000. http://content.time.com/time/world/article/0,8599,2056235,00.html (accessed June 14, 2020).

Levy, Steven. "We Are Entering the Era of the Brain Machine Interface." *Wired*. https://www.wired.com/2017/04/we-are-entering-the-era-of-the-brain-machine-interface/ (accessed July 1, 2020).

Lewis, C. S. "Bluspels and Flalansferes." *Selected Literary Essays*. Cambridge, U.K.: Cambridge University Press, 1969.

———. "First and Second Things." *God in the Dock: Essays on Theology and Ethics*, edited by Walter Hooper. Grand Rapids, Michigan: William B. Eerdmans Publishing Company, 1970.

———. *Mere Christianity*. New York: HarperCollins, 1980.

———. *Miracles*. New York: HarperCollins, 1996.

———. *That Hideous Strength*. New York: Scribner, 2003.

———. *The Abolition of Man*. New York: HarperCollins Publishers, 1974.

———. *The Weight of Glory*. New York: HarperCollins, 1980.

Linville, Mark D. "The Moral Argument." *The Blackwell Companion to Natural Theology*, edited by William Lane Craig and J. P. Moreland. West Sussex, UK: Wiley-Blackwell Publishing, 2009.

Lowe, E. J. "Causal Closure Principles and Emergentism." *Philosophy*, 75 (4), 2000. *Durham Research Online*. http://dro.dur.ac.uk/15632/ (April 9, 2020).

Ludlow, Peter, Yujin Nagasawa, and Daniel Stoljar, editors. *There's Something About Mary*. Cambridge, Massachusetts: MIT Press, 2004.

McCarthy, John. "Dartmouth AI Project Proposal," August 31, 1955. LivingInternet.com. https://www.livinginternet.com/i/ii_ai.htm (accessed March 20, 2020).

McMahon, Darrin M. *Happiness: A History*. New York: Grove Press, 2006.

Mathie, Anna. "Tolkien and the Gift of Mortality." *First Things*, Nov. 2003,https://www.firstthings.com/article/2003/11/tolkien-and-the-giftof-mortality (accessed August 15, 2020).

Meehan, James R. "TALE-SPIN, An Interactive Program That Writes Stories." Paper given at the Proceedings of the 5th International Joint Conference on Artificial Intelligence, 1977. https://www.cs.utah.edu/nlp/papers/talespin-ijcai77.pdf (accessed April 25, 2020).

Menuge, Angus. *Agents Under Fire: Materialism and the Rationality of Science*. New York: Rowman & Littlefield Publishers, Inc., 2004.

Mill, John Stuart. "On the Connection between Justice and Utility," *Utilitarianism*. London: Parker, Son, and Bourn, 1863. hedweb.com, https://www.utilitarianism.com/mill5.htm (accessed August 15, 2020).

Mirandola, Giovanni Pico della. *Oration on the Dignity of Man*, translated by A. Robert Caponigri. New York: Regnery Publishing, 1984.

Moore, G.E. "A Defence of Common Sense." *Contemporary British Philosophy (2nd series)*, edited by J. H. Muirhead, 1925. http://www.ditext.com/moore/common-sense.html (accessed May 7, 2020).

More, Max, and Natasha Vita-More, eds. *The Transhumanist Reader: Classical and Contemporary Essays on the Science, Technology, and Philosophy of the Human Future*. West Sussex, UK: John Wiley & Sons, 2013.

———. "H+: True Transhumanism." *Metanexus*, February 5, 2009, https://metanexus.net/h-true-transhumanism/ (accessed March 4, 2020).

———, "On Becoming Posthuman." Scribd (1994). https://www.scribd.com/document/354404944/On-Becoming-Posthuman (accessed August 8, 2020).

———. "The Extropian Principles Version 3.0, A Transhumanist Declaration." *Institute Incubating Positive Futures,* 1998. http://vency.com/EXtropian3.htm (accessed April 15, 2020).

———. "The Overhuman in the Transhuman." Journal of Evolution & Technology, Vol. 21, Issue 1, January 2010, https://jetpress.org/v21/more.htm (accessed March 8, 2020, 3.

———. "Transhumanism: Towards a Futurist Philosophy." more@extropy.org (accessed March 1, 2020).

Moreland, J. P. *The Recalcitrant Imago Dei: Human Persons and the Failure of Naturalism*. London, UK: SCM Press, 2009.

Moreland, J. P. and William Lane Craig. *Philosophical Foundations for a Christian Worldview*. Illinois: IVP Academic, 2003.

Mumford, Lewis. *Technics & Civilization*. Chicago: The University of Chicago Press, 2010.

Naddaf, Gerard. "The Origin and Meaning of Poetic Inspiration in Ancient Greece." The University of Sydney Seminar Presentation (November 10, 2011). Website *Academia*. https://www.academia.edu/32876708/The_Origin_and_Meaning_of_Poetic_Inspiration_in_Ancient_Greece (accessed October 15, 2020).

Nagel, Thomas. "What Is It Like to Be a Bat?" *The Philosophical Review* Vol. 83, No. 4, (1974). https://www.jstor.org/stable/2183914?seq=1#page_scan_tab_contents (accessed April 28, 2020).

Nath, Rajakishore. *Philosophy of Artificial Intelligence: a Critique of the Mechanistic Theory of Mind*. Florida: Universal-Publishers, 2009.

Niebuhr, Reinhold. *The Nature and Destiny of Man*. New York: Charles Scribner's Sons, 1941-2. Quoted in Ted Peters, "Transhumanism and the Posthuman Future." *H+/-: Transhumanism and Its Critics*, edited by Gregory R. Hansell and William Grassie. Philadelphia: Metanexus Institute, 2011.

Newell, Allen and Herbert A. Simon. "Computer Simulation of Human Thinking," April 20, 1961. http://www.bighole.nl/pub/mirror/www.bitsavers.org/pdf/rand/ipl/P-2276_Computer_Simulation_Of_Human_Thinking_Apr61.pdf (accessed March 4, 2020).

Nietzsche, Frederich. "Thus Spake Zarathustra: Part II Self-Surpassing," *Gutenberg.org,https://www.gutenberg.org/files/1998/1998-h/1998-h.htm#link2H_4_0040* (accessed on March 9, 2020).

———. "Why I Am So Wise." *On the Genealogy of Morals and Ecce Homo*, translated by Walter Kaufmann and R. J. Hollingdale. New York: Vintage Books, 1989.

Nozick, Robert. *Anarchy, State, and Utopia*. New York: Basic Books, 1974.

Nye, Naomi. "Kindness," Poets.org. https://poets.org/poem/kindness (accessed September 13, 2020).

Oderberg, David S. *Real Essentialism*. New York: Routledge, 2007.

Olds, David D. "A Semiotic Model of Mind." apa.sagepub.com. (September 18, 2016). http://citeseerx.ist.psu.edu/viewdoc/download?doi=10.1.1.1027.7291&rep=rep1&type=pdf (accessed April 19, 2020).

Ossola, Alexandra. "You Could Soon Use CRISPR to Biohack in Your Own Home." *Popular Science*, November 9, 2015. https://www.popsci.com/you-could-soon-become-biohacker-at-home-using-crispr/ (accessed September 1, 2020).

Ovid. "Daedalus and Icarus." *Metamorphosis Book VIII*, translated by Sir Samuel Garth, John Dryden, et al. The Internet Classics Archive website, http://classics.mit.edu/Ovid/Metam.mb.txt (accessed February 25, 2020).

Parfit, Derek. "Personal Identity." *The Philosophical Review* Volume 80, No. 1 (Jan. 1971). http://www.uvm.edu/~lderosse/courses/metaph/Parfit(1971).pdf (accessed March 15, 2018).

Paleo, Bruno Woltezenlogel. "Leibniz's Characteristica Universalis And Calculus Ratiocinator Today." *ResearchGate* (December 2016). https://www.researchgate.net/publication/311456139_Leibniz's_Characteristica_Universalis_and_Calculus_Ratiocinator_Today (April 1, 2020).

Papineau, David. "The Rise of Physicalism." *Core.ac.uk*. https://core.ac.uk/Download/pdf/74162.pdf (accessed April 14, 2020).

———. *Thinking about Consciousness*. Oxford: Clarendon Press, 2004.

Pearce, David. "The Abolitionist Project." *Abolitionist* website, 2007. https://www.abolitionist.com/ (accessed September 8, 2020).

———. "Brave New World? A Defense of Paradise-Engineering." *Lifeboat Foundation* website. https://lifeboat.com/ex/brave.new.world (accessed June 15, 2019).

———. *The Hedonistic Imperative*. HedWeb.com. https://www.hedweb.com/hedethic/hedon4.htm#natural (accessed June 15, 2020).

———. "Interview with Nick Bostrom and David Pearce." Cronopis, December 2007. https://www.hedweb.com/transhumanism/ (accessed April 15, 2019).

———. "What is Transhumanism? The 3 Supers." In *Institute for Ethics and Emerging Technologies*. September 16, 2014. https://ieet.org/index.php/IEET2/print/9543 (accessed March 15, 2020). Pearson, Jordan. "Forget Turing, the Lovelace Test Ha a Better Shot at Spotting AI," July 8, 2014. https://motherboard.vice.com/en_us/article/pgaany/forget-turing-the-lovelace-test-has-a-better-shot-at-spotting-ai (accessed March 20, 2020).

Peirce, Charles S. "Logic as Semiotic: The Theory of Signs." *Philosophical Writings of Peirce*, J. Buchler, editor. New York: Dover Publications, 1955. http://lchc.ucsd.edu/MCA/Mail/xmcamail.2017-05.dir/pdfAAJf6e-4SaC.pdf (accessed April 16, 2020).

Percy, Walker. *The Message in the Bottle*. Open Road Media, Kindle Edition.

———. *The Thanatos Syndrome*. New York: Picador USA, 1987.

Peters, Ted. "Progress and Provolution: Will Transhumanism Leave Sin Behind?" *Transhumanism and Transcendence: Christian Hope in an Age of Technological Enhancement*, edited by Ronald Cole-Turner, editor. Washington D.C.: Georgetown University Press, 2011.

———. "Transhumanism and the Posthuman Future: Will Technological Progress Get Us There?" In *H+/-: Transhumanism and Its Critics*, edited by Gregory R. Hansell and William Grassie, 147-175. Philadelphia: Metanexus Institute, 2011.

Pinker, Steven. *The Blank Slate: The Modern Denial of Human Nature*. New York: Penguin Books, 2002. Quoted in editors Gregory R. Hansell and William Grassie. *H+/-: Transhumanism & Its Critics*. Philadelphia: Metanexus Institute, 2011.

———. "Transhumanism, Means-End Rationality, and Cultural Appropriation." *Confessions of a Supply Side Liberal*. Interview with Steven Pinker. September 2018. https://blog.supplysideliberal.com/post/2018/2/17/steven-pinker-on-transhumanism-means-end-rationality-and-cultural-appropriation (accessed October 2, 2020).

Plato. "The Republic." "Apology." "Meno." "Parmenides." "Phaedo." "Philebus." "Symposium." "Phaedrus." *The Great Books of the Western World, Volume 6*, edited by Mortimer Adler. Chicago: Encyclopedia Britannica, Inc., 1990.

Plutarch. *Theseus*. Tufts.edu. http://www.perseus.tufts.edu/hopper/text?doc=Perseus%3Atext%3A2008.01.0067%3Achapter%3D23%3Asection%3D1 (accessed June 4, 2020).

Pollock, John. *How to Build a Person: A Prolegomenon*. Cambridge, Massachusetts: A Bradford Book, 1989.

Rana, Fazale and Kenneth Samples. *Humans 2.0: Scientific, Philosophical, and Theological Perspectives on Transhumanism*. Covina, CA: Reasons to Believe Press, 2019.

Rockoff, Marcus. "Literature.", *Post- and Transhumanism: An Introduction*, edited by Robert Ranisssch and Stefan Lorenz Sorgner. New York: Peter Lang Edition, 2014.

Roco, Mihail C., and William Sims Bainbridge, eds. "Converging Technologies for Improvement of Human Performance: Nanotechnology, Biotechnology, Information Technology and Cognitive Science." Dordrecht, The Netherlands: Springer Publishers, 2003. http://wtec.org/ConvergingTechnologies/Report/NBIC_report.pdf (accessed November 15, 2020).

Richards, Jay. *Are We Spiritual Machines: Ray Kurzweil vs. the Critics of Strong A.I.* Seattle: Discovery Institute, 2002.

Richards, Jay. *The Human Advantage: The Future of American Work in an Age of Smart Machines.* New York: Crown Forum, 2018.

Ruse, Michael. "The Biological Sciences Can Act as a Ground for Ethics." In Francisco Ayala and Robert Arp, *Contemporary Debates in Philosophy of Biology.* Oxford: Wiley-Blackwell, 2009), 1, http://philsci-archive.pitt.edu/4078/1/RusePhilSciArchive.pdf (accessed July 15, 2020).

Sandel, Michael J. *The Case Against Perfection: Ethics in the Age of GeneticEngineering.* Cambridge, Massachusetts: The Belknap Press of HarvardUniversity Press, 2007.

Sandars, Nancy Katherine, translator, *The Epic of Gilgamesh*, Assyrian International News Agency: Books Online. http://www.aina.org/books/eog/eog.pdf (accessed February 15, 2020).

Santayana, George. *The Life of Reason or The Phases of Human Progress.* New York: Charles Scribner's Sons, 1906, quoted in Charles T. Rubin, *Eclipse of Man: Human Extinction and the Meaning of Progress.* New York: Atlantis Books, 2014.

Saucy, Robert L. "Theology of Human Nature." In *Christian Perspectives on Being Human: A Multidisciplinary Approach to Integration,* edited by J.P. Moreland and David M. Ciocchi, 17-52. Grand Rapids: Baker Book House Company, 1993.

Sayers, Dorothy L. *The Mind and the Maker.* New York: HarperCollins, 1941.

———. "The Zeal of Thy House." Internet Archive. https://archive.org/stream/zealofthyhouse012297mbp/zealofthyhouse012297mbp_djvu.txt (accessed October 15, 2020). Schank, Roger. *Tell Me a Story: Narrative and Intelligence.* Evanston, Illinois: Northwestern University Press, 1998.

Schank, Roger C. "Creativity as a mechanical process." *The Nature of Creativity,* edited by Robert J. Sternberg. New York: Cambridge University Press, 1988.

―――. *Tell Me a Story: Narrative and Intelligence.* Evanston, Illinois: Northwestern University Press, 1998.

Schick, Theodore. "The Cracks of Doom: The Threat of Emerging Technologies and Tolkien's Rings of Power." *The Lord of the Rings and Philosophy: One Book to Rule Them All.* Greg Bassham and Eric Bronson, eds. Chicago: Open Court Publishing, 2003.

Schneider, Susan. *Artificial You: AI and the Future of Your Mind.* Princeton: Princeton University Press, 2019.

―――. "Future Minds: Transhumanism, Cognitive Enhancement and the

Nature of Persons." *Neuroethics Publications*, July1, 2008. https://repository.upenn.edu/cgi/viewcontent.cgi?article=1037&context=neuroethics_pubs (accessed July 15,, 2020).

Schumacher, E.F. *A Guide For The Perplexed.* New York: Harper & Row, 1977.

Searle, John R. "Minds, Brains and Programs." *The Behavioral and Brain Sciences* Vol.3 (1980). http://cogprints.org/7150/1/10.1.1.83.5248.pdf (accessed March 1, 2018).

―――. *Philosophy in a New Century: Selected Essays.* Cambridge: Cambridge University Press 2008.

Searle, John. *The Rediscovery of the Mind.* Cambridge, Massachusetts: MIT Press, 1994.

Segal, Howard P. *Technological Utopianism in American Culture.* Chicago: University of Chicago Press, 1985.

Shatzer, Jacob. *Transhumanism and the Image of God.* Downers Grove: IVP Academic, 2019.

Simon, Herbert. "Cognitive Science: the Newest Science of the Artificial." *Cognitive Science* Vol. 4 (1980). https://onlinelibrary.wiley.com/doi/pdf/10.1207/s15516709cog0401_2 (accessed February 25, 2020).

Slagle, Jim. *The Epistemological Skyhook: Determinism, Naturalism, and Self-Defeat.* New York: Routledge, 2016. Kindle edition.

Sternberg, Robert J., editor. *The Nature of Creativity: Contemporary Psychological Perspectives.* New York: Cambridge University Press, 1988.

Strawson, Galen. "The Conscious Deniers." *The New York Review of Books,* March 13, 2018. http://www.nybooks.com/daily/2018/03/13/the-consciousness-deniers/ (accessed March 20, 2020).

Swift, Jonathan. *Gulliver's Travels, Book III.* In *The Great Books of the Western World, Vol. 34,* edited by Mortimer Adler. Chicago: Encyclopedia Britannica, Inc., 1990.

Tegmark, Max. *Life 3.0: Being Human in the Age of Artificial Intelligence.* New York: Alfred A. Knopf, 2017.

Tirosh-Samuelson, Hava. "Engaging Transhumanism." In *H+/-: Transhumanism & Its Critics,* edited by Gregory R. Hansell and William Grassie, 19-52. Philadelphia: Metanexus Institute, 2011.

Tolkien, J. R. R. *Morgoth's Ring.* London: HarperCollins, 2015.

———. "On Fairy-stories." *The Tolkien Reader,* 31-99. New York: Ballantine Books, 1966.

———. *The Lord of the Rings.* New York: Houghton Mifflin Harcourt, 2004.

———. *The Silmarillion,* second edition, edited by Christopher Tolkien. New York: Ballantine Books, 1977.

Turing, Alan M. "Computing Machinery and Intelligence." Mind Vol. 49 (1950), https://home.manhattan.edu/~tina.tian/CMPT 420/Turing.pdf (accessed February 15, 2020).

Trigg, Roger. *Beyond Matter: Why Science Needs Metaphysics.* Pennsylvania: Templeton Press, 2015.

Urban, Tim. "The AI Revolution: Our Immortality or Extinction." *Wait But Why* (blog), January 27, 2015. https://waitbutwhy.com/2015/01/artificial-intelligence-revolution-2.html (accessed July 1, 2020).

Wang, Jieschu. "Symbolism vs. Connectionism: A Closing Gap in Artificial Intelligence." Blog, http://wangjieshu.com/2017/12/23/symbol-vs-connectionism-a-closing-gap-in-artificial-intelligence/ (accessed April 16, 2020).

Waters, Brent. *From Human to Posthuman: Christian Theology and Technology in a Postmodern World.* Burlington, VT: Ashgate Publishing Company, 2006.

Werskey, Gary. *The Visible College: A Collective Biography of British Scientific-Socialists in the 1930's.* London: Free Association Books, 1988.

Wilbur, Richard. *Collected Poems 1943-2004.* New York: Harcourt, Inc., 2004.

Wiley, Keith. "Transcending Biology: Reverse Engineering the Brain." Carboncopies Foundation. https://carboncopies.org/summary-of-tbreb2018-roadmap-session/ (accessed June 18, 2020).

Williams, Richard N. and Daniel N. Robinson, eds. *Scientism: The New Orthodoxy.* New York: Bloomsbury Academic, 2016.

Wilson, Edward O. *Consilience: The Unity of Knowledge.* New York: Vintage Books, 1999.

Wyer, Robert S., editor. *Knowledge and Memory: The Real Story.* New Jersey: Lawrence Erlbaum Associates, Inc, Publishers, 1995.

Young, Simon. *Designer Evolution: A Transhumanist Manifesto.* New York: Prometheus Books, 2006.

Young, Steve. "Military Uses of Nanotechnology." *The Nanoage.* December 2009. http://www.thenanoage.com/military.htm (accessed March 1, 2020).

Index

"A Defense of Common Sense", 104
A Guide for the Perplexed, 47, 48n.
Abalea, Gaelle, 184
Adler, Mortimer, 212
AGI (artificial general intelligence), 36-73, 75, 132, 139, 158, 166, 222-226
Alchemists, The, 8
Alcor Life Extension Foundation, 25, 26, 29
Allison, Henry, 61
AlphaGo, 67
Amendt-Raduege, Amy, 183, 183n.
Analytical Engine, 40, 75
Anarchy, State, and Utopia, 210
Aquinas, Thomas, 108n., 153, 216, 228-229
"Are Autonomous and Creative Machines Intrinsically Untrustworthy?", 101
Ariely, Dan, 101
Aristotle, 10, 12, 30, 105-109, 152-153, 214-217, 228-230
Aristotle's Four Causes, 105, 106-107
"Artificial and Literary: Inside the Mind of BRUTUS, a Storytelling Machine", 100
Artificial General Intelligence, 36-73, 75, 132, 139, 158, 166, 222-226
Augustine, Saint, 162

Babbitt, Irving, 43, 173
Bacon, Francis, 2, 10-14, 24, 30, 196n., 220-221
Barrett, William, 193
Basic Model, 58, 65, 71, 224
"Belief in the Singularity is Fideistic", 36
Bello, Paul, 36
Bernal, John Desmond, 20-21, 24
Bess, Michael, 117
Bezalel, son of Uri, 84
Biotechnology, 115, 228-130, 138-139, 166, 169, 205, 213
Boden, Margaret, 81-82
Boole, George, 40
Bostrom, Nick, 7, 16, 19, 27, 120, 123, 135, 140, 144, 146, 150, 158, 160-164
Brain Machine Interface (BMI), 171
Brave New World, 193-194, 198-200, 203, 205, 208, 214
Bringsjord, Alexander, 36
Bringsjord, Selmer, 67, 76-78, 89, 93, 99, 100-101, 225
BRUTUS1, 72, 76, 76n., 77, 89, 91, 94-95, 97-102, 225
Burtt, E. A., 42

Carr, Nicholas, 118
Carnap, Rudolf, 45-47
Chalmers, David, 59-60, 224
Chesterton, G. K., 43, 89
Chisholm, Roderick, 56
Christian Realism, 147
Clark, Andy, 132
Computational Theory of Mind, 39, 51, 66-68, 71, 80, 123, 223-224

"Computer Simulation of Human Thinking", 41
"Computing Machinery and Intelligence", 41, 89
Connectionist Computer System, 66
"Consciousness and its Place in Nature", 59
Consilience, 44, 48-50
Conversation between D'Alembert and Diderot, 14
Creativity (defined), 77, 89
Crick, Francis, 136, 141
CRISPR-Cas9, 129
Cryonics, 25-26, 125, 148, 158
Cyborg, 21, 24
Cyborg Engineering, 132-133, 138
Csikszentmihalyi, Mihaly, 118

Daedalus and Icarus, 7
D'Alembert's Dream, 14
d'Alembert, Jean Le Rond, 13-14
Dartmouth Conference (1956), 38, 41
Darwin, Charles, 16, 202
Data, the android, 79
Davidson, Donald, 61
de Condorcet, Marquis, 14
de Laplace, Marquis, 53
della Mirandola, Pico, 8, 10
Dembski, William, 72
Democracy and Education, 47
Dennett, Daniel, 90
Deonna, Julien, 210
Descartes, Rene, 2, 12, 39
Designer Evolution, 16, 122
Dewey, John, 46-48
Diamandis, Peter, 168-169
Diderot, Denis, 13-14
Difference Engine, 40
"Double Blur", 2, 75-77, 91, 102, 116, 135
Drexler, Eric, 26-28, 131

Elixir of Life, 8

Elliot, T. S., 43
Emerson, Ralph Waldo, 43
Encyclopédie, 13
Enemies of the Permanent Things, 165
Engines of Creation, 26
Enlightenment, 13, 212-213, 217, 220
Epic of Gilgamesh, 5, 30
Esfandiary, F. M., 24-25
Ettinger, Robert, 25-26
Eugenics, 5, 18-25, 148, 220
"Everything is Amazing and Nobody is Happy", 118
Extropy, 17, 26, 29, 146
"Extropian Principles", 27

Feser, Edward 15, 50, 58, 83, 103, 221
Fetzer, James, 58
Flamel, Nicholas, 8
FM-2030, 24-27
Fodor, Jerry, 50, 104, 223
Foresight Institute, 27, 29
Fukuyama, Francis, 116
Functionalism (see also, Functionalist Philosophy of Mind), 222-224
Functionalist Philosophy of Mind (see also, Functionalism), 57-71

Gay, Craig, 125
"Geneticists' Manifesto", 23
Gerard Naddaf, 84
Giovanni, Count, 8
George, Robert, 154
Global Brain, 132-133, 138-139
Goertzel, Ben, 34-35, 132-133, 141
Good, Irving John, 33-35
Govindarajulu, Naveen Sundar, 101
Guilford, J. P., 79
Gulliver's Travels, 191-192, 196-198

Habermas, Gary, 88
Haldane, John Burdon Sanderson, 18, 20
Happiness: A History, 212-217

Harari, Yuval Noah, 127, 160
Haugeland, John, 66, 68, 76
Hedonic Set-point, 190, 195, 203, 207
Hempel, Carl, 54
Hesiod, 84-85
Hobbes, Thomas, 39
Homer, 84-85, 174
Homo Deus, 127
Hopkins, Patrick, 165
How to Build a Person: A Prolegomenon, 59
Hughes, James J., 129, 141, 164
Humanity+, 34, 132, 143, 189
Huxley, Aldous, 191, 193-194, 198-200, 203, 205, 208, 214
Huxley, Sir Julian Sorell, 18, 21-24, 164
Hylemorphism, 106-108

Ibsen, Henrik, 94
Iliad, 85
Image and Brain, 92
International Encyclopedia of Unified Science, 47
Irrational Man, 193

Jackson, Frank, 95-98
Jefferson, Geoffrey, 89-90
John Koza's Invention Machine, 78
Jones, Randolf, 80
Joule, James, 53

Kant, Immanuel, 61-63, 65, 70, 139
"Kant's Refutation of Materialism", 62
Kirk, Russell, 8-9, 165, 173-174
Kitcher, Patricia, 61
Knowledge and Memory: The Real Story, 90
Koene, Randal A., 123-124, 134
Kosslyn, Stephen, 92-96
Kripke, Saul, 60

Kurzweil, Ray, 28-29, 76-77, 122, 126, 130, 134-135, 137-140, 161, 163, 168-172, 181, 183

Langley, Patrick, 80
"Law of Priority in Creation", 72
LeFevre, Judith, 118
Leibniz, Gottfried, 39-40, 95-96
"Letter from Utopia", 161
Levinson, Barry, 92
Lewis, C. S., 136, 144, 148, 150, 155, 197, 207, 217, 220
Lovelace, Lady Ada, 40, 72, 75-77, 99-102
Louis CK, 118
Lowe, E. J., 52

Mary's Room, 97
McCarthy, John, 38
McMahon, Darrin, 213
Meehan, James, 88-89
Menuge, Angus, 89, 98
Merkle, Ralph C., 134
Mill, John Stuart, 143
Mind uploading, 21, 123, 128, 133-135, 139-141, 163
"Minds, Brains, and Computers", 63
Minos, King, 7
Minsky, Marvin, 28
MINSTREL, 89
Monadology, 95-96
Moore, G. E., 104
Moravec, Hans, 28, 76
More, Max, 4, 8, 10-11, 17, 26-27
More, Paul Elmer, 43
Mumford, Lewis, 2
Muses, 85

Nagel, Thomas, 59-60, 95, 97-98
"Naming and Necessity", 60

Nanotechnology, 26-27, 115, 128, 130-132, 134, 138-139, 150, 158, 163, 166, 169-171, 181
Natural Law Theory, 153
New Atlantis, 13
New Bottles for New Wine, 22
Newell, Allen, 41, 66
Niebuhr, Reinhold, 147
Nietzsche, Frederick, 17-18
Novum Organum, 10
Nozick, Robert, 210
Nye, Naomi, 211

Oderberg, David, 152-153
Oholiab, 84
"On Fairy-stories", 87-166
"Oration on the Dignity of Man", 8
Origin of Species, 16
Outlines of an Historical view of the Progress of the Human Mind, 14
Ovid, 7

Page, Larry, 132, 170
Papineau, David, 51-56
Paracelsus, 8
Parfit, Derek, 124
Patent Act of 1790, 78
Pearce, David, 22, 27, 130, 149, 189-190, 194, 197, 202-211
Peirce, Charles S., 68
Percy, Walker, 191, 194-195
Perpetual Progress, 15, 26, 142, 145-146
Phaedrus, 117
Philosopher's Stone, 8
Plato, 214-215
Pollock, John, 59
Posthuman, 1-2, 25, 30, 116, 127-128, 141, 154, 219
Principle of Causal Closure, 36-37, 48, 51, 53-56, 223
Prometheus, 6

RAIR Lab (Rensselaer AI and Reasoning Laboratory), 76, 89-92, 95, 98-100, 102, 225
Religion Without Revelation, 164-165
Renaissance, 8-10, 15
Richards, Jay, 102
Rockoff, Marcus, 191-194
Rothblatt, Martine, 126
Ruse, Michael, 142
Russell, Bertrand, 40

Sandel, Michael J., 208
Santayana, George, 15, 146
Sayers, Dorothy, 85-86
Schank, Roger, 80, 88, 90
Schneider, Susan, 139
Schumacher, E. F., 47
Searle, John, 63-65, 98, 224, 225
Sellars, Wilfrid, 61
Semiotics, 68
Simon, Herbert, 41, 66
Singularity, 27-29
Singularity University, 168-169
Socrates, 117-118, 214-215
Solomon, King, 161-162
Star Trek: The Next Generation, 79
Strawson, Galen, 61
Stephen Thaler's Creativity Machine, 78
Substantial Form, 12, 106-107, 151-153
Superhappiness, 1-3, 35, 130, 189-217, 219, 221, 226-229
Superintelligence, 1-3, 29, 33-35, 132, 136, 166, 172, 184, 187, 190-191, 219, 221, 222, 226, 228
Superintelligent machine, 29, 35, 71-72, 102, 150
Superlongevity, 1-3, 30, 35, 157-160, 165-166, 172, 174-175, 177-178, 180, 184, 187
Swift, Jonathan, 191-193, 196-198

TALE-SPIN, 88-89
Techno-utopia, 1, 3, 19, 28, 30, 146, 147, 149-150, 157, 159, 172-173, 190, 194, 195, 219-220
TEMI (temporally extended mental imagery), 91-98, 225
Teroni, Fabrice, 209-211
That Hideous Strength, 155
The Abolition of Man, 44, 144, 148, 155
The Astonishing Hypothesis, 136-167
"The Bridge of Khazad-Dum", 113
The Case Against Perfection, 208
The Chinese Room Argument, 64, 74
The Distressing Principle, 101-102
The Everlasting Man, 43
"The Fable of the Dragon-Tyrant", 160
"The Future of Humanity Institute", 27, 29
The Glass Cage, 118
"The Great Silliness", 61
The Hedonistic Imperative, 22, 130, 189
The Human Advantage, 102
"The Imitation Game", 89
"The Jetsons Fallacy", 117
The Lovelace Test, 72, 77, 99-102, 225
The Metaphysical Foundations of Modern Science, 42
The Mill Analogy, 96
The Mind of the Maker, 85-86
"The Minimal Facts Approach", 87-89
The Prospect of Immortality, 25
"The Scientific Conception of the World", 45, 193
The Singularity is Near, 161, 168
The Thanatos Syndrome, 191-192, 194-195, 201-202, 205
The Theogony, 85
"The Transhumanist Declaration", 19, 27, 125, 148, 158, 164
"The Vengeful Princess", 110
The World, the Flesh, and the Devil, 20
The Zeal of Thy House, 86

Theory of Actuality and Potentiality, 105-106
Tipler, Frank, 28
Tolkien, J.R.R, 86-87, 155, 157, 159, 162, 165-166, 167, 172-174, 175-176, 178-179, 181-188, 226
"Transhumanist Values", 19, 120, 146
Treatise of Man, 12
Turing, Alan, 41, 66, 89-90
Turing Test, The, 39, 66, 72, 90, 99, 140

Ubermensch, 17
Up-Wingers, 24
Utilitarianism, 142-143
Utnapishtim, 6

Venter, Craig, 128
Vienna Circle, The, 44-46, 48, 50
Vinge, Vernor, 28-29
Vita-More, Natasha, 4
von Helmholtz, Hermann, 52

"What Is It Like to Be a Bat?", 59, 97
Whitehead, Alfred North, 40
Whole Brain Emulation, 134, 140, 186
Wilson, E. O., 44, 48-49, 50
World Transhumanist Association, 27

Young, Simon, 6, 16, 122, 144, 160
Yudkowsky, Eliezer, 150

Zarathustra, 17
Zeus, 6

www.ingramcontent.com/pod-product-compliance
Lightning Source LLC
Chambersburg PA
CBHW030034100526
44590CB00011B/199